STUDIES

IN THE

PSYCHOLOGY OF SEX

BY

HAVELOCK ELLIS

Havelock Ellis.

STUDIES IN THE PSYCHOLOGY OF SEX.

The "Studies in the Psychology of Sex" will probably be completed in five volumes. Each volume is sold separately, and is complete in itself.

This is the only edition in English published by the author's permission.

STUDIES

IN THE

PSYCHOLOGY OF SEX

SEXUAL SELECTION IN MAN

I. TOUCH.   II. SMELL.   III. HEARING.   IV. VISION

BY

HAVELOCK ELLIS

PHILADELPHIA

F. A. DAVIS COMPANY, PUBLISHERS

1911

PREFACE.

As IN many other of these *Studies,* and perhaps more than in most, the task attempted in the present volume is mainly of a tentative and preliminary character. There is here little scope yet for the presentation of definite scientific results. However it may be in the physical universe, in the cosmos of science our knowledge must be nebulous before it constellates into definitely measurable shapes, and nothing is gained by attempting to anticipate the evolutionary process. Thus it is that here, for the most part, we have to content ourselves at present with the task of mapping out the field in broad and general outlines, bringing together the facts and considerations which indicate the direction in which more extended and precise results will in the future be probably found.

In his famous *Descent of Man,* wherein he first set forth the doctrine of sexual selection, Darwin injured an essentially sound principle by introducing into it a psychological confusion whereby the physiological sensory stimuli through which sexual selection operates were regarded as equivalent to æsthetic preferences. This confusion misled many, and it is only within recent years (as has been set forth in the "Analysis of the Sexual Impulse" in the previous volume of these *Studies*) that the investigations and criticisms of numerous workers have placed the doctrine of sexual selection on a firm basis by eliminating its hazardous æsthetic element. Love springs up as a response to a number of stimuli to tumescence, the object that most adequately arouses tumescence being that which evokes love; the question of æsthetic beauty, although it develops on this basis, is not itself fundamental and need not even be consciously present at all. When we look at these phenomena in their broadest biological aspects, love is only to a limited extent a response to beauty; to a greater extent beauty is simply a name for the complexus of stimuli which most adequately arouses love. If we analyze these stimuli to tumescence as they proceed from a person of the opposite sex we find that they are all appeals which must come through the channels of four senses: touch, smell, hearing, and, above all, vision. When a man or a woman experiences sexual love for one particular person from among the multitude by which he or she is surrounded, this is due to the influences of a group of stimuli coming through the channels of one or more of these senses. There has been a sexual selection conditioned by sensory stimuli. This is true even of the finer and more spiritual influences that proceed from one person to another, although, in order to grasp the phenomena adequately, it is best to insist on the more fundamental and less complex forms which they assume. In this sense sexual selection is no longer a hypothesis concerning the truth of which it is possible to dispute; it is a self-evident fact. The difficulty is not as to its existence, but as to the methods by which it may be most precisely measured. It is fundamentally a psychological process, and should be approached from the psychological side. This is the reason for dealing with it here. Obscure as the psychological aspects of sexual selection still remain, they are full of fascination, for they reveal to us the more intimate sides of human evolution, of the process whereby man is molded into the shapes we know.

HAVELOCK ELLIS.

Carbis Water,
Lelant, Cornwall, England.

CONTENTS.

SEXUAL SELECTION IN MAN.

TOUCH.

I.

II.

III.

IV.

IV.

V.

VI.

HEARING.

I.

IV.

V.

APPENDIX A.

APPENDIX B.

SEXUAL SELECTION IN MAN.

The External Sensory Stimuli Affecting Selection in Man—The Four Senses Involved.

TUMESCENCE—the process by which the organism is brought into the physical and psychic state necessary to insure conjugation and detumescence—to some extent comes about through the spontaneous action of internal forces. To that extent it is analogous to the physical and psychic changes which accompany the gradual filling of the bladder and precede its evacuation. But even among animals who are by no means high in the zoölogical scale the process is more complicated than this. External stimuli act at every stage, arousing or heightening the process of tumescence, and in normal human beings it may be said that the process is never completed without the aid of such stimuli, for even in the auto-erotic sphere external stimuli are still active, either actually or in imagination.

The chief stimuli which influence tumescence and thus direct sexual choice come chiefly—indeed, exclusively—through the four senses of touch, smell, hearing, and sight. All the phenomena of sexual selection, so far as they are based externally, act through these four senses.[1] The reality of the influence thus exerted may be demonstrated statistically even in civil-

---

[1] Taste must, I believe, be excluded, for if we abstract the parts of touch and smell, even in those abnormal sexual acts in which it may seem to be affected, taste could scarcely have any influence. Most of our "tasting," as Waller puts it, is done by the nose, which, in man, is in specially close relationship, posteriorly, with the mouth. There are at most four taste sensations—sweet, bitter, salt, and sour—if even all of these are simple tastes. What commonly pass for taste sensations, as shown by some experiments of G. T. W. Patrick (*Psychological Review*, 1898, p. 160), are the composite results of the mingling of sensations of smell, touch, temperature, sight, and taste.

ized man, and it has been shown that, as regards, for instance, eye-color, conjugal partners differ sensibly from the unmarried persons by whom they are surrounded. When, therefore, we are exploring the nature of the influence which stimuli, acting through the sensory channels, exert on the strength and direction of the sexual impulse, we are intimately concerned with the process by which the actual form and color, not alone of living things generally, but of our own species, have been shaped and are still being shaped. At the same time, it is probable, we are exploring the mystery which underlies all the subtle appreciations, all the emotional undertones, which are woven in the web of the whole world as it appeals to us through those sensory passages by which alone it can reach us. We are here approaching, therefore, a fundamental subject of unsurpassable importance, a subject which has not yet been accurately explored save at a few isolated points and one which it is therefore impossible to deal with fully and adequately. Yet it cannot be passed over, for it enters into the whole psychology of the sexual instinct.

Of the four senses—touch, smell, hearing, and sight—with which we are here concerned, touch is the most primitive, and it may be said to be the most important, though it is usually the last to make its appeal felt. Smell, which occupies the chief place among many animals, is of comparatively less importance, though of considerable interest, in man; it is only less intimate and final than touch. Sight occupies an intermediate position, and on this account, and also on account of the very great part played by vision in life generally as well as in art, it is the most important of all the senses from the human sexual point of view. Hearing, from the same point of view, is the most remote of all the senses in its appeal to the sexual impulse, and on that account it is, when it intervenes, among the first to make its influence felt.

TOUCH.

I.

WE are accustomed to regard the skin as mainly owing its existence to the need for the protection of the delicate vessels, nerves, viscera, and muscles underneath. Undoubtedly it performs, and by its tough and elastic texture is well fitted to perform, this extremely important service. But the skin is not merely a method of protection against the external world; it is also a method of bringing us into sensitive contact with the external world. It is thus, as the organ of touch, the seat of the most widely diffused sense we possess, and, moreover, the sense which is the most ancient and fundamental of all— the mother of the other senses.

It is scarcely necessary to insist that the primitive nature of the sensory function of the skin with the derivative nature of the other senses, is a well ascertained and demonstrable fact. The lower we descend in the animal scale, the more varied we find the functions of the skin to be, and if in the higher animals much of the complexity has disappeared, that is only because the specialization of the various skin regions into distinct organs has rendered this complexity unnecessary. Even yet, however, in man himself the skin still retains, in a more or less latent condition, much of its varied and primary power, and the analysis of pathological and even normal phenomena serves to bring these old powers into clear light.

(3)

Woods Hutchinson (*Studies in Human and Comparative Pathology*, 1901, Chapters VII and VIII) has admirably set forth the immense importance of the skin, as in the first place "a tissue which is silk to the touch, the most exquisitely beautiful surface in the universe to the eye, and yet a wall of adamant against hostile attack. Impervious alike, by virtue of its wonderful responsive vitality, to moisture and drought, cold and heat, electrical changes, hostile bacteria, the most virulent of poisons and the deadliest of gases, it is one of the real Wonders of the World. More beautiful than velvet, softer and more pliable than silk, more impervious than rubber, and more durable under exposure than steel, well-nigh as resistant to electric currents as glass, it is one of the toughest and most dangerproof substances in the three kingdoms of nature" (although, as this author adds, we "hardly dare permit it to see the sunlight or breathe the open air"). But it is more than this. It is, as Woods Hutchinson expresses it, the creator of the entire body; its embryonic infoldings form the alimentary canal, the brain, the spinal cord, while every sense is but a specialization of its general organic activity. It is furthermore a kind of "skin-heart," promoting the circulation by its own energy; it is the great heat-regulating organ of the body; it is an excretory organ only second to the kidneys, which descend from it, and finally it still remains the seat of touch.

It may be added that the extreme beauty of the skin as a surface is very clearly brought out by the inadequacy of the comparisons commonly used in order to express its beauty. Snow, marble, alabaster, ivory, milk, cream, silk, velvet, and all the other conventional similes furnish surfaces which from any point of view are incomparably inferior to the skin itself. (*Cf.* Stratz, *Die Schönheit des Weiblichen Körpers*, Chapter XII.)

With reference to the extraordinary vitality of the skin, emphasized by Woods Hutchinson, it may be added that, when experimenting on the skin with the electric current, Waller found that healthy skin showed signs of life ten days or more after excision. It has been found also that fragments of skin which have been preserved in sterile fluid for even as long as nine months may still be successfully transplanted on to the body. (*British Medical Journal*, July 19. 1902.)

Everything indicates, remark Stanley Hall and Donaldson ("Motor Sensations in the Skin," *Mind*, 1885), that the skin is "not only the primeval and most reliable source of our knowledge of the external world or the archæological field of psychology," but a field in which work may shed light on some of the most fundamental problems of psychic action. Groos (*Spiele der Menschen*, pp. 8-16) also deals with the primitive character of touch sensations.

Touch sensations are without doubt the first of all the sensory impressions to prove pleasurable. We should, indeed, expect this from the fact that the skin reflexes have already appeared before birth, while a pleasurable sensitiveness of the lips is doubtless a factor in the child's response to the contact of the maternal nipple. Very early memories of sensory pleasure seem to be frequently, perhaps most frequently, tactile in character, though this fact is often disguised in recollection, owing to tactile impression being vague and diffused; there is thus in Elizabeth Potwin's "Study of Early Memories" (*Psychological Review*, November, 1901) no separate group of tactile memories, and the more elaborate investigation by Colegrove ("Individual Memories," *American Journal of Psychology*, January, 1899) yields no decisive results under this head. See, however, Stanley Hall's valuable study, "Some Aspects of the Early Sense of Self," *American Journal of Psychology*, April, 1898. Külpe has a discussion of the psychology of cutaneous sensations (*Outlines of Psychology* [English translation], pp. 87 *et seq.*).

Harriet Martineau, at the beginning of her *Autobiography*, referring to the vivid character of tactile sensations in early childhood, remarks, concerning an early memory of touching a velvet button, that "the rapture of the sensation was really monstrous." And a lady tells me that one of her earliest memories at the age of 3 is of the exquisite sensation of the casual contact of a cool stone with the vulva in the act of urinating. Such sensations, of course, cannot be termed specifically sexual, though they help to furnish the tactile basis on which the specifically sexual sensations develop.

The elementary sensitiveness of the skin is shown by the fact that moderate excitation suffices to raise the temperature, while Heidenhain and others have shown that in animals cutaneous stimuli modify the sensibility of the brain cortex, slight stimulus increasing excitability and strong stimulus diminishing it. Féré has shown that the slight stimulus to the skin furnished by placing a piece of metal on the arm or elsewhere suffices to increase the output of work with the ergograph. (Féré, *Comptes Rendus Société de Biologie*, July 12, 1902; id. *Pathologie des Emotions*, pp. 40 *et seq.*)

Féré found that the application of a mustard plaster to the skin, or an icebag, or a hot-water bottle, or even a light touch with a painter's brush, all exerted a powerful effect in increasing muscular work with the ergograph. "The tonic effect of cutaneous excitation," he remarks, "throws light on the psychology of the caress. It is always the most sensitive parts of the body which seek to give or to receive caresses. Many animals rub or lick each other. The mucous surfaces share in this irritability of the skin. The kiss is not only an expression of feeling; it is a means of provoking it. Cataglottism is by no means confined to pigeons. The tonic value of cutaneous stimulation is indeed a commonly accepted idea. Wrestlers rub their hands or limbs, and the hand-shake also is not without its physiological basis.

Cutaneous excitations may cause painful sensations to cease. Many massage practices which favor work act chiefly as sensorial stimulants; on this account many nervous persons cannot abandon them, and the Greeks and Romans found in massage not only health, but pleasure. Lauder Brunton regards many common manœuvres, like scratching the head and pulling the moustache, as methods of dilating the blood-vessels of the brain by stimulating the facial nerve. The motor reactions of cutaneous excitations favor this hypothesis." (Féré, *Travail et Plaisir*, Chapter XV, "Influence des Excitations du Toucher sur le Travail.")

The main characteristics of the primitive sense of touch are its wide diffusion over the whole body and the massive vagueness and imprecision of the messages it sends to the brain. This is the reason why it is, of all the senses, the least intellectual and the least æsthetic; it is also the reason why it is, of all the senses, the most profoundly emotional. "Touch," wrote Bain in his *Emotions and Will*, "is both the alpha and the omega of affection," and he insisted on the special significance in this connection of "tenderness"—a characteristic emotional quality of affection which is directly founded on sensations of touch. If tenderness is the alpha of affection, even between the sexes, its omega is to be found in the sexual embrace, which may be said to be a method of obtaining, through a specialized organization of the skin, the most exquisite and intense sensations of touch.

"We believe nothing is so exciting to the instinct or mere passion as the presence of the hand or those tactile caresses which mark affection," states the anonymous author of an article on "Woman in her Psychological Relations," in the *Journal of Psychological Medicine*, 1851. "They are the most general stimuli in lower animals. The first recourse in difficulty or danger, and the primary solace in anguish, for woman is the bosom of her husband or her lover. She seeks solace and protection and repose on that part of the body where she herself places the objects of her own affection. Woman appears to have the same instinctive impulse in this respect all over the world."

It is because the sexual orgasm is founded on a special adaptation and intensification of touch sensations that the sense of touch generally is to be regarded as occupying the very first place in reference to the sexual emotions. Féré, Mantegazza, Penta, and most other writers on this question are here agreed. Touch sensations constitute a vast gamut for the expression of affection, with at one end the note of minimum personal affection in the brief and limited touch involved by the conventional hand-shake and the conventional kiss, and at the other end the final and intimate contact in which passion finds the supreme satisfaction of its most profound desire. The intermediate region has its great significance for us because it offers a field in which affection has its full scope, but in which every road may possibly lead to the goal of sexual love. It is the intimacy of touch contacts, their inevitable approach to the threshold of sexual emotion, which leads to a jealous and instinctive parsimony in the contact of skin and skin and to the tendency with the increased sensitiveness of the nervous system involved by civilization to restrain even the conventional touch manifestation of ordinary affection and esteem. In China fathers leave off kissing their daughters while they are still young children. In England the kiss as an ordinary greeting between men and women—a custom inherited from classic and early Christian antiquity—still persisted to the beginning of the eighteenth century. In France the same custom existed in the seventeenth century, but in the middle of that century was beginning to be regarded as dangerous,[1] while at the present time the conventional kiss on the cheek is strictly differentiated from the kiss on the mouth, which is reserved for lovers. Touch contacts between person and person, other than those limited and defined by custom, tend to become either unpleasant—as an undesired intrusion into an intimate sphere—or else, when occurring between man and woman at some peculiar moment, they may make a powerful reverberation in the emotional and

---

[1] A. Franklin, *Les Soins de Toilette*, p. 81.

more specifically sexual sphere. One man falls in love with his future wife because he has to carry her upstairs with a sprained ankle. Another dates his love-story from a romp in which his cheek accidentally came in contact with that of his future wife. A woman will sometimes instinctively strive to attract the attention of the man who appeals to her by a peculiar and prolonged pressure of the hand—the only touch contact permitted to her. Dante, as Penta has remarked, refers to "sight or touch" as the two channels through which a woman's love is revived (*Purgatorio*, VIII, 76). Even the hand-shake of a sympathetic man is enough in some chaste and sensitive women to produce sexual excitement or sometimes even the orgasm. The cases in which love arises from the influence of stimuli coming through the sense of touch are no doubt frequent, and they would be still more frequent if it were not that the very proximity of this sense to the sexual sphere causes it to be guarded with a care which in the case of the other senses it is impossible to exercise. This intimacy of touch and the reaction against its sexual approximations leads to what James has called "the *antisexual instinct*, the instinct of personal isolation, the actual repulsiveness to us of the idea of intimate contact with most of the persons we meet, especially those of our own sex." He refers in this connection to the unpleasantness of the sensation felt on occupying a seat still warm from the body of another person.[1] The Catholic Church has always recognized the risks of voluptuous emotion involved in tactile contacts, and the facility with which even the most innocent contacts may take on a libidinous character.[2]

The following observations were written by a lady (aged 30) who has never had sexual relationships: "I am only conscious of a very sweet and pleasurable emotion when coming in contact with honorable men, and consider that a comparison can be made between the idealism of such emotions and those of music, of beauties of Nature, and of productions of art. While studying and writing articles upon a new sub-

---

[1] W. James, *Principles of Psychology*, vol. ii, p. 347.

[2] Numerous passages from the theologians bearing on this point are brought together in *Moechialogia*, pp. 221-226.

ject I came in contact with a specialist, who rendered me considerable aid, and, one day, while jointly correcting a piece of work, he touched my hand. This produced a sweet and pure sensation of thrill through the whole system. I said nothing; in fact, was too thrilled for speech; and never to this day have shown any responsive action, but for months at certain periods, generally twice a month, I have experienced the most pleasurable emotions. I have seen this friend twice since, and have a curious feeling that I stand on one side of a hedge, while he is on the other, and, as neither makes an approach, pleasure of the highest kind is experienced, but not allowed to go beyond reasonable and health-giving bounds. In some moments I feel overcome by a sense of mastery by this man, and yet, feeling that any approach would be undignified, some pleasure is experienced in restraining and keeping within proper bounds this passional emotion. All these thrills of pleasurable emotion possess a psychic value, and, so long as the nervous system is kept in perfect health, they do not seem to have the power to injure, but rather one is able to utilize the passionate emotions as weapons for pleasure and work."

Various parts of the skin surface appear to have special sexual sensitiveness, peculiarly marked in many individuals, especially women; so that, as Féré remarks (*L'Instinct Sexuel*, second edition, 1902, p. 130), contact stimulation of the lips, lobe of ear, nape of neck, little finger, knee, etc., may suffice even to produce the orgasm. Some sexually hyperæsthetic women, as has already been noted, experience this when shaking hands with a man who is attractive to them. In some neurotic persons this sensibility, as Féré shows, may exist in so morbid a degree that even the contact of the sensitive spot with unattractive persons or inanimate objects may produce the orgasm. In this connection reference may be made to the well-known fact that in some hysterical subjects there are so-called "erogenous zones" simple pressure on which suffices to evoke the complete orgasm. There is, perhaps, some significance, from our present point of view, in the fact that, as emphasized by Savill ("Hysterical Skin Symptoms," *Lancet*, January 30, 1904), the skin is one of the very best places to study hysteria.

The intimate connection between the skin and the sexual sphere is also shown in pathological conditions of the skin, especially in acne as well as simple pimples on the face. The sexual development of puberty involves a development of hair in various regions of the body which previously were hairless. As, however, the sebaceous glands on the face and elsewhere are the vestiges of former hairs and survive from a period when the whole body was hairy, they also tend to experience in an abortive manner this same impulse. Thus, we may say that, with the development of the sexual organs at puberty, there is correlated ex-

citement of the whole pilo-sebaceous apparatus. In the regions where
this apparatus is vestigial, and notably in the face, this abortive attempt of the hair-follicles and their sebaceous appendages to produce
hairs tends only to disorganization, and simple *comedones* or pustular
acne pimples are liable to occur. As a rule, acne appears about
puberty and dies out slowly during adolescence. While fairly common
in young women, it is usually much less severe, but tends to be exacer-
bated at the menstrual periods; it is also apt to appear at the change
of life. (Stephen Mackenzie, "The Etiology and Treatment of Acne Vulgaris," *British Medical Journal*, September 29, 1894. Laycock [*Nervous
Diseases of Women*, 1840, p. 23] pointed out that acne occurs chiefly in
those parts of the surface covered by sexual hair. A lucid account of
the origin of acne will be found in Woods Hutchinson's *Studies in
Human and Comparative Pathology*, pp. 179-184. G. J. Engelmann
["The Hystero-neuroses," *Gynæcological Transactions*, 1887, pp. 124 *et
seq.*] discusses various pathological disorders of the skin as reflex dis-
turbances originating in the sexual sphere.)

The influence of menstruation in exacerbating acne has been called
in question, but it seems to be well established. Thus, Bulkley ("Relation between Certain Diseases of the Skin and the Menstrual Function," *Transactions of the Medical Society of New York*, 1901, p. 328)
found that, in 510 cases of acne in women, 145, or nearly one-third,
were worse about the monthly period. Sometimes it only appeared
during menstruation. The exacerbation occurred much more frequently
just before than just after the period. There was usually some disturbance of menstruation. Various other disorders of the skin show a
similar relationship to menstruation.

It has been asserted that masturbation is a frequent or constant
cause of acne at puberty. (See, *e.g.*, discussion in *British Medical
Journal*, July, 1882.) This cannot be accepted. Acne very frequently
occurs without masturbation, and masturbation is very frequently practiced without producing acne. At the same time we may well believe
that at the period of puberty, when the pilo-sebaceous system is already
in sensitive touch with the sexual system, the shock of frequently repeated masturbation may (in the same way as disordered menstruation) have its repercussion on the skin. Thus, a lady has informed
me that at about the age of 18 she found that frequently repeated
masturbation was followed by the appearance of *comedones*.

II.

Ticklishness—Its Origin and Significance—The Psychology of Tickling—Laughter—Laughter as a Kind of Detumescence—The Sexual Relationships of Itching—The Pleasure of Tickling—Its Decrease with Age and Sexual Activity.

TOUCH, as has already been remarked, is the least intellectual of the senses. There is, however, one form of touch sensation—that is to say, ticklishness—which is of so special and peculiar a nature that it has sometimes been put aside in a class apart from all other touch sensations. Scaliger proposed to class titillation as a sixth, or separate, sense. Alrutz, of Upsala, regards tickling as a milder degree of itching, and considers that the two together constitute a sensation of distinct quality with distinct end-organs for the mediation of that quality.[1] However we may regard this extreme view, tickling is certainly a specialized modification of touch and it is at the same time the most intellectual mode of touch sensation and that with the closest connection with the sexual sphere. To regard tickling as an intellectual manifestation may cause surprise, more especially when it is remembered that ticklishness is a form of sensation which reaches full development very early in life, and it has to be admitted that, as compared even with the messages that may be sent through smell and taste, the intellectual element in ticklishness remains small. But its presence here has been independently recognized by various investigators. Groos points out the psychic factor in tickling as evidenced by the impossibility of self-tickling.[2] Louis Robinson considers that ticklishness "appears to be one of the simplest developments of mechanical and automatic nervous processes in the direction of the complex

---

[1] Alrutz's views are summarized in *Psychological Review*, Sept., 1901.

[2] *Die Spiele der Menschen*, 1899, p. 206.

functioning of the higher centres which comes within the scope of psychology."[1]   Stanley Hall and Allin remark that "these minimal touch excitations represent the very oldest stratum of psychic life in the soul."[2]   Hirman Stanley, in a somewhat similar manner, pushes the intellectual element in ticklishness very far back and associates it with "tentacular experience." "By temporary self-extension," he remarks, "even low amœboid organisms have slight, but suggestive, touch experiences that stimulate very general and violent reactions, and in higher organisms extended touch-organs, as tentacles, antennæ, hair, etc., become permanent and very delicately sensitive organs, where minimal contacts have very distinct and powerful reactions."   Thus ticklishness would be the survival of long passed ancestral tentacular experience, which, originally a stimulation producing intense agitation and alarm, has now become merely a play activity and a source of keen pleasure.[3]

We need not, however, go so far back in the zoölogical series to explain the origin and significance of tickling in the human species.   Sir J. Y. Simpson suggested, in an elaborate study of the position of the child in the womb, that the extreme excitomotory sensibility of the skin in various regions, such as the sole of the foot, the knee, the sides, which already exists before birth, has for its object the excitation and preservation of the muscular movements necessary to keep the fœtus in the most favorable position in the womb.[4]   It is, in fact, certainly the case that the stimulation of all the ticklish regions in the body tends to produce exactly that curled up position of extreme muscular flexion and general ovoid shape which is the normal position of the fœtus in the womb. We may well believe that in this early developed reflex activity

---

[1] L. Robinson, art. "Ticklishness," Tuke's *Dictionary of Psychological Medicine.*

[2] Stanley Hall and Allin, "Tickling and Laughter," *American Journal of Psychology,* October, 1897.

[3] H. M. Stanley, "Remarks on Tickling and Laughter," *American Journal of Psychology,* vol. ix, January, 1898.

[4] Simpson, "On the Attitude of the Fœtus in Utero," *Obstetric Memoirs,* 1856, vol. ii.

we have the basis of that somewhat more complex ticklishness which appears somewhat later.

The mental element in tickling is indicated by the fact that even a child, in whom ticklishness is highly developed, cannot tickle himself; so that tickling is not a simple reflex. This fact was long ago pointed out by Erasmus Darwin, and he accounted for it by supposing that voluntary exertion diminishes the energy of sensation.[1] This explanation is, however, inadmissible, for, although we cannot easily tickle ourselves by the contact of the skin with our own fingers, we can do so with the aid of a foreign body, like a feather. We may perhaps suppose that, as ticklishness has probably developed under the influence of natural selection as a method of protection against attack and a warning of the approach of foreign bodies, its end would be defeated if it involved a simple reaction to the contact of the organism with itself. This need of protection it is which involves the necessity of a minimal excitation producing a maximal effect, though the mechanism whereby this takes place has caused considerable discussion. We may, it is probable, best account for it by invoking the summation-irradiation theory of pain-pleasure, the summation of the stimuli in their course through the nerves, aided by capillary congestion, leading to irradiation due to anastomoses between the tactile corpuscles, not to speak of the much wider irradiation which is possible by means of central nervous connections.

Prof. C. L. Herrick adopts this explanation of the phenomena of tickling, and rests it, in part, on Dogiel's study of the tactile corpuscles ("Psychological Corollaries of Modern Neurological Discoveries," *Journal of Comparative Neurology*, March, 1898). The following remarks of Prof. A. Allin may also be quoted in further explanation of the same theory: "So far as ticklishness is concerned, a very important factor in the production of this feeling is undoubtedly that of the summation of stimuli. In a research of Stirling's, carried on under Ludwig's direction, it was shown that reflex contractions only occur from repeated shocks to the nerve-centres—that is, through summation of successive stimuli. That this result is also due in some degree to an alternating increase

---

[1] Erasmus Darwin, *Zoönomia*, Sect. XVII, 4.

in the sensibility of the various areas in question from altered supply of blood is reasonably certain. As a consequence of this summation-process there would result in many cases and in cases of excessive nervous discharge the opposite of pleasure, namely: pain. A number of instances have been recorded of death resulting from tickling, and there is no reason to doubt the truth of the statement that Simon de Montfort, during the persecution of the Albigenses, put some of them to death by tickling the soles of their feet with a feather. An additional causal factor in the production of tickling may lie in the nature and structure of the nervous process involved in perception in general. According to certain histological researches of recent years we know that between the sense-organs and the central nervous system there exist closely connected chains of conductors or neurons, along which an impression received by a single sensory cell on the periphery is propagated avalanchelike through an increasing number of neurons until the brain is reached. If on the periphery a single cell is excited the avalanchelike process continues until finally hundreds or thousands of nerve-cells in the cortex are aroused to considerable activity. Golgi, Ramón y Cajal, Koelliker, Held, Retzius, and others have demonstrated the histological basis of this law for vision, hearing, and smell, and we may safely assume from the phenomena of tickling that the sense of touch is not lacking in a similar arrangement. May not a suggestion be offered, with some plausibility, that even in ideal or representative tickling, where tickling results, say, from someone pointing a finger at the ticklish places, this avalanchelike process may be incited from central centres, thus producing, although in a modified degree, the pleasant phenomena in question? As to the deepest causal factor, I should say that tickling is the result of vasomotor shock." (A. Allin, "On Laughter," *Psychological Review*, May, 1903.)

The intellectual element in tickling comes out in its connection with laughter and the sense of the comic, of which it may be said to constitute the physical basis. While we are not here concerned with laughter and the comic sense,—a subject which has lately attracted considerable attention,—it may be instructive to point out that there is more than an analogy between laughter and the phenomena of sexual tumescence and detumescence. The process whereby prolonged tickling, with its nervous summation and irradiation and accompanying hyperæmia, finds sudden relief in an explosion of laughter is a real example of tumescence—as it has been defined in the study in another volume entitled "An Analysis of the Sexual Impulse"—resulting finally in the orgasm of detumescence. The reality of the connection between the sexual embrace and tickling is indicated by the fact that in some languages, as in that of the Fuegians,[1] the same word is applied to both. That ordinary tickling is not sexual is due to the circumstances of the case and the regions to which the tickling is applied. If, however, the tickling is applied within the sexual sphere, then there is a tendency for orgasm to take place instead of laughter. The connection which, through the phenomena of tickling, laughter thus bears to the sexual sphere is well indicated, as Groos has pointed out, by the fact that in sexually-minded people sexual allusions tend to produce laughter, this being the method by which they are diverted from the risks of more specifically sexual detumescence.[2]

Reference has been made to the view of Alrutz, according to which tickling is a milder degree of itching. It is more convenient and probably more correct to regard itching or pruritus, as it is termed in its pathological forms, as a distinct sensation, for it does not arise under precisely the same conditions as tickling nor is it relieved in the same way. There is interest, however, in pointing out in this connection that, like tickling, itching has a real parallelism to the specialized sexual sensations. Bronson, who has very ably interpreted the sensations of itching (New York Neurological Society, October 7, 1890; *Medical News*, February 14, 1903, and summarized in the *British Medical Journal*, March 7, 1903; and elsewhere), regards it as a perversion of the sense of touch, a dysæsthesia due to obstructed nerve-excitation with imperfect conduction of the generated force into correlated nervous energy. The scratching which relieves itching directs the nervous energy into freer channels, sometimes substituting for the pruritus either painful or voluptuous sensations. Such voluptuous sensations may be regarded as a generalized aphrodisiac sense comparable to the specialized sexual orgasm. Bronson refers to the significant fact that itching occurs so frequently in the sexual region, and states that sexual neurasthenia is sometimes the only discoverable cause of genital and anal pruritus. (*Cf.* discussion on pruritus, *British Medical Journal*,

---

[1] Hyades and Deniker, *Mission Scientifique du Cap Horn*, vol. vii, p. 296.

[2] Such an interpretation is supported by the arguments of W. McDougall ("The Theory of Laughter," *Nature*, February 5, 1903), who contends, without any reference to the sexual field, that one of the objects of laughter is automatically to "disperse our attention."

November 30, 1895.) Gilman, again (*American Journal of Psychology*, vi, p. 22), considers that scratching, as well as sneezing, is comparable to coitus.

The sexual embrace has an intimate connection with the phenomena of ticklishness which could not fail to be recognized. This connection is, indeed, the basis of Spinoza's famous definition of love,—"*Amor est titillatio quædam concomitante idea causæ externæ,*"—a statement which seems to be reflected in Chamfort's definition of love as "*l'échange de deux fantaisies, et le contact de deux epidermes.*" The sexual act, says Gowers, is, in fact, a skin reflex.[1] "The sexual parts," Hall and Allin state, "have a ticklishness as unique as their function and as keen as their importance." Herrick finds the supreme illustration of the summation and irradiation theory of tickling in the phenomena of erotic excitement, and points out that in harmony with this the skin of the sexual region is, as Dogiel has shown, that portion of the body in which the tactile corpuscles are most thoroughly and elaborately provided with anastomosing fibres. It has been pointed out[2] that, when ordinary tactile sensibility is partially abolished,—especially in hemianæsthesia in the insane,—some sexual disturbance is specially apt to be found in association.

In young children, in girls even when they are no longer children, and occasionally in men, tickling may be a source of acute pleasure, which in very early life is not sexual, but later tends to become so under circumstances predisposing to the production of erotic emotion, and especially when the nervous system is keyed up to a high tone favorable for the production of the maximum effect of tickling.

"When young," writes a lady aged 28, "I was extremely fond of being tickled, and I am to some extent still. Between the ages of 10 and 12 it gave me exquisite pleasure, which I now regard as sexual

---

[1] Even the structure of the vaginal mucous membrane, it may be noted, is analogous to that of the skin. D. Berry Hart, "Note on the Development of the Clitoris, Vagina, and Hymen," *Transactions of the Edinburgh Obstetrical Society*, vol. xxi, 1896.

[2] W. H. B. Stoddart, "Anæsthesia in the Insane," *Journal of Mental Science*, October, 1899.

in character. I used to bribe my younger sister to tickle my feet until she was tired."

Stanley Hall and Allin in their investigation of the phenomena of tickling, largely carried out among young women teachers, found that in 60 clearly marked cases ticklishness was more marked at one time than another, "as when they have been 'carrying on,' or are in a happy mood, are nervous or unwell, after a good meal, when being washed, when in perfect health, when with people they like, etc." (Hall and Allin, "Tickling and Laughter," *American Journal of Psychology*, October, 1897.) It will be observed that most of the conditions mentioned are such as would be favorable to excitations of an emotionally sexual character.

The palms of the hands may be very ticklish during sexual excitement, especially in women, and Moll (*Konträre Sexualempfindung*, p. 180) remarks that in some men titillation of the skin of the back, of the feet, and even of the forehead evokes erotic feelings.

It may be added that, as might be expected, titillation of the skin often has the same significance in animals as in man. "In some animals," remarks Louis Robinson (art. "Ticklishness," *Dictionary of Psychological Medicine*), "local titillation of the skin, though in parts remote from the reproductive organs, plainly acts indirectly upon them as a stimulus. Thus, Harvey records that, by stroking the back of a favorite parrot (which he had possessed for years and supposed to be a male), he not only gave the bird gratification,—which was the sole intention of the illustrious physiologist,—but also caused it to reveal its sex by laying an egg."

The sexual significance of tickling is very clearly indicated by the fact that the general ticklishness of the body, which is so marked in children and in young girls, greatly diminishes, as a rule, after sexual relationships have been established. Dr. Gina Lombroso, who investigated the cutaneous reflexes, found that both the abdominal and plantar reflexes, which are well marked in childhood and in young people between the ages of 15 and 18, were much diminished in older persons, and to a greater extent in women than in men, to a greater extent in the abdominal region than on the soles of the feet;[1] her results do not directly show the influence of sexual relationship, but they have an indirect bearing which is worth noting.

---

[1] Gina Lombroso, "Sur les Réflexes Cutanés," International Congress of Criminal Anthropology, Amsterdam, *Comptes Rendus*, p. 295.

The difference in ticklishness between the unmarried woman and the married woman corresponds to their difference in degree of modesty. Both modesty and ticklishness may be said to be characters which are no longer needed. From this point of view the general ticklishness of the skin is a kind of body modesty. It is so even apart from any sexual significance of tickling, and Louis Robinson has pointed out that in young apes, puppies, and other like animals the most ticklish regions correspond to the most vulnerable spots in a fight, and that consequently in the mock fights of early life skill in defending these spots is attained.

In Iceland, according to Margarethe Filhés (as quoted by Max Bartels, *Zeitschrift für Ethnologie*, 1900, ht. 2-3, p. 57), it may be known whether a youth is pure or a maid is intact by their susceptibility to tickling. It is considered a bad sign if that is lost.

I am indebted to a medical correspondent for the following communication: "Married women have told me that they find that after marriage they are not ticklish under the arms or on the breasts, though before marriage any tickling or touching in these regions, especially by a man, would make them jump or get hysterical or 'queer,' as they call it. Before coitus the sexual energy seems to be dissipated along all the nerve-channels and especially along the secondary sexual routes, —the breasts, nape of neck, eyebrows, lips, cheeks, armpits, and hair thereon, etc.,—but after marriage the surplus energy is diverted from these secondary channels, and response to tickling is diminished. I have often noted in insane cases, especially mania in adolescent girls, that they are excessively ticklish. Again, in ordinary routine practice I have observed that, though married women show no ticklishness during auscultation and percussion of the chest, this is by no means always so in young girls. Perhaps ticklishness in virgins is Nature's self-protection against rape and sexual advances, and the young girl instinctively wishing to hide the armpits, breasts, and other ticklish regions, tucks herself up to prevent these parts being touched. The married woman, being in love with a man, does not shut up these parts, as she reciprocates the advances that he makes; she no longer requires ticklishness as a protection against sexual aggression."

III.

The Secondary Sexual Skin Centres—Orificial Contacts—Cunnilingus and Fellatio—The Kiss—The Nipples—The Sympathy of the Breasts with the Primary Sexual Centres—This Connection Operative both through the Nerves and through the Blood—The Influence of Lactation on the Sexual Centres—Suckling and Sexual Emotion—The Significance of the Association between Suckling and Sexual Emotion—This Association as a Cause of Sexual Perversity.

WE have seen that the skin generally has a high degree of sensibility, which frequently tends to be in more or less definite association with the sexual centres. We have seen also that the central and specific sexual sensation, the sexual embrace itself, is, in large measure, a specialized kind of skin reflex. Between the generalized skin sensations and the great primary sexual centre of sensation there are certain secondary sexual centres which, on account of their importance, may here be briefly considered.

These secondary centres have in common the fact that they always involve the entrances and the exits of the body— the regions, that is, where skin merges into mucous membrane, and where, in the course of evolution, tactile sensibility has become highly refined. It may, indeed, be said generally of these frontier regions of the body that their contact with the same or a similar frontier region in another person of opposite sex, under conditions otherwise favorable to tumescence, will tend to produce a minimum and even sometimes a maximum degree of sexual excitation. Contact of these regions with each other or with the sexual region itself so closely simulates the central sexual reflex that channels are set up for the same nervous energy and secondary sexual centres are constituted.

It is important to remember that the phenomena we are here concerned with are essentially normal. Many of them are commonly spoken of as perversions. In so far, however, as they are aids to tumescence they must be regarded as coming

(19)

within the range of normal variation. They may be considered unæsthetic, but that is another matter. It has, moreover, to be remembered that æsthetic values are changed under the influence of sexual emotion; from the lover's point of view many things are beautiful which are unbeautiful from the point of view of him who is not a lover, and the greater the degree to which the lover is swayed by his passion the greater the extent to which his normal æsthetic standard is liable to be modified. A broad consideration of the phenomena among civilized and uncivilized peoples amply suffices to show the fallacy of the tendency, so common among unscientific writers on these subjects, to introduce normal æsthetic standards into the sexual sphere. From the normal standpoint of ordinary daily life, indeed, the whole process of sex is unæsthetic, except the earlier stages of tumescence.[1]

So long as they constitute a part of the phase of tumescence, the utilization of the sexual excitations obtainable through these channels must be considered within the normal range of variation, as we may observe, indeed, among many animals. When, however, such contacts of the orifices of the body, other than those of the male and female sexual organs proper, are used to procure not merely tumescence, but detumescence, they become, in the strict and technical sense, perversions. They are perversions in exactly the same sense as are the methods of intercourse which involve the use of checks to prevent fecundation. The æsthetic question, however, remains the same as if we were dealing with tumescence. It is necessary that this should be pointed out clearly, even at the risk of misapprehension, as confusions are here very common.

The essentially sexual character of the sensitivity of the orificial contacts is shown by the fact that it may sometimes be accidentally developed even in early childhood. This is well illustrated in a case re-

---

[1] Jonas Cohn (*Allgemeine Æsthetik*, 1901, p. 11) lays it down that psychology has nothing to do with good or bad taste. "The distinction between good and bad taste has no meaning for psychology. On this account, the fundamental conceptions of æsthetics cannot arise from psychology." It may be a question whether this view can be accepted quite absolutely.

corded by Féré. A little girl of 4, of nervous temperament and liable to fits of anger in which she would roll on the ground and tear her clothes, once ran out into the garden in such a fit of temper and threw herself on the lawn in a half-naked condition. As she lay there two dogs with whom she was accustomed to play came up and began to lick the uncovered parts of her body. It so happened that as one dog licked her mouth the other licked her sexual parts. She experienced a shock of intense sensation which she could never forget and never describe, accompanied by a delicious tension of the sexual organs. She rose and ran away with a feeling of shame, though she could not comprehend what had happened. The impression thus made was so profound that it persisted throughout life and served as the point of departure of sexual perversions, while the contact of a dog's tongue with her mouth alone afterward sufficed to evoke sexual pleasure. (Féré. *Archives de Neurologie*, 1903, No. 90.)

I do not purpose to discuss here either *cunnilingus* (the apposition of the mouth to the female pudendum) or *fellatio* (the apposition of the mouth to the male organ), the agent in the former case being, in normal heterosexual relationships, a man, in the latter a woman; they are not purely tactile phenomena, but involve various other physical and psychic elements. *Cunnilingus* was a very familiar manifestation in classic times, as shown by frequent and mostly very contemptuous references in Aristophanes, Juvenal, and many other Greek and Roman writers; the Greeks regarded it as a Phœnician practice, just as it is now commonly considered French; it tends to be especially prevalent at all periods of high civilization. *Fellatio* has also been equally well known, in both ancient and modern times, especially as practiced by inverted men. It may be accepted that both *cunnilingus* and *fellatio*, as practiced by either sex, are liable to occur among healthy or morbid persons, in heterosexual or homosexual relationships. They have little psychological significance, except to the extent that when practiced to the exclusion of normal sexual relationships they become perversions, and as such tend to be associated with various degenerative conditions, although such associations are not invariable.

The essentially normal character of *cunnilingus* and *fellatio*, when occurring as incidents in the process of tumescence, is shown by the fact that they are practiced by many animals. This is the case, for instance, among dogs. Moll points out that not infrequently the bitch, while under the dog, but before intromission, will change her position to lick the dog's penis—apparently from an instinctive impulse to heighten her own and his excitement—and then return to the normal position, while *cunnilingus* is of constant occurrence among animals, and on account of its frequency among dogs was called by the Greeks σκύλαξ (Rosenbaum, *Geschichte der Lustseuche im Altertume*, fifth edition, pp. 260-278; also notes in Moll, *Untersuchungen über die*

Libido Sexualis, Bd. 1, pp. 134, 369; and Bloch, *Beiträge zur Ætiologie der Psycopathia Sexualis*, Teil II, pp. 216 *et seq.*)

The occurrence of *cunnilingus* as a sexual episode of tumescence among lower human races is well illustrated by a practice of the natives of the Caroline Islands (as recorded by Kubary in his ethnographic study of this people and quoted by Ploss and Bartels, *Das Weib*, vol. i). It is here customary for a man to place a piece of fish between the labia, while he stimulates the latter by his tongue and teeth until under stress of sexual excitement the woman urinates; this is regarded as an indication that the proper moment for intercourse has arrived. Such a practice rests on physiologically sound facts whatever may be thought of it from an æsthetic standpoint.

The contrast between the normal æsthetic standpoint in this matter and the lover's is well illustrated by the following quotations: Dr. A. B. Holder, in the course of his description of the American Indian *bote*, remarks, concerning *fellatio*: "Of all the many varieties of sexual perversion, this, it seems to me, is the most debased that could be conceived of." On the other hand, in a communication from a writer and scholar of high intellectual distinction occurs the statement: "I affirm that, of all sexual acts, *fellatio* is most an affair of imagination and sympathy." It must be pointed out that there is no contradiction in these two statements, and that each is justified, according as we take the point of view of the ordinary onlooker or of the impassioned lover eager to give a final proof of his or her devotion. It must be added that from a scientific point of view we are not entitled to take either side.

Of the whole of this group of phenomena, the most typical and the most widespread example is certainly the kiss. We have in the lips a highly sensitive frontier region between skin and mucous membrane, in many respects analogous to the vulvo-vaginal orifice, and reinforcible, moreover, by the active movements of the still more highly sensitive tongue. Close and prolonged contact of these regions, therefore, under conditions favorable to tumescence sets up a powerful current of nervous stimulation. After those contacts in which the sexual regions themselves take a direct part, there is certainly no such channel for directing nervous force into the sexual sphere as the kiss. This is nowhere so well recognized as in France, where a young girl's lips are religiously kept for her lover, to such an extent, indeed, that young girls sometimes come to believe that the whole physical side of love is comprehended in a kiss on the mouth; so highly intelligent a woman as Madame Adam has described the agony she felt as a girl when kissed on the lips by a man, owing to the conviction that she had thereby lost her virture. Although the lips occupy this highly important position as a secondary sexual focus in the sphere of touch, the kiss is—unlike *cunnilingus* and *fellatio*—confined to man and, indeed, to a large extent, to civilized man. It is the outcome of a compound evolution which had its beginning outside the sphere of touch, and it would therefore be out of place to deal with the interesting question of its development in this place. It will be discussed elsewhere.[1]

There is yet another orificial frontier region which is a highly important tactile sexual focus: the nipple. The breasts raise, indeed, several interesting questions in their intimate connection with the sexual sphere and it may be worth while to consider them at this point.

The breasts have from the present point of view this special significance among the sexual centres that they primarily exist, not for the contact of the lover, but the contact of the child. This is doubtless, indeed, the fundamental fact on which all the touch contacts we are here concerned with have grown up. The sexual sensitivity of the lover's lips to orificial contacts has been developed from the sensitivity of the infant's lips to contact with his mother's nipple. It is on the ground of that evolution that we are bound to consider here the precise position of the breasts as a sexual centre.

As the great secreting organs of milk, the function of the breasts must begin immediately the child is cut off from the nutrition derived from direct contact with his mother's blood. It is therefore essential that the connection between the sexual organs proper, more especially the womb, and the breasts should be exceedingly intimate, so that the breasts may be in a condition to respond adequately to the demand of the child's sucking lips at the earliest moment after birth. As a matter of fact, this connection is very intimate, so intimate that it takes place in two totally distinct ways—by the nervous system and by the blood.

---

[1] See Appendix A: "The Origins of the Kiss."

The breasts of young girls sometimes become tender at puberty in sympathy with the evolution of the sexual organs, although the swelling of the breasts at this period is not normally a glandular process. At the recurring periods of menstruation, again, sensations in the breasts are not uncommon.

It is not, however, until impregnation occurs that really decisive changes take place in the breasts. "As soon as the ovum is impregnated, that is to say within a few days," as W. D. A. Griffith states it ("The Diagnosis of Pregnancy," *British Medical Journal*, April 11, 1903), "the changes begin to occur in the breast, changes which are just as well worked out as are the changes in the uterus and the vagina, which, from the commencement of pregnancy, prepare for the labor which ought to follow nine months afterward. These are changes in the direction of marked activity of function. An organ which was previously quite passive, without activity of circulation and the effects of active circulation, begins to grow and continues to grow in activity and size as pregnancy progresses."

The association between breasts and womb is so obvious that it has not escaped many savage peoples, who are often, indeed, excellent observers. Among one primitive people at least the activity of the breast at impregnation seems to be clearly recognized. The Sinangolo of British New Guinea, says Seligmann (*Journal of the Anthropological Institute*, July-December, 1902, p. 298) believe that conception takes place in the breasts; on this account they hold that coitus should never take place before the child is weaned or he might imbibe semen with the milk.

It is natural to assume that this connection between the activity of the womb and the glandular activity of the breasts is a nervous connection, by means of the spinal cord, and such a connection certainly exists and plays a very important part in the stimulating action of the breasts on the sexual organs. But that there is a more direct channel of communication even than the nervous system is shown by the fact that the secretion of milk will take place at parturition, even when the nervous connection has been destroyed. Mironoff found that, when the mammary gland is completely separated from the central nervous system, secretion, though slightly diminished, still continued. In two goats he cut the nerves shortly before parturition and after birth the breasts still swelled and functioned normally (*Archives des Sciences Biologiques*, St. Petersburg, 1895, summarized in *L'Année Biologique;* 1895, p. 329). Ribbert, again, cut out the mammary gland of a young rabbit and transplanted it into the ear; five months after the rabbit bore young and the gland secreted milk freely. The case has been reported of a woman whose spinal cord was destroyed by an accident at the level of the fifth and sixth dorsal vertebræ, yet lactation was perfectly normal (*British Medical Journal*, August 5, 1899, p. 374). We are driven to suppose that there is some chemical change in the blood, some internal secretion from the uterus or the ovaries, which acts as a direct stimulant to the breasts. (See a comprehensive discussion of the phenomena of the connection between the breasts and sexual organs, though the conclusions are not unassailable, by Temesvary, *Journal of Obstetrics and Gynæcology of the British Empire*, June, 1903). That this hypothetical secretion starts from the womb rather than the ovaries seems to be indicated by the fact that removal of both ovaries during pregnancy will not suffice to prevent lactation. In favor of the ovaries, see Beatson, *Lancet*, July, 1896; in favor of the uterus, Armand Routh, "On the Interaction between the Ovaries and the Mammary Glands," *British Medical Journal*, September 30, 1899).

While, however, the communications from the sexual organs to the breast are of a complex and at present ill understood character, the communication from the breasts to the sexual organs is without doubt mainly and chiefly nervous. When the child is put to the breast after birth the suction of the nipple causes a reflex contraction of the womb, and it is held by many, though not all, authorities that in a woman who does not suckle her child there is some risk that the womb will not return to its normal involuted size. It has also been asserted that to put a child to the breast during the early months of pregnancy causes so great a degree of uterine contraction that abortion may result.

Freund found in Germany that stimulation of the nipples by an electrical cupping apparatus brought about contraction of the pregnant uterus. At an earlier period it was recommended to irritate the nipple in order to excite the uterus to parturient action. Simpson, while pointing out that this was scarcely adequate to produce the effect desired, thought that placing a child to the breast after labor had begun might increase uterine action. (J. Y. Simpson, *Obstetric Memoirs*, vol i, p. 836; also Féré, *L'Instinct Sexuel*, second edition, p. 132).

The influence of lactation over the womb in preventing the return of menstruation during its continuance is well known. According to Remfry's investigation of 900 cases in England, in 57 per cent. of cases there is no menstruation during lactation. (L. Remfry, in paper read before Obstetrical Society of London, summarized in the *British Medical Journal*, January 11, 1896, p. 86). Bendix, in Germany, found among

140 cases that in about 40 per cent. there was no menstruation during lactation (paper read before Düsseldorf meeting of the Society of German Naturalists and Physicians, 1899). When the child is not suckled menstruation tends to reappear about six months after parturition.

It is possible that the divergent opinions of authorities concerning the necessarily favorable influence of lactation in promoting the return of the womb to its normal size may be due to a confusion of two distinct influences: the reflex action of the nipple on the womb and the effects of prolonged glandular secretion of the breasts in debilitated persons. The act of suckling undoubtedly tends to promote uterine contraction, and in healthy women during lactation the womb may even (according to Vineberg) be temporarily reduced to a smaller size than before impregnation, thus producing what is known as "lactation atrophy." In debilitated women, however, the strain of milk-production may lead to general lack of muscular tone, and involution of the womb thus be hindered rather than aided by lactation.

On the objective side, then, the nipple is to be regarded as an erectile organ, richly supplied with nerves and vessels, which, under the stimulation of the infant's lips—or any similar compression, and even under the influence of emotion or cold,—becomes firm and projects, mainly as a result of muscular contraction; for, unlike the penis and the clitoris, the nipple contains no true erectile tissue and little capacity for vascular engorgement.[1] We must then suppose that an impetus tends to be transmitted through the spinal cord to the sexual organs, setting up a greater or less degree of nervous and muscular excitement with uterine contraction. These being the objective manifestations, what manifestations are to be noted on the subjective side?

It is a remarkable proof of the general indifference with which in Europe even the fairly constant and prominent characteristics of the psychology of women have been treated until recent times that, so far as I am aware,—though I have made no special research to this end,—no one before the end of the eighteenth century had recorded the fact that the act of suckling tends to produce in women voluptuous sexual emo-

---

[1] See J. B. Hellier, "On the Nipple Reflex," *British Medical Journal*, November 7, 1896.

tions. Cabanis in 1802, in the memoir on "Influence des Sexes" in his *Rapports du Physique et du Moral de l'Homme*, wrote that several suckling women had told him that the child in sucking the breast made them experience a vivid sensation of pleasure, shared in some degree by the sexual organs. There can be no doubt that in healthy suckling women this phenomenon is exceedingly common, though in the absence of any methodical and precise investigation it cannot be affirmed that it is experienced by every woman in some degree, and it is highly probable that this is not the case. One lady, perfectly normal, states that she has had stronger sexual feelings in suckling her children than she has ever experienced with her husband, but that so far as possible she has tried to repress them, as she regards them as brutish under these circumstances. Many other women state generally that suckling is the most delicious physical feeling they have ever experienced. In most cases, however, it does not appear to lead to a desire for intercourse, and some of those who make this statement have no desire for coitus during lactation, though they may have strong sexual needs at other times. It is probable that this corresponds to the normal condition, and that the voluptuous sensations aroused by suckling are adequately gratified by the child. It may be added that there are probably many women who could say, with a lady quoted by Féré,[1] that the only real pleasures of sex they have ever known are those derived from their suckling infants.

It is not difficult to see why this normal association of sexual emotion with suckling should have come about. It is essential for the preservation of the lives of young mammals that the mothers should have an adequate motive in pleasurable sensation for enduring the trouble of suckling. The most obvious method for obtaining the necessary degree of pleasurable sensation lay in utilizing the reservoir of sexual emotion, with which channels of communication might already be said to be open through the action of the sexual organs on the breasts

---

[1] Féré, *L'Instinct Sexuel*, second edition, p. 147.

during pregnancy. The voluptuous element in suckling may thus be called a merciful provision of Nature for securing the maintenance of the child.

Cabanis seems to have realized the significance of this connection as the basis of the sympathy between mother and child, and more recently Lombroso and Ferrero have remarked (*La Donna Delinquente*, p. 438) on the fact that maternal love has a sexual basis in the element of venereal pleasure, though usually inconsiderable, experienced during suckling. Houzeau has referred to the fact that in the majority of animals the relation between mother and offspring is only close during the period of lactation, and this is certainly connected with the fact that it is only during lactation that the female animal can derive physical gratification from her offspring. When living on a farm I have ascertained that cows sometimes, though not frequently, exhibit slight signs of sexual excitement, with secretion of mucus, while being milked; so that, as the dairymaid herself observed, it is as if they were being "bulled." The sow, like some other mammals, often eats her own young after birth, mistaking them, it is thought, for the placenta, which is normally eaten by most mammals; it is said that the sow never eats her young when they have once taken the teat.

It occasionally happens that this normal tendency for suckling to produce voluptuous sexual emotions is present in an extreme degree, and may lead to sexual perversions. It does not appear that the sexual sensations aroused by suckling usually culminate in the orgasm; this however, was noted in a case recorded by Féré, of a slightly neurotic woman in whom intense sexual excitement occurred during suckling, especially if prolonged; so far as possible, she shortened the periods of suckling in order to prevent, not always successfully, the occurrence of the orgasm (Féré, *Archives de Neurologie* No. 30, 1903). Icard refers to the case of a woman who sought to become pregnant solely for the sake of the voluptuous sensations she derived from suckling, and Yellowlees (Art. "Masturbation," *Dictionary of Psychological Medicine*) speaks of the overwhelming character of "the storms of sexual feeling sometimes observed during lactation."

It may be remarked that the frequency of the association between lactation and the sexual sensations is indicated by the fact that, as Savage remarks, lactational insanity is often accompanied by fancies regarding the reproductive organs.

When we have realized the special sensitivity of the orificial regions and the peculiarly close relationships between the breasts and the sexual organs we may easily understand the considerable part which they normally play in the art of love.

As one of the chief secondary sexual characters in women, and one of her chief beauties, a woman's breasts offer themselves to the lover's lips with a less intimate attraction than her mouth only because the mouth is better able to respond. On her side, such contact is often instinctively desired. Just as the sexual disturbance of pregnancy is accompanied by a sympathetic disturbance in the breasts, so the sexual excitement produced by the lover's proximity reacts on the breasts; the nipple becomes turgid and erect in sympathy with the clitoris; the woman craves to place her lover in the place of the child, and experiences a sensation in which these two supreme objects of her desire are deliciously mingled.

The powerful effect which stimulation of the nipple produces on the sexual sphere has led to the breasts playing a prominent part in the erotic art of those lands in which this art has been most carefully cultivated. Thus in India, according to Vatsyayana, many authors are of the opinion that in approaching a woman a lover should begin by sucking the nipples of her breasts, and in the songs of the Bayaderes of Southern India sucking the nipple is mentioned as one of the natural preliminaries of coitus.

In some cases, and more especially in neurotic persons, the sexual pleasure derived from manipulation of the nipple passes normal limits and, being preferred even to coitus, becomes a perversion. In girls' schools, it is said, especially in France, sucking and titillation of the breasts are not uncommon; in men, also, titillation of the nipples occasionally produces sexual sensations (Féré, *L'Instinct Sexuel*, second edition, p. 132). Hildebrandt recorded the case of a young woman whose nipples had been sucked by her lover; by constantly drawing her breasts she became able to suck them herself and thus attained extreme sexual pleasure. A. J. Bloch, of New Orleans, has noted the case of a woman who complained of swelling of the breasts; the gentlest manipulation produced an orgasm, and it was found that the swelling had been intentionally produced for the sake of this manipulation. Moraglia in Italy knew a very beautiful woman who was perfectly cold in normal sexual relationships, but madly excited when her husband pressed or sucked her breasts. Lombroso (*Archivio di Psichiatria*, 1885, fasc. IV) has described the somewhat similar case of a woman who had no sexual sensitivity in the clitoris, vagina, or labia, and no pleasure in coitus except in very strange positions, but possessed intense sexual feelings in the right nipple as well as in the upper third of the thigh.

It is remarkable that not only is suckling apt to be accompanied by sexual pleasure in the mother, but that, in some cases, the infant also appears to have a somewhat similar experience. This is, at all events, indicated in a remarkable case recorded by Féré (*L'Instinct Sexual*, second edition, p. 257). A female infant child of slightly neurotic heredity was weaned at the age of 14 months, but so great was her affection for her mother's breasts, though she had already become accustomed to other food, that this was only accomplished with great difficulty and by allowing her still to caress the naked breasts several times a day. This went on for many months, when the mother, becoming again pregnant, insisted on putting an end to it. So jealous was the child, however, that it was necessary to conceal from her the fact that her younger sister was suckled at her mother's breasts, and once at the age of 3, when she saw her father aiding her mother to undress, she became violently jealous of him. This jealousy, as well as the passion for her mother's breasts, persisted to the age of puberty, though she learned to conceal it. At the age of 13, when menstruation began, she noticed in dancing with her favorite girl friends that when her breasts came in contact with theirs she experienced a very agreeable sensation, with erection of the nipples; but it was not till the age of 16 that she observed that the sexual region took part in this excitement and became moist. From this period she had erotic dreams about young girls. She never experienced any attraction for young men, but eventually married; though having much esteem and affection for her husband, she never felt any but the slightest sexual enjoyment in his arms, and then only by evoking feminine images. This case, in which the sensations of an infant at the breast formed the point of departure of a sexual perversion which lasted through life, is, so far as I am aware, unique.

IV.

The Bath—Antagonism of Primitive Christianity to the Cult of the Skin—Its Cult of Personal Filth—The Reasons which Justified this Attitude—The World-wide Tendency to Association between Extreme Cleanliness and Sexual Licentiousness—The Immorality Associated with Public Baths in Europe down to Modern Times.

THE hygiene of the skin, as well as its special cult, consists in bathing. The bath, as is well known, attained under the Romans a degree of development which, in Europe at all events, it has never reached before or since, and the modern visitor to Rome carries away with him no more impressive memory than that of the Baths of Caracalla. Since the coming of Christianity the cult of the skin, and even its hygiene, have never again attained the same general and unquestioned exaltation. The Church killed the bath. St. Jerome tells us with approval that when the holy Paula noted that any of her nuns were too careful in this matter she would gravely reprove them, saying that "the purity of the body and its garments means the impurity of the soul."[1] Or, as the modern monk of Mount Athos still declares: "A man should live in dirt as in a coat of mail, so that his soul may sojourn more securely within."

Our knowledge of the bathing arrangements of Roman days is chiefly derived from Pompeii. Three public baths (two for both men and women, who were also probably allowed to use the third occasionally) have so far been excavated in this small town, as well as at least three private bathing establishments (at least one of them for women), while about a dozen houses contain complete baths for private use. Even in a little farm house at Boscoreale (two miles out of Pompeii) there was an elaborate series of bathing rooms. It may be added that Pompeii was well supplied with water. All houses but the poorest had

---

[1] *"Dicens munditiam corporis atque vestitus animæ esse immunditiam."*—St. Jerome, *Ad Eustochium Virginem.*

flowing jets, and some houses had as many as ten jets. (See Mau's *Pompeii*, Chapters XXVI-XXVIII.)

The Church succeeded to the domination of imperial Rome, and adopted many of the methods of its predecessor. But there could be no greater contrast than is presented by the attitude of Paganism and of Christianity toward the bath.

As regards the tendencies of the public baths in imperial Rome, some of the evidence is brought together in the section on this subject in Rosenbaum's *Geschichte der Lustseuche im Alterthume*. As regards the attitude of the earliest Christian ascetics in this matter I may refer the reader to an interesting passage in Lecky's *History of European Morals* (vol. ii, pp. 107-112), in which are brought together a number of highly instructive examples of the manner in which many of the most eminent of the early saints deliberately cultivated personal filth.

In the middle ages, when the extreme excesses of the early ascetics had died out, and monasticism became regulated, monks generally took two baths a year when in health; in illness they could be taken as often as necessary. The rules of Cluny only allowed three towels to the community: one for the novices, one for the professed, and one for the lay brothers. At the end of the seventeenth century Madame de Mazarin, having retired to a convent of Visitandines, one day desired to wash her feet, but the whole establishment was set in an uproar at such an idea, and she received a direct refusal. In 1760 the Dominican Richard wrote that in itself the bath is permissible, but it must be taken solely for necessity, not for pleasure. The Church taught, and this lesson is still inculcated in convent schools, that it is wrong to expose the body even to one's own gaze, and it is not surprising that many holy persons boasted that they had never even washed their hands. (Most of these facts have been taken from A. Franklin, *Les Soins de Toilette*, one of the *Vie Privée d'Autrefois* series, in which further details may be found.)

In sixteenth-century Italy, a land of supreme elegance and fashion, superior even to France, the conditions were the same, and how little water found favor even with aristocratic ladies we may gather from the contemporary books on the toilet, which abound with recipes against itch and similar diseases. It should be added that Burckhardt (*Die Cultur der Renaissance in Italien*, eighth edition, volume ii, p. 92) considers that in spite of skin diseases the Italians of the Renaissance were the first nation in Europe for cleanliness.

It is unnecessary to consider the state of things in other European countries. The aristocratic conditions of former days are the plebeian conditions of to-day. So far as England is concerned, such documents as Chadwick's *Report on the Sanitary Condition of the Labouring Popu-*

lution of Great Britain (1842) sufficiently illustrate the ideas and the practices as regards personal cleanliness which prevailed among the masses during the nineteenth century and which to a large extent still prevail.

A considerable amount of opprobrium has been cast upon the Catholic Church for its direct and indirect influence in promoting bodily uncleanliness. Nietzsche sarcastically refers to the facts, and Mr. Frederick Harrison asserts that "the tone of the middle ages in the matter of dirt was a form of mental disease." It would be easy to quote many other authors to the same effect.

It is necessary to point out, however, that the writers who have committed themselves to such utterances have not only done an injustice to Christianity, but have shown a lack of historical insight. Christianity was essentially and fundamentally a rebellion against the classic world, against its vices, and against their concomitant virtues, against both its practices and its ideals. It sprang up in a different part of the Mediterranean basin, from a different level of culture; it found its supporters in a new and lower social stratum. The cult of charity, simplicity, and faith, while not primarily ascetic, became inevitably allied with asceticism, because from its point of view sexuality was the very stronghold of the classic world. In the second century the genius of Clement of Alexandria and of the great Christian thinkers who followed him seized on all those elements in classic life and philosophy which could be amalgamated with Christianity without, as they trusted, destroying its essence, but in the matter of sexuality there could be no compromise, and the condemnation of sexuality involved the condemnation of the bath. It required very little insight and sagacity for the Christians to see—though we are now apt to slur over the fact—that the cult of the bath was in very truth the cult of the flesh.[1] However profound their ignorance

---

[1] With regard to the physiological mechanism by which bathing produces its tonic and stimulating effects Woods Hutchinson has an interesting discussion (Chapter VII) in his *Studies in Human and Comparative Pathology*.

of anatomy, physiology, and psychology might be, they had before them ample evidence to show that the skin is an outlying sexual zone and that every application which promoted the purity, brilliance, and healthfulness of the skin constituted a direct appeal, feeble or strong as the case might be, to those passions against which they were warring. The moral was evident: better let the temporary garment of your flesh be soaked with dirt than risk staining the radiant purity of your immortal soul. If Christianity had not drawn that moral with clear insight and relentless logic Christianity would never have been a great force in the world.

If any doubt is felt as to the really essential character of the connection between cleanliness and the sexual impulse it may be dispelled by the consideration that the association is by no means confined to Christian Europe. If we go outside Europe and even Christendom altogether, to the other side of the world, we find it still well marked. The wantonness of the luxurious people of Tahiti when first discovered by European voyagers is notorious. The Areoi of Tahiti, a society largely constituted on a basis of debauchery, is a unique institution so far as primitive peoples are concerned. Cook, after giving one of the earliest descriptions of this society and its objects at Tahiti (Hawkesworth, *An Account of Voyages*, etc., 1775, vol. ii, p. 55), immediately goes on to describe the extreme and scrupulous cleanliness of the people of Tahiti in every respect; they not only bathed their bodies and clothes every day, but in all respects they carried cleanliness to a higher point than even "the politest assembly in Europe." Another traveler bears similar testimony: "The inhabitants of the Society Isles are, among all the nations of the South Seas, the most cleanly; and the better sort of them carry cleanliness to a very great length"; they bathe morning and evening in the sea, he remarks, and afterward in fresh water to remove the particles of salt, wash their hands before and after meals, etc. (J. R. Forster, *"Observations made during a Voyage round the World,"* 1798, p. 398.) And William Ellis, in his detailed description of the people of Tahiti (*Polynesian Researches*, 1832, vol. i, especially Chapters VI and IX), while emphasizing their extreme cleanliness, every person of every class bathing at least once or twice a day, dwells on what he considers their unspeakable moral debasement; "notwithstanding the apparent mildness of their disposition and the cheerful vivacity of their conversation, no portion of the human race was ever perhaps sunk lower in brutal licentiousness and moral degradation."

After leaving Tahiti Cook went on to New Zealand. Here he found that the people were more virtuous than at Tahiti, and also, he found, less clean.

It is, however, a mistake to suppose that physical uncleanliness ruled supreme through mediæval and later times. It is true that the eighteenth century, which saw the birth of so much that marks our modern world, witnessed a revival of the old ideal of bodily purity. But the struggle between two opposing ideals had been carried on for a thousand years or more before this. The Church, indeed, was in this matter founded on an impregnable rock. But there never has been a time when influences outside the Church have not found a shelter somewhere. Those traditions of the classic world which Christianity threw aside as useless or worse quietly reappeared. In no respect was this more notably the case than in regard to the love of pure water and the cult of the bath. Islam adopted the complete Roman bath, and made it an institution of daily life, a necessity for all classes. Granada is the spot in Europe where to-day we find the most exquisite remains of Mohammedan culture, and, though the fury of Christian conquest dragged the harrow over the soil of Granada, even yet streams and fountains spring up there and gush abundantly and one seldom loses the sound of the plash of water. The flower of Christian chivalry and Christian intelligence went to Palestine to wrest the Holy Sepulchre from the hands of pagan Mohammedans. They found there many excellent things which they had not gone out to seek, and the Crusaders produced a kind of premature and abortive Renaissance, the shadow of lost classic things reflected on Christian Europe from the mirror of Islam.

Yet it is worth while to point out, as bearing on the associations of the bath here emphasized, that even in Islam we may trace the existence of a religious attitude unfavorable to the bath. Before the time of Mohammed there were no public baths in Arabia, and it was and is believed that baths are specially haunted by the djinn—the evil spirits. Mohammed himself was at first so prejudiced against public baths that he forbade both men and women to enter them. Afterward, however, he permitted men to use them provided they wore a cloth round the loins, and women also when they could not conveniently bathe at home. Among the Prophet's sayings is found the assertion: "Whatever woman enters a bath the devil is with her," and "All the earth is given to me as a place of prayer, and as pure, except the burial ground and the bath." (See, *e.g.*, E. W. Lane, *Arabian Society in the Middle Ages*, 1883, pp. 179-183.) Although, therefore, the bath, or *hammam*, on grounds of ritual ablution, hygiene, and enjoyment speedily became universally popular in Islam among all classes and both sexes, Mohammed himself may be said to have opposed it.

Among the discoveries which the Crusaders made and brought home with them one of the most notable was that of the bath, which in its more elaborate forms seems to have been absolutely forgottten in Europe, though Roman baths might everywhere have been found underground. All authorities seem to be agreed in finding here the origin of the revival of the public bath. It is to Rome first, and later to Islam, the lineal inheritor of classic culture, that we owe the cult of water and of physical purity. Even to-day the Turkish bath, which is the most popular of elaborate methods of bathing, recalls by its characteristics and its name the fact that it is a Mohammedan survival of Roman life.

From the twelfth century onward baths have repeatedly been introduced from the East, and reintroduced afresh in slightly modified forms, and have flourished with varying degrees of success. In the thirteenth century they were very common, especially in Paris, and though they were often used, more especially in Germany, by both sexes in common, every effort was made to keep them orderly and respectable. These efforts were, however, always unsuccessful in the end. A bath always tended in the end to become a brothel, and hence either became unfashionable or was suppressed by the authorities. It is sufficient to refer to the reputation in England of "hothouses" and "bagnios." It was not until toward the end of the eighteenth century that it began to be recognized that the claims of physical cleanliness were sufficiently imperative to make it necessary that the fairly avoidable risks to morality in bathing should be avoided and the unavoidable risks bravely incurred. At the present day, now that we are accustomed to weave ingeniously together in the texture of our lives the conflicting traditions of classic and Christian days, we have almost persuaded ourselves that the pagan virtue of cleanliness comes next after godliness, and we bathe, forgetful of the great moral struggle which once went on around the bath. But we refrain from building ourselves palaces to bathe in, and for the most part we bathe with exceeding moderation.[1] It is probable that we may best harmonize our conflicting traditions by rejecting not only the Christian glorification of dirt, but also, save for definitely therapeutic purposes, the excessive heat, friction, and stimulation involved by the classic forms of bathing. Our reasonable ideal should render it easy and natural for every man, woman, and child to have a simple bath, tepid in winter, cold in summer, all the year round.

For the history of the bath in mediæval times and later Europe, see A. Franklin, *Les Soins de Toilette*, in the *Vie Privée d'Autrefois* series; Rudeck, *Geschichte der öffentlichen Sittlichkeit in Deutschland;* T. Wright, *The Homes of Other Days;* E. Dühren, *Das Geschlechtsleben in England*, bd. 1.

Outside the Church, there was a greater amount of cleanliness than we are sometimes apt to suppose. It may, indeed, be said that the uncleanliness of holy men and women would have attracted no attention if it had corresponded to the condition generally prevailing. Before public baths were established bathing in private was certainly practiced; thus Ordericus Vitalis, in narrating the murder of Mabel, the Countess de Montgomery, in Normandy in 1082, casually mentions that she was lying on the bed after her bath (*Ecclesiastical History*, Book V, Chapter XIII). In warm weather, it would appear, mediæval ladies bathed in streams, as we may still see countrywomen do in Russia, Bohemia, and occasionally nearer home. The statement of the historian Michelet, therefore, that Percival, Iseult, and the other ethereal personages of mediæval times "certainly never washed" (*La Sorcière*, p. 110) requires some qualification.

In 1292 there were twenty-six bathing establishments in Paris, and an attendant would go through the streets in the morning announcing that they were ready. One could have a vapor bath only or a hot bath to succeed it, as in the East. No woman of bad reputation,

---

[1] Thus among the young women admitted to the Chicago Normal School to be trained as teachers, Miss Lura Sanborn, the director of physical training, states (*Doctor's Magazine*, December, 1900) that a bath once a fortnight is found to be not unusual.

leper, or vagabond was at this time allowed to frequent the baths, which were closed on Sundays and feast-days. By the fourteenth century, however, the baths began to have a reputation for immorality, as well as luxury, and, according to Dufour, the baths of Paris "rivaled those of imperial Rome: love, prostitution, and debauchery attracted the majority to the bathing establishments, where everything was covered by a decent veil." He adds that, notwithstanding the scandal thus caused and the invectives of preachers, all went to the baths, young and old, rich and poor, and he makes the statement, which seems to echo the constant assertion of the early Fathers, that "a woman who frequented the baths returned home physically pure only at the expense of her moral purity."

In Germany there was even greater freedom of manners in bathing, though, it would seem, less real licentiousness. Even the smallest towns had their baths, which were frequented by all classes. As soon as the horn blew to announce that the baths were ready all hastened along the street, the poorer folk almost completely undressing themselves before leaving their homes. Bathing was nearly always in common without any garment being worn, women attendants commonly rubbed and massaged both sexes, and the dressing room was frequently used by men and women in common; this led to obvious evils. The Germans, as Weinhold points out (*Die Deutschen Frauen im Mittelalter*, 1882, bd. ii, pp. 112 *et seq.*), have been fond of bathing in the open air in streams from the days of Tacitus and Cæsar until comparatively modern times, when the police have interfered. It was the same in Switzerland. Poggio, early in the sixteenth century, found it the custom for men and women to bathe together at Baden, and said that he seemed to be assisting at the *floralia* of ancient Rome, or in Plato's Republic. Sénancour, who quotes the passage (*De l'Amour*, 1834, vol. i, p. 313), remarks that at the beginning of the nineteenth century there was still great liberty at the Baden baths.

Of the thirteenth century in England Thomas Wright (*Homes of Other Days*, 1871, p. 271) remarks: "The practice of warm bathing prevailed very generally in all classes of society, and is frequently alluded to in the mediæval romances and stories. For this purpose a large bathing-tub was used. People sometimes bathed immediately after rising in the morning, and we find the bath used after dinner and before going to bed. A bath was also often prepared for a visitor on his arrival from a journey; and, what seems still more singular, in the numerous stories of amorous intrigues the two lovers usually began their interviews by bathing together."

In England the association between bathing and immorality was established with special rapidity and thoroughness. Baths were here officially recognized as brothels, and this as early as the twelfth century, under Henry II. These organized bath-brothels were confined to Southwark, outside the walls of the city, a quarter which was also given up to various sports and amusements. At a later period, "hot-houses," bagnios, and hummums (the eastern *hammam*) were spread all over London and remained closely identified with prostitution, these names, indeed, constantly tending to become synonymous with brothels. (T. Wright, *Homes of Other Days*, 1871, pp. 494-496, gives an account of them.)

In France the baths, being anathematized by both Catholics and Huguenots, began to lose vogue and disappear. "Morality gained," remarks Franklin, "but cleanliness lost." Even the charming and elegant Margaret of Navarre found it quite natural for a lady to mention incidentally to her lover that she had not washed her hands for a week. Then began an extreme tendency to use cosmetics, essences, perfumes, and a fierce war with vermin, up to the seventeenth century, when some progress was made, and persons who desired to be very elegant and refined were recommended to wash their faces "nearly every day." Even in 1782, however, while a linen cloth was advised for the purpose of cleaning the face and hands, the use of water was still somewhat discountenanced. The use of hot and cold baths was now, however, beginning to be established in Paris and elsewhere, and the bathing establishments at the great European health resorts were also beginning to be put on the orderly footing which is now customary. When Casanova, in the middle of the eighteenth century, went to the public baths at Berne he was evidently somewhat surprised when he found that he was invited to choose his own attendant from a number of young women, and when he realized that these attendants were, in all respects, at the disposition of the bathers. It is evident that establishments of this kind were then already dying out, although it may be added that the customs described by Casanova appear to have persisted in Budapest and St. Petersburg almost or quite up to the present. The great European public baths have long been above suspicion in this respect (though homosexual practices are not quite excluded), while it is well recognized that many kinds of hot baths now in u-e produce a powerfully stimulating action upon the sexual system, and patients taking such baths for medical purposes are frequently warned against giving way to these influences.

The struggle which in former ages went on around bathing establishments has now been in part transferred to massage establishments. Massage is an equally powerful stimulant to the skin and the sexual sphere,—acting mainly by friction instead of mainly by heat,—and it has not yet attained that position of general recognition and popularity which, in the case of bathing establishments, renders it bad policy to court disrepute.

Like bathing, massage is a hygienic and therapeutic method of influencing the skin and subjacent tissues which, together with its advantages, has certain concomitant disadvantages in its liability to affect the sexual sphere. This influence is apt to be experienced by individuals of both sexes, though it is perhaps specially marked in women. Jouin (quoted in Paris *Journal de Médecine*, April 23, 1893) found that of 20 women treated by massage, of whom he made inquiries, 14 declared that they experienced voluptuous sensations; 8 of these belonged to respectable families; the other 6 were women of the *demimonde* and gave precise details; Jouin refers in this connection to the *aliptes* of Rome. It is unnecessary to add that the gynæcological massage introduced in recent years by the Swedish teacher of gymnastics, Thure-Brandt, as involving prolonged rubbing and kneading of the pelvic regions, *"pression glissante du vagin,"* etc. (*Massage Gynéeologique*, by G. de Frumerie, 1897), whatever its therapeutic value, cannot fail in a large proportion of cases to stimulate the sexual emotions. (Eulenburg remarks that for sexual anæsthesia in women the Thure-Brandt system of massage may "naturally" be recommended, *Sexuale Neuropathie*, p. 78.) I have been informed that in London and elsewhere massage establishments are sometimes visited by women who seek sexual gratification by massage of the genital regions by the *masseuse.*

V.

Summary—Fundamental Importance of Touch—The Skin the Mother of All the Other Senses.

THE sense of touch is so universally diffused over the whole skin, and in so many various degrees and modifications, and it is, moreover, so truly the Alpha and the Omega of affection, that a broken and fragmentary treatment of the subject has been inevitable.

The skin is the archæological field of human and prehuman experience, the foundation on which all forms of sensory perception have grown up, and as sexual sensibility is among the most ancient of all forms of sensibility, the sexual instinct is necessarily, in the main, a comparatively slightly modified form of general touch sensibility. This primitive character of the great region of tactile sensation, its vagueness and diffusion, the comparatively unintellectual as well as unæsthetic nature of the mental conceptions which arise on the tactile basis make it difficult to deal precisely with the psychology of touch. The very same qualities, however, serve greatly to heighten the emotional intensity of skin sensations. So that, of all the great sensory fields, the field of touch is at once the least intellectual and the most massively emotional. These qualities, as well as its intimate and primitive association with the apparatus of tumescence and detumescence, make touch the readiest and most powerful channel by which the sexual sphere may be reached.

In disentangling the phenomena of tactile sensibility ticklishness has been selected for special consideration as a kind of sensation, founded on reflexes developing even before birth, which is very closely related to sexual phenomena. It is, as it were, a play of tumescence, on which laughter supervenes as a play of detumescence. It leads on to the more serious phenomena of tumescence, and it tends to die out after adolescence,

(41)

at the period during which sexual relationships normally begin. Such a view of ticklishness, as a kind of modesty of the skin, existing merely to be destroyed, need only be regarded as one of its aspects. Ticklishness certainly arose from a nonsexual starting-point, and may well have protective uses in the young animal.

The readiness with which tactile sensibility takes on a sexual character and forms reflex channels of communication with the sexual sphere proper is illustrated by the existence of certain secondary sexual foci only inferior in sexual excitability to the genital region. We have seen that the chief of these normal foci are situated in the orificial regions where skin and mucous membrane meet, and that the contact of any two orificial regions between two persons of different sex brought together under favorable conditions is apt, when prolonged, to produce a very intense degree of sexual erethism. This is a normal phenomenon in so far as it is a part of tumescence, and not a method of obtaining detumescence. The kiss is a typical example of these contacts, while the nipple is of special interest in this connection, because we are thereby enabled to bring the psychology of lactation into intimate relationship with the psychology of sexual love.

The extreme sensitiveness of the skin, the readiness with which its stimulation reverberates into the sexual sphere, clearly brought out by the present study, enable us to understand better a very ancient contest—the moral struggle around the bath. There has always been a tendency for the extreme cultivation of physical purity to lead on to the excessive stimulation of the sexual sphere; so that the Christian ascetics were entirely justified, on their premises, in fighting against the bath and in directly or indirectly fostering a cult of physical uncleanliness. While, however, in the past there has clearly been a general tendency for the cult of physical purity to be associated with moral licentiousness, and there are sufficient grounds for such an association, it is important to remember that it is not an inevitable and fatal association; a scrupulously clean person is by no means necessarily impelled to licentiousness; a physically unclean person is by no means necessarily morally pure. When we have eliminated certain forms of the bath which must be regarded as luxuries rather than hygienic necessities, though they occasionally possess therapeutic virtues, we have eliminated the most violent appeals of the bath to the sexual impulse. So imperative are the demands of physical purity now becoming, in general opinion, that such small risks to moral purity as may still remain are constantly and wisely disregarded, and the immoral traditions of the bath now, for the most part, belong to the past.

SMELL.

I.

The Primitiveness of Smell—The Anatomical Seat of the Olfactory Centres.—Predominance of Smell among the Lower Mammals—Its Diminished Importance in Man—The Attention Paid to Odors by Savages.

THE first more highly organized sense to arise on the diffused tactile sensitivity of the skin is, in most cases, without doubt that of smell. At first, indeed, olfactory sensibility is not clearly differentiated from general tactile sensibility; the pit of thickened and ciliated epithelium or the highly mobile antennæ which in many lower animals are sensitive to odorous stimuli are also extremely sensitive to tactile stimuli; this is, for instance, the case with the snail, in whom at the same time olfactive sensibility seems to be spread over the whole body.[1] The sense of smell is gradually specialized, and when taste also begins to develop a kind of chemical sense is constituted. The organ of smell, however, speedily begins to rise in importance as we ascend the zoölogical scale. In the lower vertebrates, when they began to adopt a life on dry land, the sense of smell seems to have been that part of their sensory equipment which proved most useful under the new conditions, and it developed with astonishing rapidity. Edinger finds that in the brain of reptiles the "area olfactoria" is of enormous extent, covering, indeed, the greater part of the cortex, though it may be quite true, as Herrick remarks, that, while smell is preponderant, it is perhaps not correct to attribute an exclusively olfactory tone to the cerebral activities of the *Sauropsida* or even the

---

[1] Émile Yung, "Le Sens Olfactif de l'Escargot (Helix Pomata)," *Archives de Psychologie*, November, 1903.

Ichthyopsida. Among most mammals, however, in any case, smell is certainly the most highly developed of the senses; it gives the first information of remote objects that concern them; it gives the most precise information concerning the near objects that concern them; it is the sense in terms of which most of their mental operations must be conducted and their emotional impulses reach consciousness. Among the apes it has greatly lost importance and in man it has become almost rudimentary, giving place to the supremacy of vision.

Prof. G. Elliot Smith, a leading authority on the brain, has well summarized the facts concerning the predominance of the olfactory region in the mammal brain, and his conclusions may be quoted. It should be premised that Elliot Smith divides the brain into rhinencephalon and neopallium. Rhinencephalon designates the regions which are pre-eminently olfactory in function: the olfactory bulb, its peduncle, the tuberculum olfactorium and locus perforatus, the pyriform lobe, the paraterminal body, and the whole hippocampal formation. The neopallium is the dorsal cap of the brain, with frontal, parietal, and occipital areas, comprehending all that part of the brain which is the seat of the higher associative activities, reaching its fullest development in man.

"In the early mammals the olfactory areas form by far the greater part of the cerebral hemisphere, which is not surprising when it is recalled that the forebrain is, in the primitive brain, essentially an appendage, so to speak, of the smell apparatus. When the cerebral hemisphere comes to occupy such a dominant position in the brain it is perhaps not unnatural to find that the sense of smell is the most influential and the chief source of information to the animal; or, perhaps, it would be more accurate to say that the olfactory sense, which conveys general information to the animal such as no other sense can bring concerning its prey (whether near or far, hidden or exposed), is much the most serviceable of all the avenues of information to the lowly mammal leading a terrestrial life, and therefore becomes predominant; and its particular domain—the forebrain—becomes the ruling portion of the nervous system.

"This early predominance of the sense of smell persists in most mammals (unless an aquatic mode of life interferes and deposes it: compare the *Cetacea, Sirenia,* and *Pinnipedia,* for example) even though a large neopallium develops to receive visual, auditory, tactile, and other impressions pouring into the forebrain. In the *Anthropoidea* alone of nonaquatic mammals the olfactory regions undergo an absolute (and not only relative, as in the *Carnivora* and *Ungulata*) dwindling, which is equally shared by the human brain, in common with those of the other *Simiidæ*, the *Cercopithecidæ*, and the *Cebidæ*. But all the parts of the rhinencephalon, which are so distinct in macrosmatic mammals, can also be recognized in the human brain. The small ellipsoidal olfactory bulb is moored, so to speak, on the cribriform plate of the ethmoid bone by the olfactory nerves; so that, as the place of attachment of the olfactory peduncle to the expanding cerebral hemisphere becomes removed (as a result of the forward extension of the hemisphere) progressively farther and farther backward, the peduncle becomes greatly stretched and elongated. And, as this stretching involves the gray matter without lessening the number of nerve-fibres in the olfactory tract, the peduncle becomes practically what it is usually called—*i.e.*, the olfactory 'tract.' The tuberculum olfactorium becomes greatly reduced and at the same time flattened; so that it is not easy to draw a line of demarcation between it and the anterior perforated space. The anterior rhinal fissure, which is present in the early human fœtus, vanishes (almost, if not altogether) in the adult. Part of the posterior rhinal fissure is always present in the 'incisura temporalis,' and sometimes, especially in some of the non-European races, the whole of the posterior rhinal fissure is retained in that typical form which we find in the anthropoid apes." (G. Elliot Smith, in *Descriptive and Illustrated Catalogue of the Physiological Series of Comparative Anatomy Contained in the Museum of the Royal College of Surgeons of England*, second edition, vol. ii.) A full statement of Elliot Smith's investigations, with diagrams, is given by Bullen, *Journal of Mental Science*, July, 1899. It may be added that the whole subject of the olfactory centres has been thoroughly studied by Elliot Smith, as well as by Edinger, Mayer, and C. L. Herrick. In the *Journal of Comparative Neurology*, edited by the last named, numerous discussions and summaries bearing on the subject will be found from 1896 onward. Regarding the primitive sense-organs of smell in the various invertebrate groups some information will be found in A. B. Griffiths's *Physiology of the Invertebrata*, Chapter XI.

The predominance of the olfactory area in the nervous system of the vertebrates generally has inevitably involved intimate psychic associations between olfactory stimuli and the sexual impulse. For most mammals not only are all sexual associations mainly olfactory, but the impressions received by this sense suffice to dominate all others. An animal not only receives adequate sexual excitement from olfactory stimuli, but those stimuli often suffice to counterbalance all the evidence of the other senses.

We may observe this very well in the case of the dog. Thus, a young dog, well known to me, who had never had connection with a bitch, but was always in the society of its father, once met the latter directly after the elder dog had been with a bitch. He immediately endeavored to behave toward the elder dog, in spite of angry repulses, exactly as a dog behaves toward a bitch in heat. The messages received by the sense of smell were sufficiently urgent not only to set the sexual mechanism in action, but to overcome the experiences of a lifetime. There is an interesting chapter on the sense of smell in the mental life of the dog in Giessler's *Psychologie des Geruches*, 1894, Chapter XI. Passy (in the appendix to his memoir on olfaction, *L'Année Psychologique*, 1895) gives the result of some interesting experiments as to the effects of perfume on dogs; civet and castoreum were found to have the most powerfully exciting effect.

The influences of smell are equally omnipotent in the sexual life of many insects. Thus, Féré has found that in cockchafers sexual coupling failed to take place when the antennæ, which are the organs of smell, were removed; he also found that males, after they had coupled with females, proved sexually attractive to other males (*Comptes Rendus de la Société de Biologie*, May 21, 1898). Féré similarly found that, in a species of *Bombyx*, males after contact with females sometimes proved attractive to other males, although no abnormal relationships followed. (*Soc. de Biol*, July 30, 1898.)

With the advent of the higher apes, and especially of man, all this has been changed. The sense of smell, indeed, still persists universally and it is still also exceedingly delicate, though often neglected.[1] It is, moreover, a useful auxiliary in the exploration of the external world, for, in contrast to the very few sensations furnished to us by touch and by taste, we are acquainted with a vast number of smells, though the information they give us is frequently vague. An experienced perfumer, says Piesse, will have two hundred odors in his laboratory and can distinguish them all. To a sensitive nose nearly everything smells. Passy goes so far as to state that he has "never met with any object that is really inodorous when one pays attention to it, not even excepting glass," and, though we can scarcely accept this statement absolutely,—especially in

---

[1] The sensitiveness of smell in man generally exceeds that of chemical reaction or even of spectral analysis; see Passy, *L'Année Psychologique*, second year, 1895, p. 380.

view of the careful experiments of Ayrton, which show that, contrary to a common belief, metals when perfectly clean and free from traces of contact with the skin or with salt solutions have no smell,—odor is still extremely widely diffused. This is especially the case in hot countries, and the experiments of the Cambridge Anthropological Expedition on the sense of smell of the Papuans were considerably impeded by the fact that at Torres Straits everything, even water, seemed to have a smell. Savages are often accused more or less justly of indifference to bad odors. They are very often, however, keenly alive to the significance of smells and their varieties, though it does not appear that the sense of smell is notably more developed in savage than in civilized peoples. Odors also continue to play a part in the emotional life of man, more especially in hot countries. Nevertheless both in practical life and in emotional life, in science and in art, smell is, at the best, under normal conditions, merely an auxiliary. If the sense of smell were abolished altogether the life of mankind would continue as before, with little or no sensible modification, though the pleasures of life, and especially of eating and drinking, would be to some extent diminished.

In New Ireland, Duffield remarks (*Journal of the Anthropological Institute*, 1886, p. 118), the natives have a very keen sense of smell; unusual odors are repulsive to them, and "carbolic acid drove them wild."

The New Caledonians, according to Foley (*Bulletin de la Société d'Anthropologie*, November 6, 1879), only like the smells of meat and fish which are becoming "high," like *popoya*, which smells of fowl manure, and *kava*, of rotten eggs. Fruits and vegetables which are beginning to go bad seem the best to them, while the fresh and natural odors which we prefer seem merely to say to them: "We are not yet eatable." (A taste for putrefying food, common among savages, by no means necessarily involves a distaste for agreeable scents, and even among Europeans there is a widespread taste for offensively smelling and putrid foods, especially cheese and game.)

The natives of Torres Straits were carefully examined by Dr. C. S. Myers with regard to their olfactory acuteness and olfactory preferences. It was found that acuteness was, if anything, slightly greater than among Europeans. This appeared to be largely due to the careful attention they pay to odors. The resemblances which they detected among different odorous substances were frequently found to rest on real chemical affinities. The odors they were observed to dislike most frequently were asafœtida, valerianic acid, and civet, the last being regarded as most repulsive of all on account of its resemblance to fæcal odor, which these people regard with intense disgust. Their favorite odors were musk, thyme, and especially violet. (*Report of the Cambridge Anthropological Expedition to Torres Straits*, vol. ii, Part II, 1903.)

In Australia Lumholtz (*Among Cannibals*, p. 115) found that the blacks had a keener sense of smell than he possessed.

In New Zealand the Maoris, as W. Colenso shows, possessed, formerly at all events, a very keen sense of smell or else were very attentive to smell, and their taste as regarded agreeable and disagreeable odors corresponded very closely to European taste, although it must be added that some of their common articles of food possessed a very offensive odor. They are not only sensitive to European perfumes, but possessed various perfumes of their own, derived from plants and possessing a pleasant, powerful, and lasting odor; the choicest and rarest was the gum of the *taramea (Aciphylla Colensoi)*, which was gathered by virgins after the use of prayers and charms. Sir Joseph Banks noted that Maori chiefs wore little bundles of perfumes around their necks, and Cook made the same observation concerning the young women. References to the four chief Maori perfumes are contained in a stanza which is still often hummed to express satisfaction, and sung by a mother to her child:—

> "My little neck-satchel of sweet-scented moss,
> My little neck-satchel of fragrant fern,
> My little neck-satchel of odoriferous gum,
> My sweet-smelling neck-locket of sharp-pointed *taramea*."

In the summer season the sleeping houses of Maori chiefs were often strewed with a large, sweet-scented, flowering grass of powerful odor. (W. Colenso, *Transactions of the New Zealand Institute*, vol. xxiv, reprinted in *Nature*, November 10, 1892.)

Javanese women rub themselves with a mixture of chalk and strong essence which, when rubbed off, leaves a distinct perfume on the body. (Stratz, *Die Frauenkleidung*, p. 84.)

The Samoans, Friedländer states (*Zeitschrift für Ethnologie*, 1899, p. 52), are very fond of fragrant and aromatic odors. He gives a list of some twenty odorous plants which they use, more especially as garlands for the head and neck, including ylang-ylang and gardenia; he remarks that of one of these plants (cordyline) he could not himself detect the odor.

The Nicobarese, Man remarks (*Journal of the Anthropological Institute*, 1889, p. 377), like the natives of New Zealand, particularly dislike the smell of carbolic acid. Both young men and women are very partial to scents; the former say they find their use a certain passport to the favor of their wives, and they bring home from the jungle the scented leaves of a certain creeper to their sweethearts and wives.

Swahili women devote much attention to perfuming themselves. When a woman wishes to make herself desirable she anoints herself all over with fragrant ointments, sprinkles herself with rose-water, puts perfume into her clothes, strews jasmine flowers on her bed as well as binding them round her neck and waist, and smokes *ûdi*, the perfumed wood of the aloe; "every man is glad when his wife smells of *ûdi*" (Velten, *Sitten und Gebraüche der Suahili*, pp. 212-214).

II.

Rise of the Study of Olfaction—Cloquet—Zwaardemaker—The Theory of Smell—The Classification of Odors—The Special Characteristics of Olfactory Sensation in Man—Smell as the Sense of Imagination—Odors as Nervous Stimulants—Vasomotor and Muscular Effects—Odorous Substances as Drugs.

DURING the eighteenth century a great impetus was given to the physiological and psychological study of the senses by the philosophical doctrines of Locke and the English school generally which then prevailed in Europe. These thinkers had emphasized the immense importance of the information derived through the senses in building up the intellect, so that the study of all the sensory channels assumed a significance which it had never possessed before. The olfactory sense fully shared in the impetus thus given to sensory investigation. At the beginning of the nineteenth century a distinguished French physician, Hippolyte Cloquet, a disciple of Cabanis, devoted himself more especially to this subject. After publishing in 1815 a preliminary work, he issued in 1821 his *Osphrésiologie, ou Traité des odeurs, du sens et des organes de l'Olfaction,* a complete monograph on the anatomy, physiology, psychology, and pathology of the olfactory organ and its functions, and a work that may still be consulted with profit, if indeed it can even yet be said to be at every point superseded. After Cloquet's time the study of the sense of smell seems to have fallen into some degree of discredit. For more than half a century no important progress was made in this field. Serious investigators seemed to have become shy of the primitive senses generally, and the subject of smell was mainly left to those interested in "curious" subjects. Many interesting observations were, however, incidentally made; thus Laycock, who was a pioneer in so many by-paths of psychology and anthropology, showed a special interest in the olfactory sense, and frequently

(51)

touched on it in his *Nervous Diseases of Women* and elsewhere. The writer who more than any other has in recent years restored the study of the sense of smell from a by-path to its proper position as a highway for investigation is without doubt Professor Zwaardemaker, of Utrecht. The invention of his first olfactometer in 1888 and the appearance in 1895 of his great work *Die Physiologie des Geruchs* have served to give the physiology of the sense of smell an assured status and to open the way anew for much fruitful investigation, while a number of inquirers in many countries have had their attention directed to the elucidation of this sense.

Notwithstanding, however, the amount of work which has been done in this field during recent years, it cannot be said that the body of assured conclusions so far reached is large. The most fundamental principles of olfactory physiology and psychology are still somewhat vague and uncertain. Although sensations of smell are numerous and varied, in this respect approaching the sensations of vision and hearing, smell still remains close to touch in the vagueness of its messages (while the most sensitive of the senses, remarks Passy, it is the least precise), the difficulty of classifying them, the impossibility of so controlling them as to found upon them any art. It seems better, therefore, not to attempt to force the present study of a special aspect of olfaction into any general scheme which may possibly not be really valid.

The earliest and most general tendency in regard to the theory of smell was to regard it as a kind of chemical sense directly stimulated by minute particles of solid substance. A vibratory theory of smell, however, making it somewhat analogous to hearing, easily presents itself. When I first began the study of physiology in 1881, a speculation of this kind presented itself to my mind. Long before, Philipp von Walther, a professor at Landshut, had put forward a dynamic theory of olfaction (*Physiologie des Menschen*, 1807-8, vol. ii, p. 278). "It is a purely dynamic operation of the odorous substance in the olfactory organ," he stated. Odor is conveyed by the air, he believed, in the same way as heat. It must be added that his reasons for this theory will not always bear examination. More recently a similar theory has been seriously put forward in various quarters. Sir William Ramsay tentatively suggested such a theory (*Nature*, vol. xxv, p. 187) in analogy with light and sound. Haycraft (*Proceedings of the Royal Society of Edinburgh,* 1883-87, and *Brain,* 1887-88), largely starting from Mendelieff's law of periodicity, similarly sought to bring smell into line with the higher senses, arguing that molecules with the same vibration have the same smell. Rutherford (*Nature,* August 11, 1892, p. 343), attaching importance to the evidence brought forward by von Brunn showing that the olfactory cells terminate in very delicate short hairs, also stated his belief that the different qualities of smell result from differences in the frequency and form of the vibrations initiated by the action of the chemical molecules on these olfactory cells, though he admitted that such a conception involved a very subtle conception of molecular vibration. Vaschide and Van Melle (Paris Academy of Sciences, December 26, 1899) have, again, argued that smell is produced by rays of short wave-lengths, analogous to light-rays, Röntgen rays, etc. Chemical action is however, a very important factor in the production of odors; this has been well shown by Ayrton (*Nature,* September 8, 1898). We seem to be forced in the direction of a chemico-vibratory theory, as pointed out by Southerden (*Nature,* March 26, 1903), the olfactory cells being directly stimulated, not by the ordinary vibrations of the molecules, but by the agitations accompanying chemical changes.

The vibratory hypothesis of the action of odors has had some influence on the recent physiologists who have chiefly occupied themselves with olfaction. "It is probable," Zwaardemaker writes (*L'Année Psychologique,* 1898), "that aroma is a physico-chemical attribute of the molecules"; he points out that there is an intimate analogy between color and odor, and remarks that this analogy leads us to suppose in an aroma ether vibrations of which the period is determined by the structure of the molecule.

Since the physiology of olfaction is yet so obscure it is not surprising that we have no thoroughly scientific classification of smells, notwithstanding various ambitious attempts to reach a classification. The classification adopted by Zwaardemaker is founded on the ancient scheme of Linnæus, and may here be reproduced:—

I. Ethereal odors (chiefly esters; Rimmel's fruity series).

II. Aromatic odors (terpenes, camphors, and the spicy, herbaceous, rosaceous, and almond series; the chemical types are well determined: cineol, eugenol, anethol, geraniol, benzaldehyde).

III. The balsamic odors (chiefly aldehydes, Rimmel's jasmin, violet, and balsamic series, with the chemical types: terpineol, ionone, vanillin).

IV. The ambrosiacal odors (ambergris and musk).

V. The alliaceous odors, with the cacodylic group (asafœtida, ichthyol, etc.).

VI. Empyreumatic odors.

VII. Valerianaceous odors (Linnæus's *Odores hircini*, the capryl group, largely composed of sexual odors).

VIII. Narcotic odors (Linnæus's *Odores tetri*).

IX. Stenches.

A valuable and interesting memoir, "Revue Générale sur les Sensations Olfactives," by J. Passy, the chief French authority on this subject, will be found in the second volume of *L'Année Psychologique*, 1895. In the fifth issue of the same year-book (for 1898) Zwaardemaker presents a full summary of his work and views, "Les Sensations Olfactives, leurs Combinaisons et leurs Compensations." A convenient, but less authoritative, summary of the facts of normal and pathological olfaction will be found in a little volume of the "Actualités Médicales" series by Dr. Collet, *L'Odorat et ses Troubles*, 1904. In a little book entitled *Wegweiser zu einer Psychologie des Geruches* (1894) Giessler has sought to outline a psychology of smell, but his sketch can only be regarded as tentative and provisional.

At the outset, nevertheless, it seems desirable that we should at least have some conception of the special characteristics which mark the great and varied mass of sensations reaching the brain through the channel of the olfactory organ. The main special character of olfactory images seems to be conditioned by the fact that they are intermediate in character between those of touch or taste and those of sight or sound, that they have much of the vagueness of the first and something of the richness and variety of the second. Æsthetically, also, they occupy an intermediate position between the higher and the lower senses.[1] They are, at the same time, less practically useful than either the lower or the higher senses. They furnish us with a great mass of what we may call by-sensations, which are of little practical use, but inevitably become intimately mixed with the experiences of life by association and thus acquire an emotional significance which is often very considerable. Their emotional force, it may well be, is connected with the fact that their anatomical seat is the

---

[1] The opinions of psychologists concerning the æsthetic significance of smell, not on the whole very favorable, are brought together and discussed by J. V. Volkelt, "Der Æsthetische Wert der niederen Sinne," *Zeitschrift für Psychologie und Physiologie der Sinnesorgane*, 1902, ht. 3.

most ancient part of the brain. They lie in a remote and almost disused storehouse of our minds and show the fascination or the repulsiveness of all vague and remote things. It is for this reason that they are—to an extent that is remarkable when we consider that they are much more precise than touch sensations—subject to the influence of emotional associations. The very same odor may be at one moment highly pleasant, at the next moment highly unpleasant, in accordance with the emotional attitude resulting from its associations. Visual images have no such extreme flexibility; they are too definite to be so easily influenced. Our feelings about the beauty of a flower cannot oscillate so easily or so far as may our feelings about the agreeableness of its odor. Our olfactory experiences thus institute a more or less continuous series of by-sensations accompanying us through life, of no great practical significance, but of considerable emotional significance from their variety, their intimacy, their associational facility, their remote ancestral reverberations through our brains.

It is the existence of these characteristics—at once so vague and so specific, so useless and so intimate—which led various writers to describe the sense of smell as, above all others, the sense of imagination. No sense has so strong a power of suggestion, the power of calling up ancient memories with a wider and deeper emotional reverberation, while at the same time no sense furnishes impressions which so easily change emotional color and tone, in harmony with the recipient's general attitude. Odors are thus specially apt both to control the emotional life and to become its slaves. With the use of incense religions have utilized the imaginative and symbolical virtues of fragrance. All the legends of the saints have insisted on the odor of sanctity that exhales from the bodies of holy persons, especially at the moment of death. Under the conditions of civilization these primitive emotional associations of odor tend to be dispersed, but, on the other hand, the imaginative side of the olfactory sense becomes accentuated, and personal idiosyncrasies of all kinds tend to manifest themselves in the sphere of smell.

Rousseau (in *Émile*, Bk. II) regarded smell as the sense of the imagination. So, also, at an earlier period, it was termed (according to Cloquet) by Cardano. Cloquet frequently insisted on the qualities of odors which cause them to appeal to the imagination; on their irregular and inconstant character; on their power of intoxicating the mind on some occasions; on the curious individual and racial preferences in the matter of odors. He remarked on the fact that the Persians employed asafœtida as a seasoning, while valerian was accounted a perfume in antiquity. (Cloquet, *Osphrésiologie*, pp. 28, 45, 71, 112.) It may be added, as a curious example familiar to most people of the dependence of the emotional tone of a smell on its associations, that, while the exhalations of other people's bodies are ordinarily disagreeable to us, such is not the case with our own; this is expressed in the crude and vigorous dictum of the Elizabethan poet, Marston, "Every man's dung smells sweet i' his own nose." There are doubtless many implications, moral as well as psychological, in that statement.

The modern authorities on olfaction, Passy and Zwaardemaker, both alike insist on the same characteristics of the sense of smell: its extreme acuity and yet its vagueness. "We live in a world of odor," Zwaardemaker remarks (*L'Année Psychologique*, 1898, p. 203), "as we live in a world of light and of sound. But smell yields us no distinct ideas grouped in regular order, still less that are fixed in the memory as a grammatical discipline. Olfactory sensations awake vague and half-understood perceptions, which are accompanied by very strong emotion. The emotion dominates us, but the sensation which was the cause of it remains unperceived." Even in the same individual there are wide variations in the sensitiveness to odors at different times, more especially as regards faint odors; Passy (*L'Année Psychologique*, 1895, p. 387) brings forward some observations on this point.

Maudsley noted the peculiarly suggestive power of odors; "there are certain smells," he remarked, "which never fail to bring back to me instantly and visibly scenes of my boyhood"; many of us could probably say the same. Another writer (E. Dillon, "A Neglected Sense," *Nineteenth Century*, April, 1894) remarks that "no sense has a stronger power of suggestion."

Ribot has made an interesting investigation as to the prevalence and nature of the emotional memory of odors (*Psychology of the Emotions*, Chapter XI). By "emotional memory" is meant the spontaneous or voluntary revivability of the image, olfactory or other. (For the general question, see an article by F. Pillon, "La Mémoire Affective, son Importance Théorique et Pratique," *Revue Philosophique*, February, 1901; also Paulhan, "Sur la Mémoire Affective," *Revue Philosophique*, December, 1902 and January, 1903.) Ribot found that 40 per cent. of persons are unable to revive any such images of taste or smell; 48

per cent. could revive some; 12 per cent. declared themselves capable of reviving all, or nearly all, at pleasure. In some persons there is no necessary accompanying revival of visual or tactile representations, but in the majority the revived odor ultimately excites a corresponding visual image. The odors most frequently recalled were pinks, musk, violets, heliotrope, carbolic acid, the smell of the country, of grass, etc. Piéron (*Revue Philosophique*, December, 1902) has described the special power possessed by vague odors, in his own case, of evoking ancient impressions.

Dr. J. N. Mackenzie (*American Journal of the Medical Sciences*, January, 1886) considers that civilization exerts an influence in heightening or encouraging the influence of olfaction as it affects our emotions and judgment, and that, in the same way, as we ascend the social scale the more readily our minds are influenced and perhaps perverted by impressions received through the sense of smell.

Odors are powerful stimulants to the whole nervous system, causing, like other stimulants, an increase of energy which, if excessive or prolonged, leads to nervous exhaustion. Thus, it is well recognized in medicine that the aromatics containing volatile oils (such as anise, cinnamon, cardamoms, cloves, coriander, and peppermint) are antispasmodics and anæsthetics, and that they stimulate digestion, circulation, and the nervous system, in large doses producing depression. The carefully arranged plethysmographic experiments of Shields, at the Johns Hopkins University, have shown that olfactory sensations, by their action on the vasomotor system, cause an increase of blood in the brain and sometimes in addition stimulation of the heart; musk, wintergreen, wood violet, and especially heliotrope were found to act strongly in these ways.[1]

Féré's experiments with the dynamometer and the ergograph have greatly contributed to illustrate the stimulating effects of odors. Thus, he found that smelling musk suffices to double muscular effort. With a number of odorous substances he has found that muscular work is temporarily heightened; when taste stimulation was added the increase of energy,

[1] T. E. Shields, "The Effect of Odors, etc., upon the Blood-flow," *Journal of Experimental Medicine*, vol. i, November, 1896. In France, C. Henry and Tardif have made somewhat similar experiments on respiration and circulation. See the latter's *Les Odeurs et les Parfums*, Chapter III.

notably when using lemon, was "colossal." A kind of "sensorial intoxication" could be produced by the inhalation of odors and the whole system stimulated to greater activity; the visual acuity was increased, and electric and general excitability heightened.[1] Such effects may be obtained in perfectly healthy persons, though both Shields and Féré have found that in highly nervous persons the effects are liable to be much greater. It is doubtless on this account that it is among civilized peoples that attention is chiefly directed to perfumes, and that under the conditions of modern life the interest in olfaction and its study has been revived.

It is the genuinely stimulant qualities of odorous substances which led to the widespread use of the more potent among them by ancient physicians, and has led a few modern physicians to employ them still. Thus, vanilla, according to Eloy, deserves to be much more frequently used therapeutically than it is, on account of its excitomotor properties; he states that its qualities as an excitant of sexual desire have long been recognized and that Fonssagrives used to prescribe it for sexual frigidity.[2]

---

[1] Féré, *Sensation et Mouvement*, Chapter VI; *ib.*, *Comptes Rendus de la Société de Biologie*, November 3, December 15 and 22, 1900.

[2] Eloy, art. "Vanille," *Dictionnaire Encyclopédique des Sciences Médicales.*

III.

The Specific Body Odors of Various Peoples—The Negro, etc.—
The European—The Ability to Distinguish Individuals by Smell—The
Odor of Sanctity—The Odor of Death—The Odors of Different Parts
of the Body—The Appearance of Specific Odors at Puberty—The Odors
of Sexual Excitement—The Odors of Menstruation—Body Odors as a
Secondary Sexual Character—The Custom of Salutation by Smell—The
Kiss—Sexual Selection by Smell—The Alleged Association between
Size of Nose and Sexual Vigor—The Probably Intimate Relationship
between the Olfactory and Genital Spheres—Reflex Influences from
the Nose—Reflex Influences from the Genital Sphere—Olfactory Hallucinations in Insanity as Related to Sexual States—The Olfactive Type—
The Sense of Smell in Neurasthenic and Allied States—In Certain Poets
and Novelists—Olfactory Fetichism—The Part Played by Olfaction in
Normal Sexual Attraction—In the East, etc.—In Modern Europe—The
Odor of the Armpit and its Variations—As a Sexual and General Stimulant—Body Odors in Civilization Tend to Cause Sexual Antipathy unless
some Degree of Tumescence is Already Present—The Question whether
Men or Women are more Liable to Feel Olfactory Influences—Women
Usually more Attentive to Odors—The Special Interest in Odors Felt by
Sexual Inverts.

In approaching the specifically sexual aspect of odor in the
human species we may start from the fundamental fact—a fact
we seek so far as possible to disguise in our ordinary social
relations—that all men and women are odorous. This is
marked among all races. The powerful odor of many, though
not all, negroes is well known; it is by no means due to un-
cleanly habits, and Joest remarks that it is even increased by
cleanliness, which opens the pores of the skin; according to Sir
H. Johnston, it is most marked in the armpits and is stronger
in men than in women. Pruner Bey describes it as "am-
moniacal and rancid; it is like the odor of the he-goat." The
odor varies not only individually, but according to the tribe;
Castellani states that the negress of the Congo has merely a
slight *"goût de noisette"* which is agreeable rather than otherwise. Monbuttu women, according to Parke, have a strong Gor-
gonzola perfume, and Emin told Parke that he could distin-

guish the members of different tribes by their characteristic
odor. In the same way the Nicobarese, according to Man, can
distinguish a member of each of the six tribes of the archipelago
by smell. The odor of Australian blacks is less strong than
that of negroes and has been described as of a phosphoric character. The South American Indians, d'Orbigny stated, have
an odor stronger than that of Europeans, though not as strong
as most negroes; it is marked, Latcham states, even among
those who, like the Araucanos, bathe constantly. The Chinese
have a musky odor. The odor of many peoples is described as
being of garlic.[1]

A South Sea Islander, we are told by Charles de Varigny,
on coming to Sydney and seeing the ladies walking about the
streets and apparently doing nothing, expressed much astonish-
ment, adding, with a gesture of contempt, "and they have no
smell!" It is by no means true, however, that Europeans are
odorless. They are, indeed, considerably more odorous than
are many other races,—for instance, the Japanese,—and there
is doubtless some association between the greater hairiness of
Europeans and their marked odor, since the sebaceous glands
are part of the hair apparatus. A Japanese anthropologist,
Adachi, has published an interesting study on the odor of
Europeans,[2] which he describes as a strong and pungent smell,
—sometimes sweet, sometimes bitter,—of varying strength in
different individuals, absent in children and the aged, and having its chief focus in the armpits, which, however carefully
they are washed, immediately become odorous again. Adachi
has found that the sweat-glands are larger in Europeans than
in the Japanese, among whom a strong personal odor is so

[1] R. Andree, "Völkergeruch," in *Ethnographische Parallelen*, Neue
Folge, 1889, pp. 213-222, brings together many passages describing the
odors of various peoples. Hagen, *Sexuelle Osphresiologie*, pp. 166 *et
seq.*, has a chapter on the subject; Joest, supplement to *International
Archiv für Ethnographie*, 1893, p. 53, has an intertesting passage on the
smells of various races, as also Waitz, *Introduction to Anthropology*,
p. 103. *Cf.* Sir H. H. Johnston, *British Central Africa*, p. 395; T. H.
Parke, *Experiences in Equatorial Africa*, p. 409; E. H. Man, *Journal of
the Anthropological Institute*, 1889, p. 391; Brough Smyth, *Aborigines
of Victoria*, vol. i, p. 7; d'Orbigny, *L'Homme Américain*, vol. i, p. 87, etc.
[2] B. Adachi "Geruch der Europaer," *Globus*, 1903, No. 1.

uncommon that "armpit stink" is a disqualification for the army. It is certainly true that the white races smell less strongly than most of the dark races, odor seeming to be correlated to some extent with intensity of pigmentation, as well as with hairiness; but even the most scrupulously clean Europeans all smell. This fact may not always be obvious to human nostrils, apart from intimate contact, but it is well known to dogs, to whom their masters are recognizable by smell. When Huc traveled in Tibet in Chinese disguise he was not detected by the natives, but the dogs recognized him as a foreigner by his smell and barked at him. Many Chinese can tell by smell when a European has been in a room.[1] There are, however, some Europeans who can recognize and distinguish their friends by smell. The case has been recorded of a man who with bandaged eyes could recognize his acquaintances, at the distance of several paces, the moment they entered the room. In another case a deaf and blind mute woman in Massachusetts knew all her acquaintances by smell, and could sort linen after it came from the wash by the odor alone. Governesses have been known to be able when blindfolded to recognize the ownership of their pupils' garments by smell; such a case is known to me. Such odor is usually described as being agreeable, but not one person in fifty, it is stated, is able to distinguish it with sufficient precision to use it as a method of recognition. Among some races, however, this aptitude would appear to be better developed. Dr. C. S. Myers at Sarawak noted that his Malay boy sorted the clean linen according to the skin-odor of the wearer.[2] Chinese servants are said to do the same, as well as Australians and natives of Luzon.[3]

Although the distinctively individual odor of most persons is not sufficiently marked to be generally perceptible, there are cases in which

---

[1] Hagen quotes testimonies on this point, *Sexuelle Osphresiologie*, p. 173. The negro, Castellani states, considers that Europeans have a smell of death.

[2] *Reports of the Cambridge Anthropological Expedition*, vol. ii, p. 181.

[3] Waitz, *Introduction to Anthropology*, p. 103.

it is more distinct to all nostrils. The most famous case of this kind
is that of Alexander the Great, who, according to Plutarch, exhaled
so sweet an odor that his tunics were soaked with aromatic perfume
(*Convivalium Disputationum*, lib. I, quest. 6). Malherbe, Cujas, and
Haller are said to have diffused a musky odor. The agreeable odor of
Walt Whitman has been remarked by Kennedy and others. The perfume
exhaled by many holy men and women, so often noted by ancient writers
(discussed by Görres in the second volume of his *Christliche Mystik*) and
which has entered into current phraseology as a merely metaphorical
"odor of sanctity," was doubtless due, as Hammond first pointed out, to
abnormal nervous conditions, for it is well known that such conditions
affect the odor, and in insanity, for instance, the presence is noted of
bodily odors which have sometimes even been considered of diagnostic
importance. J. B. Friedreich, *Allgemeine Diagnostik der Psychischen
Krankheiten*, second edition, 1832, pp. 9-10, quotes passages from various authors on this point, which he accepts; various writers of more
recent date have made similar observations.

The odor of sanctity was specially noted at death, and was doubtless confused with the *odor mortis*, which frequently precedes death
and by some is regarded as an almost certain indication of its approach.
In the *British Medical Journal*, for May and June, 1898, will be found
letters from several correspondents substantiating this point. One of
these correspondents (Dr. Tuckey, of Tywardwreath, Cornwall) mentions
that he has in Cornwall often seen ravens flying over houses in which
persons lay dying, evidently attracted by a characteristic odor.

It must be borne in mind, however, that, while every person has, to a sensitive nose, a distinguishing odor, we must
regard that odor either as but one of the various sensations
given off by the body, or else as a combination of two or more
of these emanations. The body in reality gives off a number of
different odors. The most important of these are: (1) the
general skin odor, a faint, but agreeable, fragrance often to be
detected on the skin even immediately after washing; (2) the
smell of the hair and scalp; (3) the odor of the breath; (4)
the odor of the armpit; (5) the odor of the feet; (6) the
perineal odor; (7) in men the odor of the preputial smegma;
(8) in women the odor of the mons veneris, that of vulvar
smegma, that of vaginal mucus, and the menstrual odor. All
these are odors which may usually be detected, though sometimes only in a very faint degree, in healthy and well-washed

persons under normal conditions. It is unnecessary here to take into account the special odors of various secretions and excretions.[1]

It is a significant fact, both as regards the ancestral sexual connections of the body odors and their actual sexual associations to-day, that, as Hippocrates long ago noted, it is not until puberty that they assume their adult characteristics. The infant, the adult, the aged person, each has his own kind of smell, and, as Monin remarks, it might be possible, within certain limits, to discover the age of a person by his odor. Jorg in 1832 pointed out that in girls the appearance of a specific smell of the excreta indicates the establishment of puberty, and Kaan, in his *Psychopathia Sexualis*, remarked that at puberty "the sweat gives out a more acrid odor resembling musk." In both sexes puberty, adolescence, early manhood and womanhood are marked by a gradual development of the adult odor of skin and excreta, in general harmony with the secondary sexual developments of hair and pigment. Venturi, indeed, has, not without reason, described the odor of the body as a secondary sexual character.[2] It may be added that, as is the case with the pigment in various parts of the body in woman, some of these odors tend to become exaggerated in sympathy with sexual and other emotional states.

The odor of the infant is said to be of butyric acid; that of old people to resemble dry leaves. Continent young men have been said by many ancient writers to smell more strongly than the unchaste, and some writers have described as "seminal odor"—an odor resembling that of animals in heat, faintly recalling that of the he-goat, according to Venturi—the exhalations of the skin at such times.

During sexual excitement, as women can testify, a man very frequently, if not normally, gives out an odor which, as usually described, proceeds from the skin, the breath, or both. Grimaldi states that it is as of rancid butter; others say it resembles chloroform. It is said to be sometimes perceptible for a distance of several feet and to last for several hours after coitus. (Various quotations are given by Gould

---

[1] Monin, *Les Odeurs du Corps Humain*, second edition, Paris, 1886, discusses briefly but comprehensively the normal and more especially the pathological odors of the body and of its secretions and excretions.

[2] Venturi, *Degenerazione Psicho-sessuale*, p. 417.

and Pyle, *Anomalies and Curiosities of Medicine*, section on "Human Odors," pp. 397-403.) St. Philip Neri is said to have been able to recognize a chaste man by smell.

During menstruation girls and young women frequently give off an odor which is quite distinct from that of the menstrual fluid, and is specially marked in the breath, which may smell of chloroform or violets. Pouchet (confirmed by Raciborski, *Traité de la Menstruation*, 1868, p. 74) stated that about a day before the onset of menstruation a characteristic smell is exuded. Menstruating girls are also said sometimes to give off a smell of leather. Aubert, of Lyons (as quoted by Galopin), describes the odor of the skin of a woman during menstruation as an agreeable aromatic or acidulous perfume of chloroform character. By some this is described as emanating especially from the armpits. Sandras (quoted by Raciborski) knew a lady who could always tell by a sensation of faintness and *malaise*—apparently due to a sensation of smell—when she was in contact with a menstruating woman. I am acquainted with a man, having strong olfactory sympathies and antipathies, who detects the presence of menstruation by smell. It is said that Hortense Baré, who accompanied her lover, the botanist Commerson, to the Pacific disguised as a man, was recognized by the natives as a woman by means of smell.

Women, like men, frequently give out an odor during coitus or strong sexual excitement. This odor may be entirely different from that normally emanating from the woman, of an acid or hircine character, and sufficiently strong to remain in a room for a considerable period. Many of the ancient medical writers (as quoted by Schurigius, *Parthenologia*, p. 286) described the goaty smell produced by venery, especially in women; they regarded it as specially marked in harlots and in the newly married, and sometimes even considered it a certain sign of defloration. The case has been recorded of a woman who emitted a rose odor for two days after coitus (McBride, quoted by Kiernan in an interesting summary, "Odor in Pathology," *Doctor's Magazine*, December, 1900). There was, it is said (*Journal des Savans*, 1684, p. 39, quoting from the *Journal d'Angleterre*) a monk in Prague who could recognize by smell the chastity of the women who approached him. (This monk, it is added, when he died, was composing a new science of odors.)

Gustav Klein (as quoted by Adler, *Die Mangelhafte Geschlechtsempfindungen des Weibes*, p. 25) argues that the special function of the glands at the vulvar orifice—the *glandulæ vestibulares majores*—is to give out an odorous secretion to act as an attraction to the male, this relic of sexual periodicity no longer, however, playing an important part in the human species. The vulvar secretion, however, it may be added, still has a more aromatic odor than the vaginal secretion, with its simple mucous odor, very clearly perceived during parturition.

It may be added that we still know extremely little concerning the sexual odors of women among primitive peoples. Ploss and Bartels are only able to bring forward (*Das Weib*, 1901, bd. 1, p. 218) a statement concerning the women of New Caledonia, who, according to Moncelon, when young and ardent, give out during coitus a powerful odor which no ablution will remove. In abnormal states of sexual excitement such odor may be persistent, and, according to an ancient observation, a nymphomaniac, whose periods of sexual excitement lasted all through the spring-time, at these periods always emitted a goatlike odor. It has been said (G. Tourdes, art. "Aphrodisie," *Dictionnaire Encyclopédique des Sciences Médicales*) that the erotic temperament is characterized by a special odor.

If the body odors tend to develop at puberty, to be maintained during sexual life, especially in sympathy with conditions of sexual disturbance, and to become diminished in old age, being thus a kind of secondary sexual character, we should expect them to be less marked in those cases in which the primary sexual characters are less marked. It is possible that this is actually the case. Hagen, in his *Sexuelle Osphrésiologie*, quotes from Roubaud's *Traité de l'Impuissance* the statement that the body odor of the castrated differs from that of normal individuals. Burdach had previously stated that the odor of the eunuch is less marked than that of the normal man.

It is thus possible that defective sexual development tends to be associated with corresponding olfactory defect. Heschl[1] has reported a case in which absence of both olfactory nerves coincided with defective development of the sexual organs. Féré remarks that the impotent show a repugnance for sexual odors. Dr. Kiernan informs me that in women after oöphorectomy he has noted a tendency to diminished (and occasionally increased) sense of smell. These questions, however, await more careful and extended observation.

A very significant transition from the phenomena of personal odor to those of sexual attraction by personal odor is to be found in the fact that among the peoples inhabiting a large part of the world's surface the ordinary salutation between friends is by mutual smelling of the person. In some form or

---

[1] Quoted by Féré, *L'Instinct Sexuel*, 1902, p. 133.

another the method of salutation by applying the nose to the nose, face, or hand of a friend in greeting is found throughout a large part of the Pacific, among the Papuans, the Eskimo, the hill tribes of India, in Africa, and elsewhere.[1] Thus, among a certain hill tribe in India, according to Lewin, they smell a friend's cheek: "in their language, they do not say, 'Give me a kiss,' but they say 'Smell me.'" And on the Gambia, according to F. Moore, "When the men salute the women, they, instead of shaking their hands, put it up to their noses, and smell twice to the back of it." Here we have very clearly a recognition of the emotional value of personal odor widely prevailing throughout the world. The salutation on an olfactory basis may, indeed, be said to be more general than the salutation on a tactile basis on which European handshaking rests, each form involving one of the two most intimate and emotional senses. The kiss may be said to be a development proceeding both from the olfactory and the tactile bases, with perhaps some other elements as well, and is too complex to be regarded as a phenomenon of either purely tactile or purely olfactory origin.[2]

As the sole factor in sexual selection olfaction must be rare. It is said that Asiatic princes have sometimes caused a number of the ladies to race in the seraglio garden until they were heated; their garments have then been brought to the prince, who has selected one of them solely by the odor.[3] There was here a sexual selection mainly by odor. Any exclusive efficacy of the olfactory sense is rare, not so much because the impressions of this sense are inoperative, but because agreeable personal odors are not sufficiently powerful, and the olfactory organ is too obtuse, to enable smell to take precedence of sight. Nevertheless, in many people, it is probable that certain odors, especially those that are correlated with a healthy and sexually desirable person, tend to be agreeable; they are fortified by

---

[1] H. Ling Roth, "On Salutations," *Journal of the Anthropological Institute*, November, 1889.

[2] See Appendix A: "The Origins of the Kiss."

[3] See, *e. g.*, passage quoted by I. Bloch, *Beiträge zur Ätiologie der Psychopathia Sexualis*, Teil II, p. 205.

their association with the loved person, sometimes to an irresistible degree; and their potency is doubtless increased by the fact, to which reference has already been made, that many odors, including some bodily odors, are nervous stimulants.

It is possible that the sexual associations of odors have been still further fortified by a tendency to correlation between a high development of the olfactory organ and a high development of the sexual apparatus. An association between a large nose and a large male organ is a very ancient observation and has been verified occasionally in recent times. There is normally at puberty a great increase in the septum of the nose, and it is quite conceivable, in view of the sympathy, which, as we shall see, certainly exists between the olfactory and sexual region, that the two regions may develop together under a common influence.

The Romans firmly believed in the connection between a large nose and a large penis. "Noscitur e naso quanta sit hasta viro," stated Ovid. This belief continued to prevail, especially in Italy, through the middle ages; the physiognomists made much of it, and licentious women (like Joanna of Naples) were, it appears, accustomed to bear it in mind, although disappointment is recorded often to have followed. (See, e.g., the quotations and references given by J. N. Mackenzie, "Physiological and Pathological Relations between the Nose and the Sexual Apparatus in Man." *Johns Hopkins Hospital Bulletin*, No. 82, January, 1898; also Hagen, *Sexuelle Osphresiologie*, pp. 15-19.) A similar belief as to the association between the sexual impulse in women and a long nose was evidently common in England in the sixteenth century, for in Massinger's *Emperor of the East* (Act II, Scene 1) we read,

"Her nose, which by its length assures me
Of storms at midnight if I fail to pay her
The tribute she expects."

At the present day, a proverb of the Venetian people still embodies the belief in the connection between a large nose and a large sexual member.

The probability that such an association tends in many cases to prevail is indicated not only by the beliefs of antiquity, when more careful attention was paid to these matters, but by the testimony of various modern observers, although it does not appear that any series of exact observations have yet been made.

It may be noted that Marro, in his careful anthropological study of criminals (*I Caratteri dei Delinquenti*), found no class of criminals with so large a proportion alike of anomalies of the nose and anomalies of the genital organs as sexual offenders.

However this may be, it is less doubtful that there is a very intimate relation both in men and women between the olfactory mucous membrane of the nose and the whole genital apparatus, that they frequently show a sympathetic action, that influences acting on the genital sphere will affect the nose, and occasionally, it is probable, influences acting on the nose reflexly affect the genital sphere. To discuss these relationships would here be out of place, since specialists are not altogether in agreement concerning the matter. A few are inclined to regard the association as extremely intimate, so that each region is sensitive even to slight stimuli applied to the other region, while, on the other hand, many authorities ignore altogether the question of the relationship. It would appear, however, that there really is, in a considerable number of people at all events, a reflex connection of this kind. It has especially been noted that in many cases congestion of the nose precedes menstruation.

Bleeding of the nose is specially apt to occur at puberty and during adolescence, while in women it may take the place of menstruation and is sometimes more apt to occur at the menstrual periods; disorders of the nose have also been found to be aggravated at these periods. It has even been possible to control bleeding of the nose, both in men and women, by applying ice to the sexual regions. In both men and women, again, cases have been recorded in which sexual excitement, whether of coitus or masturbation, has been followed by bleeding of the nose. In numerous cases it is followed by slight congestive conditions of the nasal passages and especially by sneezing. Various authors have referred to this phenomenon; I am acquainted with a lady in whom it is fairly constant.[1]

---

[1] It must at the same time be remembered that the more or less degree of exposure involved by sexual intercourse is itself a cause of nasal congestion and sneezing.

Féré records the case of a lady, a nervous subject, who began to experience intense spontaneous sexual excitement shortly after marriage, accompanied by much secretion from the nose.[1] J. N. Mackenzie is acquainted with a number of such cases, and he considers that the popular expression "bride's cold" indicates that this effect of strong sexual excitement is widely recognized.

The late Professor Hack, of Freiburg, in 1884, called general medical attention to the intimate connection between the nose and states of nervous hyperexcitability in various parts of the body, although such a connection had been recognized for many centuries in medical literature. While Hack and his disciples thus gave prominence to this association, they undoubtedly greatly exaggerated its importance and significance. (Sir Felix Semon, *British Medical Journal*, November 9, 1901.) Even many workers who have more recently further added to our knowledge have also, as sometimes happens with enthusiasts, unduly strained their own data. Starting from the fact that in women during menstruation examination of the nose reveals a degree of congestion not found during the rest of the month, Fliess (*Die Beziehungen zwischen Nase und Weiblichen Geschlechtsorganen*, 1897), with the help of a number of elaborate and prolonged observations, has reached conclusions which, while they seem to be hazardous at some points, have certainly contributed to build up our knowledge of this obscure subject. Schiff (*Wiener klinische Wochenschrift*, 1900, p. 58, summarized in *British Medical Journal*, February 16, 1901), starting from a skeptical standpoint, has confirmed some of Fliess's results, and in a large number of cases controlled painful menstruation by painting with cocaine the so-called "genital spots" in the nose, all possibility of suggestion being avoided. Ries, of Chicago, has been similarly successful with the method of Fliess (*American Gynæcology*, vol. iii, No. 4, 1903). Benedikt (*Wiener medicinische Wochenschrift*, No. 8, 1901, summarized in *Journal of Medical Science*, October, 1901), while pointing out that the nose is not the only organ in sympathetic relation with the sexual sphere, suggests that the mechanism of the relationship is involved in the larger problem of the harmony in growth and in nutrition of the different parts of the organism. In this way, probably, we may attach considerable significance to the existence of a kind of erectile tissue in the nose.

An interesting example of a reflex influence from the nose affecting the genital sphere has been brought forward by Dr. E. S. Tal-

---

[1] Féré, *Pathologie des Emotions*, p. 81.

bot, of Chicago: "A 56-year-old man was operated on (September 1, 1903) for the removal of the left cartilage of the septum of the nose owing to a previous traumatic fracture at the sixteenth year. No pain was experienced until two years ago, when a continual soreness occurred at the apical end of the fracture during the winter months. The operation was decided upon fearing more serious complications. The parts were cocainized. No pain was experienced in the operation except at one point at the lower posterior portion near the floor of the nose. A profound shock to the general system followed. The reflex influence of the pain upon the genital organs caused semen to flow continually for three weeks. Treatment of general motor irritability with camphor monobromate and conium, on consultation with Dr. Kiernan, checked the flow. The discharge produced spinal neurasthenia. The legs and feet felt heavy. Erythromelalgia caused uneasiness. The patient walked with difficulty. The tired feeling in the feet and limbs was quite noticeable four months after the operation, although the pain had, to a great extent diminished." (Chicago Academy of Medicine, January, 1904, and private letter.)

J. N. Mackenzie has brought together a great many original observations, together with interesting quotations from old medical literature, in his two papers: "The Pathological Nasal Reflex" (*New York Medical Journal*, August 20, 1887) and "The Physiological and Pathological Relations between the Nose and the Sexual Apparatus of Man" (*Johns Hopkins Hospital Bulletin*, January 1, 1898). A number of cases have also been brought together from the literature by G. Endriss in his Inaugural Dissertation, *Die bisherigen Beobachtungen von Physiologischen und Pathologischen Beziehungen der oberen Luftwege zu den Sexualorganen*, Teil. II, Würzburg, 1892.

The intimate association between the sexual centers and the olfactory tract is well illustrated by the fact that this primitive and ancient association tends to come to the surface in insanity. It is recognized by many alienists that insanity of a sexual character is specially liable to be associated with hallucinations of smell.

Many eminent alienists in various countries are very decidedly of the opinion that there is a special tendency to the association of olfactory hallucinations with sexual manifestations, and, although one or two authorities have expressed doubt on the matter, the available evidence clearly indicates such an association. Hallucinations of smell are comparatively rare as compared to hallucinations of sight and hearing; they are commoner in women than in men and they not infrequently occur at periods of sexual disturbance, at adolescence, in puerperal fever, at the change of life, in women with ovarian troubles, and in old people troubled with sexual desires or remorse for such desires. They have often been noted as specially frequent in cases of excessive masturbation.

Krafft-Ebing, who found olfactory hallucinations common in various sexual states, considers that they are directly dependent on sexual excitement (*Allgemeine Zeitschrift für Psychiatrie*, bd. 34, ht. 4, 1877). Conolly Norman believes in a distinct and frequent association between olfactory hallucinations and sexual disturbance (*Journal of Mental Science*, July, 1899, p. 532). Savage is also impressed by the close association between sexual disturbance or changes in the reproductive organs and hallucinations of smell as well as of touch. He has found that persistent hallucinations of smell disappeared when a diseased ovary was removed, although the patient remained insane. He considers that such hallucinations of smell are allied to reversions. (G. H. Savage, "Smell, Hallucinations of," Tuke's *Dictionary of Psychological Medicine*; cf. the same author's manual of *Insanity and Allied Neuroses*.) Matusch, while not finding olfactory hallucinations common at the climacteric, states that when they are present they are connected with uterine trouble and sexual craving. He finds them more common in young women. (Matusch, Der Einfluss des Climacterium auf Entstehung und Form der Geistesstörung," *Allgemeine Zeitschrift für Psychiatrie*, vol. xlvi, ht. 4). Féré has related a significant case of a young man in whom hallucinations of smell accompanied the sexual orgasm; he subsequently developed epilepsy, to which the hallucination then constituted the aura (*Comptes Rendus de la Société de Biologie*, December, 1896). The prevalence of a sexual element in olfactory hallucinations has been investigated by Bullen, who examined into 95 cases of hallucinations of smell among the patients in several asylums. (In a few cases there were reasons for believing that peripheral conditions existed which would render these hallucinations more strictly illusions). Of these, 64 were women. Sixteen of the women were climacteric cases, and 3 of them had sexual hallucinations or delusions. Fourteen other women (chiefly cases of chronic delusional insanity) had sexual delusions. Altogether, 31 men and women had sexual delusions. This is a large proportion. Bullen is not, however, inclined to admit any direct connection between the reproductive system and the sense of smell. He finds that other hallucinations are very frequently associated with the olfactory hallucinations, and considers that the co-existence of olfactory and sexual troubles simply indicates a very deep and widespread nervous disturbance. (F. St. John Bullen, "Olfactory Hallucinations in the Insane", *Journal of Mental Science*, July, 1899.) In order to elucidate the matter fully we require further precise inquiries on the lines Bullen has laid down.

It may be of interest to note, in this connection, that smell and taste hallucinations appear to be specially frequent in forms of religious insanity. Thus, Dr. Zurcher, in her inaugural dissertation on Joan of Arc (*Jeanne d'Arc*, Leipzig, 1895, p. 72), estimates that on the average in such insanity nearly 50 per cent. of the hallucinations affect smell and taste; she refers also to the olfactory hallucinations of great religious leaders, Francis of Assisi, Katherina Emmerich, Lazzaretti, and the Anabaptists.

It may well be, as Zwaardemaker has suggested in his *Physiologie des Geruchs,* that the nasal congestion at menstruation and similar phenomena are connected with that association of smell and sexuality which is observable throughout the whole animal world, and that the congestion brings about a temporary increase of olfactory sensitiveness during the stage of sexual excitation.[1] Careful investigation of olfactory acuteness would reveal the existence of such menstrual heightening of its acuity.

In a few exceptional, but still quite healthy people, smell would appear to possess an emotional predominance which it cannot be said to possess in the average person. These exceptional people are of what Binet in his study of sexual fetichism calls olfactive type; such persons form a group which, though of smaller size and less importance, is fairly comparable to the well-known groups of visual type, of auditory type, and of psychomotor type. Such people would be more attentive to odors, more moved by olfactory sympathies and antipathies, than are ordinary people. For these, it may well be, the supremacy accorded to olfactory influences in Jäger's *Entdeckung der Seele,* though extravagantly incorrect for ordinary persons, may appear quite reasonable.

It is certain also that a great many neurasthenic people, and particularly those who are sexually neurasthenic, are peculiarly susceptible to olfactory influences. A number of eminent

---

[1] J. N. Mackenzie similarly suggests (*Johns Hopkins Hospital Bulletin*, No. 82, 1898) that "irritation and congestion of the nasal mucous membrane precede, or are the excitants of, the olfactory impression that forms the connecting link between the sense of smell and erethism of the reproductive organs exhibited in the lower animals."

poets and novelists--especially, it would appear, in France--seem to be in this case. Baudelaire, of all great poets, has most persistently and most elaborately emphasized the imaginative and emotional significance of odor; the *Fleurs du Mal* and many of the *Petits Poèmes en Prose* are, from this point of view, of great interest. There can be no doubt that in Baudelaire's own imaginative and emotional life the sense of smell played a highly important part; and that, in his own words, odor was to him what music is to others. Throughout Zola's novels--and perhaps more especially in *La Faute de l'Abbé Mouret*--there is an extreme insistence on odors of every kind. Prof. Leopold Bernard wrote an elaborate study of this aspect of Zola's work[1]; he believed that underlying Zola's interest in odors there was an abnormally keen olfactory sensibility and large development of the olfactory region of the brain. Such a supposition is, however, unnecessary, and, as a matter of fact, a careful examination of Zola's olfactory sensibility, conducted by M. Passy, showed that it was somewhat below normal.[2] At the same time it was shown that Zola was really a person of olfactory psychic type, with a special attention to odors and a special memory for them; as is frequently the case with perfumers with less than normal olfactory acuity he possessed a more than normal power of discriminating odors; it is possible that in early life his olfactory acuity may also have been above normal. In the same way Nietzsche, in his writings, shows a marked sensibility, and especially antipathy, as regards odors, which has by some been regarded as an index to a real physical sensibility of abnormal keenness; according to Möbius, however, there was no reason for supposing this to be the case.[3] Huysmans, who throughout his books reveals a very intense pre-occupation with the exact shades of many kinds of sensory impressions, and an apparently abnormally keen sensibility to them, has shown a great interest in odors, more especially in an oft-quoted passage in *A Rebours*. The blind Milton of "Para-

[1] *Les Odeurs dans les Romans de Zola*, Montpellier, 1889.
[2] Toulouse, *Emile Zola*, pp. 163-165, 173-175.
[3] P. J. Möbius, *Das Pathologische bei Nietzsche*.

dise Lost" (as the late Mr. Grant Allen once remarked to me), dwells much on scents; in this case it is doubtless to the blindness and not to any special organic predisposition that we must attribute this direction of sensory attention.[1] Among our older English poets, also, Herrick displays a special interest in odors with a definite realization of their sexual attractiveness.[2] Shelley, who was alive to so many of the unusual æsthetic aspects of things, often shows an enthusiastic delight in odors, more especially those of flowers. It may, indeed, be said that most poets—though to a less degree than those I have mentioned—devote a special attention to odors, and, since it has been possible to describe smell as the sense of imagination, this need not surprise us. That Shakespeare, for instance, ranked this sense very high indeed is shown by various passages in his works and notably by Sonnet LIV: "O, how much more doth beauty beauteous seem!"—in which he implicitly places the attraction of odor on at least as high a level as that of vision.[3]

A neurasthenic sensitiveness to odors, specially sexual odors, is frequently accompanied by lack of sexual vigor. In this way we may account for the numerous cases in which old men in whom sexual desire survives the loss of virile powers—probably somewhat abnormal persons at the outset—find satisfaction in sexual odors. Here, also, we have the basis for olfactory fetichism. In such fetichism the odor of the woman alone, whoever she may be and however unattractive she may be, suffices to furnish complete sexual satisfaction. In many, although not all, of those cases in which articles of women's

---

[1] Moll has a passage on the sense of smell in the blind, more especially in sexual respects, *Untersuchungen über die Libido Sexualis*, bd. 1, pp. 137 *et seq.*

[2] See, for instance, his poem, "Love Perfumes all Parts," in which he declares that "Hands and thighs and legs are all richly aromatical." And compare the lyrics entitled "A Song to the Maskers," "On Julia's Breath," "Upon Julia's Unlacing Herself," "Upon Julia's Sweat," and "To Mistress Anne Soame."

[3] There are various indications that Goethe was attentive to the attraction of personal odors; and that he experienced this attraction himself is shown by the fact that, as he confessed, when he once had to leave Weimar on an official journey for two days he took a bodice of Frau von Stein's away in order to carry the scent of her body with him.

clothing become the objects of fetichistic attraction, there is certainly an olfactory element due to the personal odor attaching to the garments.[1]

Olfactory influences play a certain part in various sexually abnormal tendencies and practices which do not proceed from an exclusively olfactory fascination. Thus, *cunnilingus* and *fellatio* derive part of their attraction, more especially in some individuals, from a predilection for the odors of the sexual parts. (See, *e. g.*, Moll, *Untersuchungen über die Libido Sexualis*, bd. 1, p. 134.) In many cases smell plays no part in the attraction; "I enjoy *cunnilingus*, if I like the girl very much," a correspondent writes, "*in spite* of the smell." We may associate this impulse with the prevalence of these practices among sexual inverts, in whom olfactory attractions are often specially marked. Those individuals, also, who are sexually affected by the urinary and alvine excretions ("*renifleurs*," "*stercoraires*," etc.) are largely, though not necessarily altogether, moved by olfactory impressions. The attraction was, however, exclusively olfactory in the case of the young woman recorded by Moraglia (*Archivio di Psichiatria*, 1892, p. 267), who was irresistibly excited by the odor of the fermented urine of men, and possibly also in the case narrated to Moraglia by Prof. L. Bianchi (*ib.* p. 568), in which a wife required flatus from her husband.

The sexual pleasure derived from partial strangulation (discussed in the study of "Love and Pain" in a previous volume) may be associated with heightened olfactory sexual excitation. Dr. Kiernan, who points this out to me, has investigated a few neuropathic patients who like to have their necks squeezed, as they express it, and finds that in the majority the olfactory sensibility is thus intensified.

Even in ordinary normal persons, however, there can be no doubt that personal odor tends to play a not inconsiderable part in sexual attractions and sexual repulsions. As a sexual excitant, indeed, it comes far behind the stimuli received through the sense of sight. The comparative bluntness of the sense of smell in man makes it difficult for olfactory influence to be felt, as a rule, until the preliminaries of courtship are already over; so that it is impossible for smell ever to possess the same significance in sexual attraction in man that it

---

[1] Hagen has brought together from the literature of the subject a number of typical cases of olfactory fetichism, *Sexuelle Osphresiologie*, 1901, pp. 82 *et seq.*

possesses in the lower animals. With that reservation there can be no doubt that odor has a certain favorable or unfavorable influence in sexual relationships in all human races from the lowest to the highest. The Polynesian spoke with contempt of those women of European race who "have no smell," and in view of the pronounced personal odor of so many savage peoples as well as of the careful attention which they so often pay to odors, we may certainly assume, even in the absence of much definite evidence, that smell counts for much in their sexual relationships. This is confirmed by such practices as that found among some primitive peoples—as, it is stated, in the Philippines—of lovers exchanging their garments to have the smell of the loved one about them. In the barbaric stages of society this element becomes self-conscious and is clearly avowed; personal odors are constantly described with complacency, sometimes as mingled with the lavish use of artificial perfumes, in much of the erotic literature produced in the highest stages of barbarism, especially by Eastern peoples living in hot climates; it is only necessary to refer to the *Song of Songs,* the *Arabian Nights,* and the Indian treatises on love. Even in some parts of Europe the same influence is recognized in the crudest animal form, and Krauss states that among the Southern Slavs it is sometimes customary to leave the sexual parts unwashed because a strong odor of these parts is regarded as a sexual stimulant. Under the usual conditions of life in Europe personal odor has sunk into the background ; this has been so equally under the conditions of classic, mediæval, and modern life. Personal odor has been generally regarded as unæsthetic; it has, for the most part, only been mentioned to be reprobated, and even those poets and others who during recent centuries have shown a sensitive delight and interest in odors—Herrick, Shelley, Baudelaire, Zola, and Huysmans—have seldom ventured to insist that a purely natural and personal odor can be agreeable. The fact that it may be so, and that for most people such odors cannot be a matter of indifference in the most intimate of all relationships, is usually only to be learned casually and incidentally. There can be no doubt, however, that, as Kiernan points out, the extent to which olfaction influences the sexual sphere in civilized man has been much underestimated. We need not, therefore, be surprised at the greater interest which has recently been taken in this subject. As usually happens, indeed, there has been in some writers a tendency to run to the opposite extreme, and we cannot, with Gustav Jäger, regard the sexual instinct as mainly or altogether an olfactory matter.

Of the Padmini, the perfect woman, the "lotus woman," Hindu writers say that "her sweat has the odor of musk," while the vulgar woman, they say, smells of fish *(Kama Sutra of Vatsyayana)*. Ploss and Bartels *(Das Weib*, 1901, p. 218) bring forward a passage from the Tamil *Kokkôgam*, minutely describing various kinds of sexual odor in women, which they regard as resting on sound observation.

Four things in a woman, says the Arab, should be perfumed: the mouth, the armpits, the pudenda, and the nose. The Persian poets, in describing the body, delighted to use metaphors involving odor. Not only the hair and the down on the face, but the chin, the mouth, the beauty spots, the neck, all suggested odorous images. The epithets applied to the hair frequently refer to musk, ambergris, and civet. *(Anis el Ochchaq*, translated by Huart, *Bibliothèque de l'Ecole des Hautes Etudes*, fasc. 25, 1875.)

The Hebrew *Song of Songs* furnishes a typical example of a very beautiful Eastern love-poem in which the importance of the appeal to the sense of smell is throughout emphasized. There are in this short poem as many as twenty-four fairly definite references to odors,—personal odors, perfumes, and flowers,—while numerous other references to flowers, etc., seem to point to olfactory associations. Both the lover and his sweetheart express pleasure in each other's personal odor.

> "My beloved is unto me," she sings, "as a bag of myrrh
>   That lieth between my breasts;
>   My beloved is unto me as a cluster of henna flowers
>   In the vineyard of En-gedi."

And again: "His cheeks are as a bed of spices [or balsam], as banks of sweet herbs." While of her he says: "The smell of thy breath [or nose] is like apples."

Greek and Roman antiquity, which has so largely influenced the traditions of modern Europe, was lavish in the use of perfumes, but showed no sympathy with personal odors. For the Roman satirists, like Martial, a personal odor is nearly always an unpleasant odor,

though there are a few allusions in classic literature recognizing
bodily smell as a sexual attraction. Ovid, in his *Ars Amandi* (Book
III), says it is scarcely necessary to remind a lady that she must not
keep a goat in her armpits: *"ne trux caper iret in alas."* *"Mulier tum
bene olet ubi nihil olet"* is an ancient dictum, and in the sixteenth century Montaigne still repeated the same saying with complete approval.

A different current of feeling began to appear with the new
emotional movement during the eighteenth century. Rousseau called
attention to the importance of the olfactory sense, and in his educa-
tional work, *Emile* (Bk. II), he referred to the odor of a woman's
"cabinet de toilette" as not so feeble a snare as is commonly supposed.
In the same century Casanova wrote still more emphatically concerning
the same point; in the preface to his *Mémoires* he states: "I have
always found sweet the odor of the women I have loved"; and elsewhere: "There is something in the air of the bedroom of the woman
one loves, something so intimate, so balsamic, such voluptuous emanations, that if a lover had to choose between Heaven and this place
of delight his hesitation would not last for a moment" (*Mémoires*,
vol. iii). In the previous century, in England, Sir Kenelm Digby, in
his interesting and remarkable *Private Memoirs*, when describing a visit
to Lady Venetia Stanley, afterward his wife, touches on personal odor
as an element of attraction; he had found her asleep in bed and on
her breasts "did glisten a few drops of sweatlike diamond sparks, and
had a more fragrant odor than the violets or primroses whose season
was newly passed."

In 1821 Cadet-Devaux published, in the *Revue Encyclopédique*,
a study entitled "De l'atmosphère de la Femme et de sa Puissance,"
which attracted a great deal of attention in Germany as well as in
France; he considered that the exhalations of the feminine body are
of the first importance in sexual attraction.

Prof. A. Galopin in 1886 wrote a semiscientific book, *Le Parfum
de la Femme*, in which the sexual significance of personal odor is developed to its fullest. He writes with enthusiasm concerning the sweet
and health-giving character of the natural perfume of a beloved
woman, and the mischief done both to health and love by the use of
artificial perfumes. "The purest marriage that can be contracted between a man and a woman," he asserts (p. 157) "is that engendered by
olfaction and sanctioned by a common assimilation in the brain of the
animated molecules due to the secretion and evaporation of two bodies
in contact and sympathy."

In a book written during the first half of the nineteenth century
which contains various subtle observations on love we read, with
reference to the sweet odor which poets have found in the breath of
women: "In reality many women have an intoxicatingly agreeable

breath which plays no small part in the love-compelling atmosphere which they spread around them" (*Eros oder Wörterbuch über die Physiologie*, 1849, Bd. I, p. 45).

Most of the writers on the psychology of love at this period, however, seem to have passsed over the olfactory element in sexual attraction, regarding it probably as too unæsthetic. It receives no emphasis either in Sénancour's *De l'Amour* or Stendhal's *De l'Amour* or Michelet's *L'Amour*.

The poets within recent times have frequently referred to odors, personal and other, but the novelists have more rarely done so. Zola and Huysmans, the two novelists who have most elaborately and insistently developed the olfactory side of life, have dwelt more on odors that are repulsive than on those that are agreeable. It is therefore of interest to note that in a few remarkable novels of recent times the attractiveness of personal odor has been emphasized. This is notably so in Tolstoy's *War and Peace*, in which Count Peter suddenly resolves to marry Princess Helena after inhaling her odor at a ball. In d'Annunzio's *Trionfo della Morte* the seductive and consoling odor of the beloved woman's skin is described in several passages; thus, when Giorgio kissed Ippolita's arms and shoulders, we are told, "he perceived the sharp and yet delicate perfume of her, the perfume of the skin that in the hour of joy became intoxicating as that of the tuberose, and a terrible lash to desire."

When we are dealing with the sexual significance of personal odors in man there is at the outset an important difference to be noticed in comparison with the lower mammals. Not only is the significance of odor altogether very much less, but the focus of olfactory attractiveness has been displaced. The centre of olfactory attractiveness is not, as usually among animals, in the sexual region, but is transferred to the upper part of the body. In this respect the sexual olfactory allurement in man resembles what we find in the sphere of vision, for neither the sexual organs of man nor of woman are usually beautiful in the eyes of the opposite sex, and their exhibition is not among us regarded as a necessary stage in courtship. The odor of the body, like its beauty, in so far as it can be regarded as a possible sexual allurement, has in the course of development been transferred to the upper parts. The careful concealment of the sexual region has doubtless favored this transfer. It has thus happened that when personal odor acts as a sexual allurement it is the armpit, in any case normally the chief focus of odor in the body, which mainly comes into play, together with the skin and the hair.

Aubert, of Lyons, noted that during menstruation the odor of the armpits may become more powerful, and describes it as being at this time an aromatic odor of acidulous or chloroform character. Galopin remarks that, while some women's armpits smell of sheep in rut, others, when exposed to the air, have a fragrance of ambergris or violet. Dark persons (according to Gould and Pyle) are said sometimes to exhale a prussic acid odor, and blondes more frequently musk; Galopin associates the ambergris odor more especially with blondes.

While some European poets have faintly indicated the woman's armpit as a centre of sexual attraction, it is among Eastern poets that we may find the idea more directly and naturally expressed. Thus, in a Chinese drama ("The Transmigration of Yo-Chow," *Mercure de France*, No. 8, 1901) we find a learned young doctor addressing the following poem to his betrothed:—

"When I have climbed to the bushy summit of Mount Chao,
I have still not reached to the level of your odorous armpit.
I must needs mount to the sky
Before the breeze brings to me
The perfume of that embalsamed nest!"

This poet seems, however, to have been carried to a pitch of enthusiasm unusual even in China, for his future mother-in-law, after expressing her admiration for the poem, remarks: "But who would have thought one could find so many beautiful things under my daughter's armpit!"

The odor of the armpit is the most powerful in the body, sufficiently powerful to act as a muscular stimulant even in the absence of any direct sexual association. This is indicated by an observation made by Féré, who noticed, when living opposite a laundry, that an old woman who worked near the window would, toward the close of the day, introduce her right hand under the sleeve of the other to the armpit and then hold it to her nose; this she would do about every five minutes. It was evident that the odor acted as a stimulant to her failing energies. Féré has been informed by others who have had occasion to frequent workrooms that this proceeding is by no means uncommon among persons of both sexes. (Féré, *L'Instinct Sexuel*, second edition, p. 135.) I have myself noticed the same gesture very deliberately made in the street by a young English woman of the working class, under circumstances which suggested that it acted as an immediate stimulant in fatigue.

Huysmans—who in his novels has insisted on odors, both those of a personal kind and perfumes, with great precision—has devoted one of the sketches, "Le Gousset," in his *Croquis Parisiens* (1880) to the varying odors of women's armpits. "I have followed this fragrance in the country," he remarks, "behind a group of women gleaners under the bright sun. It was excessive and terrible; it stung your nostrils like an unstoppered bottle of alkali; it seized you, irritating your mucous membrane with a rough odor which had in it something of the relish of wild duck cooked with olives and the sharp odor of the shallot. On the whole, it was not a vile or repugnant emanation; it united, as an anticipated thing, with the formidable odors of the landscape; it was the pure note, completing with the human animals' cry of heat the odorous melody of beasts and woods." He goes on to speak of the perfume of feminine arms in the ball-room. "There the aroma is of ammoniated valerian, of chlorinated urine, brutally accentuated sometimes, even with a slight scent of prussic acid about it, a faint whiff of overripe peaches." These "spice-boxes," however, Huysmans continues, are more seductive when their perfume is filtered through the garments. "The appeal of the balsam of their arms is then less insolent, less cynical, than at the ball where they are more naked, but it more easily uncages the animal in man. Various as the color of the hair, the odor of the armpit is infinitely divisible; its gamut covers the whole keyboard of odors, reaching the obstinate scents of syringa and elder, and sometimes recalling the sweet perfume of the rubbed fingers that have held a cigarette. Audacious and sometimes fatiguing in the brunette and the black woman, sharp and fierce in the red woman, the armpit is heady as some sugared wines in the blondes." It will be noted that this very exact description corresponds at various points with the remarks of more scientific observers.

Sometimes the odor of the armpit may even become a kind of fetich which is craved for its own sake and in itself suffices to give pleasure. Féré has recorded such a case, in a friend of his own, a man of 60, with whom at one time he used to hunt, of robust health and belonging to a healthy family. On these hunting expeditions he used to tease the girls and women he met (sometimes even rather old women) in a surprising manner, when he came upon them walking in the fields with their short-sleeved chemises exposed. When he had succeeded in introducing his hand into the woman's armpit he went away satisfied, and frequently held the hand to his nose with evident pleasure. After long hesitation Féré asked for an explanation, which was frankly given. As a child he had liked the odor, without knowing why. As a young man women with strong odors had stimulated him to extraordinary sexual exploits, and now they were the only women who had any influence on him. He professed to be able to recognize continence by the odor, as well as the most favorable moment for approaching a woman. Throughout life a cold in the head had always been accompanied by persistent general excitement. (Féré, *L'Instinct Sexuel*, 1902, p. 134.)

We not only have to recognize that in the course of evolution the specific odors of the sexual region have sunk into the background as a source of sexual allurements, we have further to recognize the significant fact that even those personal odors which are chiefly liable under normal circumstances to come occasionally within the conscious sexual sphere, and indeed purely personal odors of all kinds, fail to exert any attraction, but rather tend to cause antipathy, unless some degree of tumescence has already been attained. That is to say, our olfactory experiences of the human body approximate rather to our tactile experiences of it than to our visual experiences. Sight is our most intellectual sense, and we trust ourselves to it with comparative boldness without any undue dread that its messages will hurt us by their personal intimacy; we even court its experiences, for it is the chief organ of our curiosity, as smell is of a dog's. But smell with us has ceased to be a leading channel of intellectual curiosity. Personal odors do not, as vision does, give us information that is very largely intellectual; they make an appeal that is mainly of an intimate, emotional, imaginative character. They thus tend, when we are in our normal condition, to arouse what James calls the antisexual instinct.

"I cannot understand how people do not see how the senses are connected," said Jenny Lind to J. A. Symonds (Horatio Brown, *J. A. Symonds*, vol. i, p. 207). "What I have suffered from my sense of smell! My youth was misery from my acuteness of sensibility."

Mantegazza discusses the strength of olfactory antipathies (*Fisiologia dell' Odio*, p. 101), and mentions that once when ill in Paraguay he was nursed by an Indian girl of 16, who was fresh as a peach and extremely clean, but whose odor—"a mixture of wild beast's lair and decayed onions"—caused nausea and almost made him faint.

Moll (*Untersuchungen über die Libido Sexualis*, bd. i, p. 135) records the case of a neuropathic man who was constantly rendered impotent by his antipathy to personal body odors. It had very frequently happened to him to be attracted by the face and appearance of a girl, but at the last moment potency was inhibited by the perception of personal odor.

In the case of a man of distinguished ability known to me, belonging to a somewhat neuropathic family, there is extreme sensitiveness to the smell of a woman, which is frequently the most obvious thing to him about her. He has seldom known a woman whose natural perfume entirely suits him, and his olfactory impressions have frequently been the immediate cause of a rupture of relationships.

It was formerly discussed whether strong personal odor constituted adequate ground for divorce. Hagen, who brings forward references on this point (*Sexuelle Osphresiologie*, pp. 75-83), considers that the body odors are normally and naturally repulsive because they are closely associated with the capryl group of odors, which are those of many of the excretions.

Olfactory antipathies are, however, often strictly subordinated to the individual's general emotional attitude toward the object from which they emanate. This is illustrated in the case, known to me, of a man who on a hot day entering a steamboat with a woman to whom he was attached seated himself between her and a man, a stranger. He soon became conscious of an axillary odor which he concluded to come from the man and which he felt as disagreeable. But a little later he realized that it proceeded from his own companion, and with this discovery the odor at once lost its disagreeable character.

In this respect a personal odor resembles a personal touch. Two intimate touches of the hand, though of precisely similar physical quality, may in their emotional effects be separated by an immeasurable interval, in dependence on our attitude toward the person from whom they proceed.

Personal odor, in order to make its allurement felt, and not to arouse antipathy, must, in normal persons, have been preceded by conditions which have inhibited the play of the antisexual instinct. A certain degree of tumescence must already have been attained. It is even possible, when we bear in mind the intimate sympathy between the sexual sphere and the nose, that the olfactory organ needs to have its sensibility modified in a form receptive to sexual messages, though such an assumption is by no means necessary. It is when such a faint preliminary degree of tumescence has been attained, however it may have been attained,—for the methods of tumescence, as we know, are innumerable,—that a sympathetic personal

odor is enabled to make its appeal. If we analyze the cases in
which olfactory perceptions have proved potent in love, we
shall nearly always find that they have been experienced under
circumstances favorable for the occurrence of tumescence.
When this is not the case we may reasonably suspect the presence of some degree of perversion.

In the oft-quoted case of the Austrian peasant who found that
he was aided in seducing young women by dancing with them and then
wiping their faces with a handkerchief he had kept in his armpit, we
may doubtless regard the preliminary excitement of the dance as an
essential factor in the influence produced.

In the same way, I am acquainted with the case of a lady not
usually sensitive to simple body odors (though affected by perfumes
and flowers) who on one occasion, when already in a state of sexual
erethism, was highly excited when perceiving the odor of her lover's
axilla.

The same influence of preliminary excitement may be seen in
another instance known to me, that of a gentleman who when traveling
abroad fell in with three charming young ladies during a long railway
journey. He was conscious of a pleasurable excitement caused by the
prolonged intimacy of the journey, but this only became definitely
sexual when the youngest of the ladies, stretching before him to look
out of the window and holding on to the rack above, accidentally
brought her axilla into close proximity with his face, whereupon erection
was caused, although he himself regards personal odors, at all events
when emanating from strangers, as indifferent or repulsive.

A medical correspondent, referring to the fact that with many
men (indeed women also) sexual excitement occurs after dancing for
a considerable time, remarks that he considers the odor of the woman's
sweat is here a considerable factor.

The characteristics of olfaction which our investigation
has so far revealed have not, on the whole, been favorable to
the influence of personal odors as a sexual attraction in civilized men. It is a primitive sense which had its flowering time
before men arose; it is a comparatively unæsthetic sense; it is
a somewhat obtuse sense which among Europeans is usually
incapable of perceiving the odor of the "human flower"—to
use Goethe's phrase—except on very close contact, and on this
account, and on account of the fact that it is a predominantly

emotional sense, personal odors in ordinary social intercourse are less likely to arouse the sexual instinct than the antisexual instinct. If a certain degree of tumescence is required before a personal odor can exert an attractive influence, a powerful personal odor, strong enough to be perceived before any degree of tumescence is attained, will tend to cause repulsion, and in so doing tend, consciously or unconsciously, to excite prejudice against personal odor altogether. This is actually the case in civilization, and most people, it would appear, view with more or less antipathy the personal odors of those persons to whom they are not sexually attracted, while their attitude is neutral in this respect toward the individuals to whom they are sexually attracted.[1] The following statement by a correspondent seems to me to express the experience of the majority of men in this respect: "I do not notice that different people have different smells. Certain women I have known have been in the habit of using particular scents, but no associations could be aroused if I were to smell the same scent now, for I should not identify it. As a boy I was very fond of scent, and I associate this with my marked sexual proclivities. I like a woman to use a little scent. It rouses my sexual feelings, but not to any large extent. I dislike the smell of a woman's vagina." While the last statement seems to express the feelings of many if not most men, it may be proper to add that there seems no natural reason why the vulvar odor of a clean and healthy woman should be other than agreeable to a normal man who is her lover.

In literature it is the natural odor of women rather than men which receives attention. We should expect this to be the case since literature is chiefly produced by men. The question as to whether men or women are really more apt to be sexually influenced in this way cannot thus be decided. Among animals, it seems probable, both sexes are alike influenced by odors, for, while it is usually the male whose sexual regions

---

[1] Moll's inquiries among normal persons have also shown that few people are conscious of odor as a sexual attraction. (*Untersuchungen über die Libido Sexualis.* Bd. 1, p. 133.)

are furnished with special scent glands, when such occur, the peculiar odor of the female during the sexual season is certainly not less efficacious as an allurement to the male. If we compare the general susceptibility of men and women to agreeable odors, apart from the question of sexual allurement, there can be little doubt that it is most marked among women. As Groos points out, even among children little girls are more interested in scents than boys, and the investigations of various workers, especially Garbini, have shown that there is actually a greater power of discriminating odors among girls than among boys. Marro has gone further, and in an extended series of observations on girls before and after the establishment of puberty—which is of considerable interest from the point of view of the sexual significance of olfaction—he has shown reason to believe that girls acquire an increased susceptibility to odors when sexual life begins, although they show no such increased powers as regards the other senses.[1] On the whole, it would appear that, while women are not apt to be seriously affected, in the absence of any preliminary excitation, by crude body odors, they are by no means insusceptible to the sexual influence of olfactory impressions. It is probable, indeed, that they are more affected, and more frequently affected, in this way, than are men.

Edouard de Goncourt, in his novel *Chérie*—the intimate history of a young girl, founded, he states, on much personal observation—describes (Chapter LXXXV) the delight with which sensuous, but chaste young girls often take in strong perfumes. "Perfume and love," he remarks, "impart delights which are closely allied." In an earlier chapter (XLIV) he writes of his heroine at the age of 15: "The intimately happy emotion which the young girl experienced in reading *Paul et Virginie* and other honestly amorous books she sought to make more complete and intense and penetrating by soaking the book with scent, and the love-story reached her senses and imagination through pages moist with liquid perfume."

---

[1] Marro, *La Pubertà*, 1898, Chapter II. Tardif found in boys that perfumes exerted little or no influence on circulation and respiration before puberty, though his observations on this point were too few to carry weight.

Garbini (*Archivio per l'Antropologia*, 1896, fasc. 3) in a very thorough investigation of a large number of children, found that the earliest osmo-gustative sensations occurred in the fourth week in girls, the fifth week in boys; the first real and definite olfactory sensations appeared in the fifteenth month in girls, in the sixteenth in boys; while experiments on several hundred children between the ages of 3 and 6 years showed the girls slightly, but distinctly, superior to the boys. It may, of course, be argued that these results merely show a somewhat greater precocity of girls. I have summarized the main investigations into this question in *Man and Woman*, revised and enlarged edition, 1904, pp. 134-138. On the whole, they seem to indicate greater olfactory acuteness on the part of women, but the evidence is by no means altogether concordant in this sense. Popular and general scientific opinion is also by no means always in harmony. Thus, Tardif, in his book on odors in relation to the sexual instinct, throughout assumes, as a matter of course, that the sense of smell is most keen in men; while, on the other hand, I note that in a pamphlet by Mr. Martin Perls, a manufacturing perfumer, it is stated with equal confidence that "it is a well-known fact that ladies have, even without a practice of long standing, a keener sense of smell than men," and on this account he employs a staff of young ladies for testing perfumes by smell in the laboratory by the glazed paper test.

It is sometimes said that the use of strong perfumes by women indicates a dulled olfactory organ. On the other hand, it is said that the use of tobacco deadens the sensitiveness of the masculine nose. Both these statements seem to be without foundation. The use of a large amount of perfume is rather a question of taste than a question of sensory acuteness (not to mention that those who live in an atmosphere of perfume are, of course, only faintly conscious of it), and the chemist perfumer in his laboratory surrounded by strong odors can distinguish them all with great delicacy. As regards tobacco, in Spain the *cigarreras* are women and girls who live perpetually in an atmosphere of tobacco, and Señora Pardo Bazan, who knows them well, remarks in her novel, *La Tribuna*, which deals with life in a tobacco factory, that "the acuity of the sense of smell of the *cigarreras* is notable, and it would seem that instead of blunting the nasal membrane the tobacco makes the olfactory nerves keener."

"It was the same as if I was in a sweet apple garden, from the sweetness that came to me when the light wind passed over them and stirred their clothes," a woman is represented as saying concerning a troop of handsome men in the Irish sagas (*Cuchulain of Muirthemne*, p. 161). The pleasure and excitement experienced by a woman in the odor of her lover is usually felt concerning a vague and mixed odor which may be characteristic, but is not definitely traceable to any specific bodily sexual odor. The general odor of the man she loves, one woman states, is highly, sometimes even overwhelmingly, attractive to her; but the specific odor of the male sexual organs which she describes as fishy has no attraction. A man writes that in his relations with women he has never been able to detect that they were influenced by the axillary or other specific odors. A woman writes: "To me any personal odor, as that of perspiration, is very disagreeable, and the healthy *naked* human body is very free from any odor. Fresh perspiration has no disagreeable smell; it is only by retention in the clothing that it becomes objectionable. The faint smell of smoke which lingers round men who smoke much is rather exciting to me, but only when it is *very* faint. If at all strong it becomes disagreeable. As most of the men who have attracted me have been great smokers, there is doubtless a direct association of ideas. It has only once occurred to me that an indifferent unpleasant smell became attractive in connection with some particular person. In this case it was the scent of stale tobacco, such as comes from the end of a cold cigar or cigarette. It was, and is now, very disagreeable to me, but, for the time and in connection with a particular person, it seemed to me more delightful and exciting than the most delicious perfume. I think, however, only a very strong attraction could overcome a dislike of this sort, and I doubt if I could experience such a twist-round if it had been a personal odor. Stale tobacco, though nasty, conveys no mentally disagreeable idea. I mean it does not suggest dirt or unhealthiness."

It is probably significant of the somewhat considerable part which, in one way or another, odors and perfumes play in the emotional life of women, that, of the 4 women whose sexual histories are recorded in Appendix B of vol. iii of these *Studies*, all are liable to experience sexual effects from olfactory stimuli, 3 of them from personal odors (though this fact is not in every case brought out in the histories as recorded), while of the 8 men not one has considered his olfactory experiences in this respect as worthy of mention.

The very marked sexual fascination which odor, associated with the men they love, exerts on women has easily passed unperceived, since women have not felt called upon to proclaim it. In sexual inversion, however, when the woman takes a more active and outspoken part than in normal love, it may very clearly be traced. Here, indeed, it is often exaggerated, in consequence of the common tendency for neurotic and neurasthenic persons to be more than normally susceptible to the influence of odors. In the majority of inverted women, it may safely be said, the odor of the beloved person plays a very considerable part. Thus, one inverted woman asks the woman she loves to send her some of her hair that she may intoxicate herself in solitude with its perfume (*Archivio di Psicopatie Sessuali*, vol. i, fasc. 3, p. 36). Again, a young girl with some homosexual tendencies, was apt to experience sexual emotions when in ordinary contact with schoolfellows whose body odor was marked (Féré, *L'Instinct Sexuel*, p. 260). Such examples are fairly typical.

That the body odor of men may in a large number of cases be highly agreeable and sexually attractive is shown by the testimony of male sexual inverts. There is abundant evidence to this effect. Raffalovich (*L'Uranisme et l'Unisexualité*, p. 126) insists on the importance of body odors as a sexual attraction to the male invert, and is inclined to think that the increased odor of the man's own body during sexual excitement may have an auto-aphrodisiacal effect which is reflected on the body of the loved person. The odor of peasants, of men who work in the open air, is specially apt to be found attractive. Moll mentions the case of an inverted man who found the "forest, mosslike odor" of a schoolfellow irresistibly attractive.

The following passage from a letter written by an Italian marquis has been sent to me: "Bonifazio stripped one evening, to give me pleasure. He has the full, rounded flesh and amber coloring which painters of the Giorgione school gave to their S. Sebastians. When he began to dress, I took up an old *fascia*, or girdle of netted silk, which was lying under his breeches, and which still preserved the warmth of his body. I buried my face in it, and was half inebriated by its exquisite aroma of young manhood and fresh hay. He told me he had worn it for two years. No wonder it was redolent of him. I asked him to let me keep it as a souvenir. He smiled and said: 'You like it because it has lain so long upon my *pancia*.' 'Yes, just so,' I replied; 'whenever I kiss it, thus and thus, it will bring you back to me.' Sometimes I tie it round my naked waist before I go to bed. The smell of it is enough to cause a powerful erection, and the contact of its fringes with my testicles and phallus has once or twice produced an involuntary emission."

I may here reproduce a communication which has reached me concerning the attractiveness of the odor of peasants: "One predominant attraction of these men is that they are pure and clean; their bodies in a state of healthy normal function. Then they possess, if they are temperate, what the Greek poet Straton called the φυδικὴ χρωτὸs (a quality which, according to this authority, is never found in women). This 'natural fair perfume of the flesh' is a peculiar attribute of young men who live in the open air and deal with natural objects. Even their perspiration has an odor very different from that of girls in ball-rooms: more refined, ethereal, pervasive, delicate, and difficult to seize. When they have handled hay—in the time of hay-harvest, or in winter, when they bring hay down from mountain huts—the youthful peasants carry about with them the smell of 'a field the

Lord hath blesssed.' Their bodies and their clothes exhale an in-definable fragrance of purity and sex combined. Every gland of the robust frame seems to have accumulated scent from herbs and grasses, which slowly exudes from the cool, fresh skin of the lad. You do not perceive it in a room. You must take the young man's hands and bury your face in them, or be covered with him under the same blanket in one bed, to feel this aroma. No sensual impression on the nerves of smell is more poignantly impregnated with spiritual poetry—the poetry of adolescence, and early hours upon the hills, and labor cheerfully ac-complished, and the harvest of God's gifts to man brought home by human industry. It is worth mentioning that Aristophanes, in his description of the perfect Athenian Ephebus, dwells upon his being redolent of natural perfumes."

In a passage in the second part of *Faust* Goethe (who appears to have felt considerable interest in the psychology of smell) makes three women speak concerning the ambrosiacal odor of young men.

In this connection, also, I note a passage in a poem ("Appleton House") by our own English poet Marvell, which it is of interest to quote:—

> "And now the careless victors play,
> Dancing the triumphs of the hay,
> When every mower's wholesome heat
> Smells like an Alexander's sweat.
> Their females fragrant as the mead
> Which they in fairy circles tread,
> When at their dance's end they kiss,
> Their new-mown hay not sweeter is."

IV.

The Influence of Perfumes—Their Aboriginal Relationship to Sexual Body Odors—This True even of the Fragrance of Flowers—The Synthetic Manufacture of Perfumes—The Sexual Effects of Perfumes—Perfumes perhaps Originally Used to Heighten the Body Odors—The Special Significance of the Musk Odor—Its Wide Natural Diffusion in Plants and Animals and Man—Musk a Powerful Stimulant—Its Widespread Use as a Perfume—Peau d'Espagne—The Smell of Leather and its Occasional Sexual Effects—The Sexual Influence of the Odors of Flowers—The Identity of many Plant Odors with Certain Normal and Abnormal Body Odors—The Smell of Semen in this Connection.

So FAR we have been mainly concerned with purely personal odors. It is, however, no longer possible to confine the discussion of the sexual significance of odor within the purely animal limit. The various characteristics of personal odor which have been noted—alike those which tend to make it repulsive and those which tend to make it attractive—have led to the use of artificial perfumes, to heighten the natural odor when it is regarded as attractive, to disguise it when it is regarded as repellent; while at the same time, happily covering both of these impulses, has developed the pure delight in perfume for its own agreeableness, the æsthetic side of olfaction. In this way—although in a much less constant and less elaborate manner—the body became adorned to the sense of smell just as by clothing and ornament it is adorned to the sense of sight.

But—and this is a point of great significance from our present standpoint—we do not really leave the sexual sphere by introducing artificial perfumes. The perfumes which we extract from natural products, or, as is now frequently the case, produce by chemical synthesis, are themselves either actually animal sexual odors or allied in character or composition to the personal odors they are used to heighten or disguise. Musk is the product of glands of the male *Moschus moschiferus* which correspond to preputial sebaceous glands;

castoreum is the product of similar sexual glands in the beaver, and civet likewise from the civet; ambergris is an intestinal calculus found in the rectum of the cachelot.[1] Not only, however, are nearly all the perfumes of animal origin, in use by civilized man, odors which have a specifically sexual object among the animals from which they are derived, but even the perfumes of flowers may be said to be of sexual character. They are given out at the reproductive period in the lives of plants, and they clearly have very largely as their object an appeal to the insects who secure plant fertilization, such appeal having as its basis the fact that among insects themselves olfactory sensibility has in many cases been developed in their own mating.[2] There is, for example, a moth in which both sexes are similarly and inconspicuously marked, but the males diffuse an agreeable odor, said to be like pineapple, which attracts the females.[3] If, therefore, the odors of flowers have developed because they proved useful to the plant by attracting insects or other living creatures, it is obvious that the advantage would lie with those plants which could put forth an animal sexual odor of agreeable character, since such an odor would prove fascinating to animal creatures. We here have a very simple explanation of the fundamental identity of odors in the animal and vegetable worlds. It thus comes about that from a psychological point of view we are not really entering a new field when we begin to discuss the influence of perfumes other than those of the animal body. We are merely concerned with somewhat more complex or somewhat more refined sexual odors; they are not specifically different from the human odors and they mingle with them harmoniously. Popular language

---

[1] H. Beauregard, *Matière Médicale Zoölogique: Histoire des Drogues d'origine Animale*, 1901.

[2] Professor Plateau, of Ghent, has for many years carried on a series of experiments which would even tend to show that insects are scarcely attracted by the colors of flowers at all, but mainly influenced by a sense which would appear to be smell. His experiments have been recorded during recent years (from 1887) in the *Bulletins de l'Académie Royale de Belgique*, and have from time to time been summarized in *Nature*, e.g., February 5, 1903.

[3] David Sharp, *Cambridge Natural History: Insects*, Part II, p. 398.

bears witness to the truth of this statement, and the normal and abnormal human odors, as we have already seen, are constantly compared to artificial, animal, and plant odors, to chloroform, to musk, to violet, to mention only those similitudes which seem to occur most frequently.

The methods now employed for obtaining the perfumes universally used in civilized lands are three: (1) the extraction of odoriferous compounds from the neutral products in which they occur; (2) the artificial preparation of naturally occurring odoriferous compounds by synthetic processes; (3) the manufacture of materials which yield odors resembling those of pleasant smelling natural objects. (See, *e.g.*, "Natural and Artificial Perfumes," *Nature*, December 27, 1900.) The essential principles of most of our perfumes belong to the complex class of organic compounds known as terpenes. During recent years a number of the essential elements of natural perfumes have been studied, in many cases the methods of preparing them artificially discovered, and they are largely replacing the use of natural perfumes not only for soaps, etc., but for scent essences, though it appears to be very difficult to imitate exactly the delicate fragrance achieved by Nature. Artificial musk was discovered accidentally by Bauer when studying the butyltoluenes contained in a resin extractive. Vanillin, the odoriferous principle of the vanilla bean, is an aldehyde which was first artificially prepared by Tiemann and Haarmann in 1874 by oxidizing coniferin, a glucoside contained in the sap of various coniferæ, but it now appears to be usually manufactured from eugenol, a phenol contained in oil of cloves. Piperonal, an aldehyde closely allied to vanillin, is used in perfumery under the name of heliotropin and is prepared from oil of sassafras and oil of camphor. Cumarine, the material to which tonka bean, sweet woodruff, and new-mown hay owe their characteristic odors, was synthetically prepared by W. H. Parkin in 1868 by heating sodiosalicylic aldehyde with acetic anhydride, though now more cheaply prepared from an herb growing in Florida. Irone, which has the perfume of violets, was isolated in 1893 from a ketone contained in orris-root; and ionone, another ketone which has a very closely similar odor of fresh violets and was isolated after some years' further work, is largely used in the preparation of violet perfume. Irone and ionone are closely similar in composition to oil of turpentine which when taken into the body is partly converted into perfume and gives a strong odor of violets to the urine. "Little has yet been accomplished toward ascertaining the relation between the odor and the chemical constitution of substances in general. Hydrocarbons as a class possess considerable similarity in odor, so also do the organic sulphides and,

to a much smaller extent, the ketones. The subject waits for some
one to correlate its various physiological, psychological and physical
aspects in the same way that Helmholtz did for sound. It seems, as
yet, impossible to assign any probable reason to the fact that many
substances have a pleasant odor. It may, however, be worth suggesting that certain compounds, such as the volatile sulphides and
the indoles, have very unpleasant odors because they are normal con-
stituents of mammalian excreta and of putrefied animal products; the
repulsive odors may be simply necessary results of evolutionary processes." (*Loc. cit., Nature,* December 27, 1900.)

Many of the perfumes in use are really combinations of a great
many different odors in varying proportions, such as oil of rose, lavender oil, ylang-ylang, etc. The most highly appreciated perfumes are
often made up of elements which in stronger proportion would be regarded as highly unpleasant.

In the study and manufacture of perfumes Germany and France
have taken the lead in recent times. The industry is one of great importance. In France alone the trade in perfumes amounts to £4,000,000.

It is doubtless largely owing to the essential and fundamental identity of odors—to the chemical resemblances even
of odors from the most widely remote sources—that we find
that perfumes in many cases have the same sexual effects as
are primitively possessed by the body odors. In northern countries, where the use of perfumes is chiefly cultivated by women,
it is by women that this sexual influence is most liable to be
felt. In the South and in the East it appears to be at least
equally often experienced by men. Thus, in Italy Mantegazza
remarks that "many men of strong sexual temperament cannot
visit with impunity a laboratory of essences and perfumes."[1]
In the East we find it stated in the Islamic book entitled *The
Perfumed Garden of Sheik Nefzaoui* that the use of perfumes by
women, as well as by men, excites to the generative act. It is
largely in reliance on this fact that in many parts of the world,
especially among Eastern peoples and occasionally among ourselves in Europe, women have been accustomed to perfume the
body and especially the vulva.[2]

----

[1] Mantegazza, *Fisiologia dell' Amore,* 1873, p. 176.
[2] Mantegazza (*L'Amour dans l'Humanité,* p. 94) refers to various
peoples who practice this last custom. Egypt was a great centre of the
practice more than 3000 years ago.

It seems highly probable that, as has been especially emphasized by Hagen, perfumes were primitively used by women, not as is sometimes the case in civilization, with the idea of disguising any possible natural odor, but with the object of heightening and fortifying the natural odor.[1] If the primitive man was inclined to disparage a woman whose odor was slight or imperceptible,—turning away from her with contempt, as the Polynesian turned away from the ladies of Sydney: "They have no smell!"—women would inevitably seek to supplement any natural defects in this respect, and to accentuate their odorous qualities, in the same way as by corsets and bustles, even in civilization, they have sought to accentuate the sexual saliencies of their bodies. In this way we may, as Hagen suggests, explain the fact that until recent times the odors preferred by women have not been the most delicate or exquisite, but the strongest, the most animal, the most sexual: musk, castoreum, civet, and ambergris.

In that interesting novel—dealing with the adventures of a Jewish maiden at the Persian court of Xerxes—which under the title of *Esther* has found its way into the Old Testament we are told that it was customary in the royal harem at Shushan to submit the women to a very prolonged course of perfuming before they were admitted to the king: "six months with oil of myrrh and six months with sweet odors." (*Esther*, Chapter II, v. 12.)

In the *Arabian Nights* there are many allusions to the use of perfumes by women with a more or less definitely stated aphrodisiacal intent. Thus we read in the story of Kamaralzaman: "With fine incense I will perfume my breasts, my belly, my whole body, so that my skin may melt more sweetly in thy mouth, O apple of my eye!"

Even among savages the perfuming of the body is sometimes practiced with the object of inducing love in the partner. Schellong states that the Papuans of Kaiser Wilhelm's Land rub various fragrant plants into their bodies for this purpose. (*Zeitschrift für Ethnologie*, 1899, ht. i, p. 19.) The significance of this practice is more fully revealed by Haddon when studying the Papuans of Torres Straits, among whom the initiative in courtship is taken by the women. It was by scenting

---

[1] Hagen, *Sexuelle Osphrésiologie*, 1901, p. 226. It has been suggested to me by a medical correspondent that one of the primitive objects of the hair, alike on head, mons veneris, and axilla, was to collect sweat and heighten its odor to sexual ends.

himself with a pungent odorous substance that a young man indicated that he was ready to be sued by the girls. A man would wear this scent at the back of his neck during a dance in order to attract the attention of a particular girl; it was believed to act with magical certainty, after the manner of a charm (*Reports of the Cambridge Anthropological Expedition to Torres Straits*, vol. v, pp. 211, 222, and 328).

The perfume which is of all perfumes the most interesting from the present point of view is certainly musk. With ambergris, musk is the chief member of Linnæus's group of *Odores ambrosiacæ*, a group which in sexual significances, as Zwaardemaker remarks, ranks besides the capryl group of odors. It is a perfume of ancient origin; its name is Persian[1] (indicating doubtless the channel whence it reached Europe) and ultimately derived from the Sanskrit word for testicle in allusion to the fact that it was contained in a pouch removed from the sexual parts of the male musk-deer. Musk odors, however, often of considerable strength, are very widely distributed in Nature, alike among animals and plants. This is indicated by the frequency with which the word "musk" forms part of the names of animals and plants which are by no means always nearly related. We have the musk-ox, the musky mole, several species called musk-rat, the musk-duck, the musk-beetle; while among plants which have received their names from a real or supposed musky odor are, besides several that are called musk-plant, the musk-rose, the musk-hyacinth, the musk-mallow, the musk-orchid, the musk-melon, the musk-cherry, the musk-pear, the musk-plum, muskat and muscatels, musk-seed, musk-tree, musk-wood, etc.[2] But a musky odor is not merely widespread in Nature among plants and the lower animals, it is peculiarly associated with man. Incidentally we have already seen how it is regarded as characteristic of some races of man, especially the Chinese. Moreover, the smell of the negress is said to be musky in character, and

---

[1] The names of all our chief perfumes are Arabic or Persian: civet, musk, ambergris, attar, camphor, etc.

[2] Cloquet (*Osphrésiologie*, pp. 73-76) has an interesting passage on the prevalence of the musk odor in animals, plants, and even mineral substances.

among Europeans a musky odor is said to be characteristic of blondes. Laycock, in his *Nervous Diseases of Women*, stated his opinion that "the musk odor is certainly the sexual odor of man"; and Féré states that the musk odor is that among natural perfumes most nearly approaching the odor of the sexual secretions. We have seen that the Chinese poet vaunts the musky odor of his mistress's armpits, while another Oriental saying concerning the attractive woman is that "her navel is filled with musk." Persian literature contains many references to musk as an attractive body odor, and Firdusi speaks of a woman's hair as "a crown of musk," while the Arabian poet Motannabi says of his mistress that "her hyacinthine hair smells sweeter than Scythian musk." Galopin stated that he knew women whose natural odor of musk (and less frequently of ambergris) was sufficiently strong to impart to a bath in less than an hour a perfume due entirely to the exhalations of the musky body; it must be added that Galopin was an enthusiast in this matter.

The special significance of musk from our present point of view lies not only in the fact that we here have a perfume, widely scattered throughout nature and often in an agreeable form, which is at the same time a very frequent personal odor in man. Musk is the odor which not only in the animals to which it has given a name, but in many others, is a specifically sexual odor, chiefly emitted during the sexual season. The sexual odors, indeed, of most animals seem to be modifications of musk. The Sphinx moth has a musky odor which is confined to the male and is doubtless sexual. Some lizards have a musky odor which is heightened at the sexual season; crocodiles during the pairing season emit from their submaxillary glands a musky odor which pervades their haunts. In the same way elephants emit a musky odor from their facial glands during the rutting season. The odor of the musk-duck is chiefly confined to the breeding season.[1] The musky odor of the negress is said to be heightened during sexual excitement.

---

[1] Laycock brings together various instances of the sexual odors of animals, insisting on their musky character (*Nervous Diseases of*

The predominance of musk as a sexual odor is associated with the fact that its actual nervous influence, apart from the presence of sexual associations, is very considerable. Féré found it to be a powerful muscular stimulant. In former times musk enjoyed a high reputation as a cardiac stimulant; it fell into disuse, but in recent years its use in asthenic states has been revived, and excellent results, it has been claimed, have followed its administration in cases of collapse from Asiatic cholera. For sexual torpor in women it still has (like vanilla and sandal) a certain degree of reputation, though it is not often used, and some of the old Arabian physicians (especially Avicenna) recommended it, with castoreum and myrrh, for amenorrhœa. Its powerful action is indicated by the experience of Esquirol, who stated that he had seen cases in which sensory stimulation by musk in women during lactation had produced mania. It has always had the reputation, more especially in the Mohammedan East, of being a sexual stimulant to men; "the noblest of perfumes," it is called in *El Ktab*, "and that which most provokes to venery."

It is doubtless a fact significant of the special sexual effects of musk that, as Laycock remarked, in cases of special idiosyncrasy to odors, musk appears to be that odor which is most liked or disliked. Thus, the old English physician Whytt remarked that "several delicate women who could easily bear the stronger smell of tobacco have been thrown into fits by musk, ambergris, or a pale rose."[1] It may be remarked that in the *Perfumed Garden of Sheik Nefzaoui* it is stated that it is by their sexual effects that perfumes tend to throw women into a kind of swoon, and Lucretius remarks that a woman who smells castoreum, another animal sexual perfume, at the time of her menstrual period may swoon.[2]

Women; section, "Odors"). See also a section in the *Descent of Man* (Part II, Chapter XVIII), in which Darwin argues that "the most odoriferous males are the most successful in winning the females." Distant also has an interesting paper on this subject, "Biological Suggestions," *Zoölogist*, May, 1902; he points out the significant fact that musky odors are usually confined to the male, and argues that animal odors generally are more often attractive than protective.

[1] R. Whytt, *Works*, 1768, p. 543.
[2] Lucretius, VI, 790-5.

Not only is musk the most cherished perfume of the Islamic world, and the special favorite of the Prophet himself, who greatly delighted in perfumes ("I love your world," he is reported to have said in old age, "for its women and its perfumes"),[1] it is the only perfume generally used by the women of a land in which the refinements of life have been carried so far as Japan, and they received it from the Chinese.[2]

Moreover, musk is still the most popular of European perfumes. It is the perfumes containing musk, Piesse states in his well-known book on the *Art of Perfumery*, which sell best. It is certainly true that in its simple form the odor of musk is not nowadays highly considered in Europe. This fact is connected with the ever-growing refinement in accordance with which the specific odors of the sexual regions in human beings tend to lose their primitive attractiveness and bodily odors generally become mingled with artificial perfumes and so disguised. But, although musk in its simple form, and under its ancient name, has lost its hold in Europe, it is an interesting and significant fact that it is still the perfumes which contains musk that are the most widely popular.

Peau d'Espagne may be mentioned as a highly complex and luxurious perfume, often the favorite scent of sensuous persons, which really owes a large part of its potency to the presence of the crude animal sexual odors of musk and civet. It consists of wash-leather steeped in ottos of neroli, rose, santal, lavender, verbena, bergamot, cloves, and cinnamon, subsequently smeared with civet and musk. It is said by some, probably with a certain degree of truth, that Peau d'Espagne is of

---

[1] Mohammed, said Ayesha, was very fond of perfumes, especially "men's scents," musk and ambergris. He used also to burn camphor on odoriferous wood and enjoy the fragrant smell, while he never refused perfumes when offered them as a present. The things he cared for most, said Ayesha, were women, scents, and foods. Muir, *Life of Mahomet*, vol. iii, p. 297.

[2] H. ten Kate, *International Centralblatt für Anthropologie*, Ht. 6, 1902. This author, who made observations on Japanese with Zwaardemaker's olfactometer, found that, contrary to an opinion sometimes stated, they have a somewhat defective sense of smell. He remarks that there are no really native Japanese perfumes.

all perfumes that which most nearly approaches the odor of a woman's skin; whether it also suggests the odor of leather is not so clear.

There is, however, no doubt that the smell of leather has a curiously stimulating sexual influence on many men and women. It is an odor which seems to occupy an intermediate place between the natural body odors and the artificial perfumes for which it sometimes serves as a basis; possibly it is to this fact that its occasional sexual influence is owing, for, as we have already seen, there is a tendency for sexual allurement to attach to odors which are not the specific personal body odors but yet are related to them. Moll considers, no doubt rightly, that shoe fetichism, perhaps the most frequent of sexual fetichistic perversions, is greatly favored, if, indeed, it does not owe its origin to, the associated odor of the feet and of the shoes.[1] He narrates a case of shoe fetichism in a man in which the perversion began at the age of 6, when for the first time he wore new shoes, having previously used only the left-off shoes of his elder brother; he felt and smelt these new shoes with sensations of unmeasured pleasure; and a few years later began to use shoes as a method of masturbation.[2] Näcke has also recorded the case of a shoe fetichist who declared that the sexual attraction of shoes (usually his wife's) lay largely in the odor of the leather.[3] Krafft-Ebing, again, brings forward a case of shoe fetichism in which the significant fact is mentioned that the subject bought a pair of leather cuffs to smell while masturbating.[4] Restif de la Bretonne, who was somewhat of a shoe fetichist, appears to have enjoyed smelling shoes. It is not probable that the odor of leather explains the whole of shoe fetichism,—as we shall see when, in another "Study," this question comes before us—and in many cases it cannot be said to enter at all; it is, however, one of the factors. Such a con-

---

[1] Moll: *Die Konträre Sexualempfindung*, third edition, 1890, p. 306.
[2] Moll: *Libido Sexualis*, bd. 1, p. 284.
[3] P. Näcke, "Un Cas de Fetichisme de Souliers," *Bulletin de la Société de Médecine Mentale de Belgique*, 1894.
[4] *Psychopathia Sexualis*, English edition, p. 167.

clusion is further supported by the fact that by many the odor of new shoes is sometimes desired as an adjuvant to coitus. It is in the experience of prostitutes that such a device is not infrequent. Näcke mentions that a colleague of his was informed by a prostitute that several of her clients desired the odor of new shoes in the room, and that she was accustomed to obtain the desired perfume by holding her shoes for a moment over the flame of a spirit lamp.

The direct sexual influence of the odor of leather is, however, more conclusively proved by those instances in which it exists apart from shoes or other objects having any connection with the human body. I have elsewhere in these "Studies"[1] recorded the case of a lady, entirely normal in sexual and other respects, who is conscious of a considerable degree of pleasurable sexual excitement in the presence of the smell of leather objects, more especially of leather-bound ledgers and in shops where leather objects are sold. She thinks this dates from the period when, as a child of 9, she was sometimes left alone for a time on a high stool in an office. A possible explanation in this case lies in the supposition that on one of these early occasions sexual excitement was produced by the contact with the stool (in a way that is not infrequent in young girls) and that the accidentally associated odor of leather permanently affected the nervous system, while the really significant contact left no permanent impression. Even on such a supposition it might, however, still be maintained that a real potency of the leather odor is illustrated by this case, and this is likewise suggested by the fact that the same subject is also sexually affected by various perfumes and odorous flowers not recalling leather.[2]

---

[1] *Studies in the Psychology of Sex*, vol. iii, "Appendix B, History VIII."

[2] Philip Salmuth (*Observationes Medicæ*, Centuria II, no. 63) in the seventeenth century recorded a case in which a young girl of noble birth (whose sister was fond of eating chalk, cinnamon, and cloves) experienced extreme pleasure in smelling old books. It would appear, however, that in this case the fascination lay not so much in the odor of the leather as in the mouldy odor of worm-eaten books; "*fœtore veterum librorum, a blattis et tineis exesorum, situque prorsus corruptorum*" are Salmuth's words.

It has been suggested to me by a lady that the odor of leather suggests that of the sexual organs. The same suggestion is made by Hagen,[1] and I find it stated by Gould and Pyle that menstruating girls sometimes smell of leather. The secret of its influence may thus be not altogether obscure; in the fact that leather is animal skin, and that it may thus vaguely stir the olfactory sensibilities which had been ancestrally affected by the sexual stimulus of the skin odor lies the probable foundation of the mystery.

In the absence of all suggestion of personal or animal odors, in its most exquisite forms in the fragrance of flowers, olfactory sensations are still very frequently of a voluptuous character. Mantegazza has remarked that it is a proof of the close connection between the sense of smell and the sexual organs that the expression of pleasure produced by olfaction resembles the expression of sexual pleasures.[2] Make the chastest woman smell the flowers she likes best, he remarks, and she will close her eyes, breathe deeply, and, if very sensitive, tremble all over, presenting an intimate picture which otherwise she never shows, except perhaps to her lover. He mentions a lady who said: "I sometimes feel such pleasure in smelling flowers that I seem to be committing a sin."[3] It is really the case that in many persons—usually, if not exclusively, women—the odor of flowers produces not only a highly pleasurable, but a distinctly and specifically sexual, effect. I have met with numerous cases in which this effect was well marked. It is usually white flowers with heavy, penetrating odors which exert this influence. Thus, one lady (who is similarly affected by various perfumes, forget-me-not, ylang-ylang,

---

[1] *Sexuelle Osphrésiologie*, p. 106.

[2] Mantegazza, *Fisiologia dell' Amore*, p. 176.

[3] In this connection I may quote the remark of the writer of a thoughtful article in the *Journal of Psychological Medicine*, 1851: "The use of scents, especially those allied to the musky, is one of the luxuries of women, and in some constitutions cannot be indulged without some danger to the morals, by the excitement to the ovaria which results. And although less potent as aphrodisiacs in their action on the sexual system of women than of men, we have reason to think that they cannot be used to excess with impunity by most."

etc.) finds that a number of flowers produce on her a definite sexual effect, with moistening of the pudenda. This effect is especially produced by white flowers like the gardenia, tuberose, etc. Another lady, who lives in India, has a similar experience with flowers. She writes: "A scent to cause me sexual excitement must be somewhat heavy and *penetrating*. Nearly all white flowers so affect me and many Indian flowers with heavy, almost pungent scents. (All the flower scents are quite unconnected with me with any individual). Tuberose, lilies of the valley, and frangipani flowers have an almost intoxicating effect on me. Violets, roses, mignonette, and many others, though very delicious, give me no sexual feeling at all. For this reason the line, 'The lilies and langours of virtue for the roses and raptures of vice' seems all wrong to me. The lily seems to me a very sensual flower, while the rose and its scent seem very good and countrified and virtuous. Shelley's description of the lily of the valley, 'whom youth makes so fair and *passion* so pale,' falls in much more with my ideas. I can quite understand," she adds, "that leather, especially of books, might have an exciting effect, as the smell has this *penetrating* quality, but I do not think it produces any special feeling in me." This more sensuous character of white flowers is fairly obvious to many persons who do not experience from them any specifically sexual effects. To some people lilies have an odor which they describe as sexual, although these persons may be quite unaware that Hindu authors long since described the vulvar secretion of the *Padmini*, or perfect woman, during coitus, as "perfumed like the lily that has newly burst."[1] It is noteworthy that it was more especially the white flowers—lily, tuberose, etc.—which were long ago noted by Cloquet as liable to cause various unpleasant nervous effects, cardiac oppression and syncope.[2]

When we are concerned with the fragrances of flowers it would seem that we are far removed from the human sexual field, and that their sexual effects are inexplicable. It is not

---

[1] *Kama Sutra* of Vatsyayana, 1883, p. 5.
[2] Cloquet, *Osphrésiologie*, p. 95.

so. The animal and vegetable odors, as, indeed, we have already seen, are very closely connected. The recorded cases are very numerous in which human persons have exhaled from their skins—sometimes in a very pronounced degree—the odors of plants and flowers, of violets, of roses, of pine-apple, of vanilla. On the other hand, there are various plant odors which distinctly recall, not merely the general odor of the human body, but even the specifically sexual odors. A rare garden weed, the stinking goosefoot, *Chenopodium vulvaria*, it is well known, possesses a herring brine or putrid fish odor —due, it appears, to propylamin, which is also found in the flowers of the common white thorn or mayflower *(Cratægus oxyacantha)* and many others of the *Rosaceæ*—which recalls the odor of the animal and human sexual regions.[1] The reason is that both plant and animal odors belong chemically to the same group of capryl odors (Linnæus's *Odores hircini*), so called from the goat, the most important group of odors from the sexual point of view. Caproic and capryl acid are contained not only in the odor of the goat and in human sweat, and in animal products as many cheeses, but also in various plants, such as Herb Robert *(Geranium robertianum)*, and the Stinking St. John's worts *(Hypericum hircinum)*, as well as the *Chenopodium*. Zwaardemaker considers it probable that the odor of the vagina belongs to the same group, as well as the odor of semen (which Haller called *odor aphrodisiacus*), which last odor is also found, as Cloquet pointed out, in the flowers of the common berberry *(Berberis vulgaris)* and in the chestnut. A very remarkable and significant example of the same odor seems to occur in the case of the flowers of the henna plant, the white-flowered Lawsonia *(Lawsonia inermis)*, so widely used in some Mohammedan lands for dyeing the nails and other parts of the body. "These flowers diffuse the sweetest odor," wrote Sonnini in Egypt a century ago; "the women delight to

---

[1] In Normandy the *Chenopodium*, it is said, is called "conio," and in Italy erba connina (con, cunnus), on account of its vulvar odor. The attraction of dogs to this plant has been noted. In the same way cats are irresistibly attracted to preparations of valerian because their own urine contains valerianic acid.

wear them, to adorn their houses with them, to carry them to the baths, to hold them in their hands, and to perfume their bosoms with them. They cannot patiently endure that Christian and Jewish women shall share the privilege with them. It is very remarkable that the perfume of the henna flowers, when closely inhaled, is almost entirely lost in a very decided spermatic odor. If the flowers are crushed between the fingers this odor prevails, and is, indeed, the only one perceptible. It is not surprising that so delicious a flower has furnished Oriental poetry with many charming traits and amorous similes." Such a simile Sonnini finds in the *Song of Songs*, i, 13-14.[1]

The odor of semen has not been investigated, but, according to Zwaardemaker, artificially produced odors (like cadaverin) resemble it. The odor of the leguminous fenugreek, a botanical friend considers, closely approaches the odor given off in some cases by the armpit in women. It is noteworthy that fenugreek contains cumarine, which imparts its fragrance to new-mown hay and to various flowers of somewhat similar odor. On some persons these have a sexually exciting effect, and it is of considerable interest to observe that they recall to many the odor of semen. "It seems very natural," a lady writes, "that flowers, etc., should have an exciting effect, as the original and by far the pleasanest way of love-making was in the open among flowers and fields; but a more purely physical reason may, I think, be found in the exact resemblance between the scent of semen and that of the pollen of flowering grasses. The first time I became aware of this resemblance it came on me with a rush that here was the explanation of the very exciting effect of a field of flowering grasses and, perhaps through them, of the scents of other flowers. If I am right, I suppose flower scents should affect women more powerfully than men in a sexual way. I do not think anyone would be likely to notice the odor of semen in this connection unless they had been greatly struck by the exciting effects of the pollen of grasses. I had often noticed it and puzzled over it." As pollen

---

[1] Sonnini, *Voyage dans la Haute et Basse Egypte*, 1799, vol. i, p. 298.

is the male sexual element of flowers, its occasionally stimulating effect in this direction is perhaps but an accidental result of a unity running through the organic world, though it may be perhaps more simply explained as a special form of that nasal irritation which is felt by so many persons in a hay-field. Another correspondent, this time a man, tells me that he has noted the resemblance of the odor of semen to that of crushed grasses. A scientific friend who has done much work in the field of organic chemistry tells me he associates the odor of semen with that produced by diastasic action on mixing flour and water, which he regards as sexual in character. This again brings us to the starchy products of the leguminous plants. It is evident that, subtle and obscure as many questions in the physiology and psychology of olfaction still remain, we cannot easily escape from their sexual associations.

V.

The Evil Effects of Excessive Olfactory Stimulation—The Symptoms of Vanillism—The Occasional Dangerous Results of the Odors of Flowers—Effects of Flowers on the Voice.

THE reality of the olfactory influences with which we have been concerned, however slight they may sometimes appear, is shown by the fact that odors, both agreeable and disagreeable, are stimulants, obeying the laws which hold good for stimulants generally. They whip up the nervous energies momentarily, but in the end, if the excitation is excessive and prolonged, they produce fatigue and exhaustion. This is clearly shown by Féré's elaborate experiments on the influences of odors, as compared with other sensory stimulants, on the amount of muscular work performed with the ergograph.[1] Commenting on the remark of Bernardin de Saint-Pierre, that "man uses perfumes to impart energy to his passion," Féré remarks: "But perfumes cannot keep up the fires which they light." Their prolonged use involves fatigue, which is not different from that produced by excessive work, and reproduces all the bodily and psychic accompaniments of excessive work.[2] It is well known that workers in perfumes are apt to suffer from the inhalation of the odors amid which they live. Dealers in musk are said to be specially liable to precocious dementia. The symptoms generally experienced by the men and women who work in vanilla factories where the crude fruit is prepared for commerce have often been studied and are well known. They are due to the inhalation of the scent, which has all the properties of the aromatic aldehydes, and include

---

[1] Féré, *Travail et Plaisir*, Chapter XIII.

[2] *Travail et Plaisir*, p. 175. It is doubtless true of the effects of odors on the sexual sphere. Féré records the case of a neurasthenic lady whose sexual coldness toward her husband only disappeared after the abandonment of a perfume (in which heliotrope was apparently the chief constituent) she had been accustomed to use in excessive amounts.

(107)

skin eruptions,[1] general excitement, sleeplessness, headache, excessive menstruation, and irritable bladder. There is nearly always sexual excitement, which may be very pronounced.[2]

We are here in the presence, it may be insisted, not of a nervous influence only, but of a direct effect of odor on the vital processes. The experiments of Tardif on the influence of perfumes on frogs and rabbits showed that a poisonous effect was exerted[3]; while Féré, by incubating fowls' eggs in the presence of musk, found repeatedly that many abnormalities occurred, and that development was retarded even in the embryos that remained normal; while he obtained somewhat similar results by using essences of lavender, cloves, etc.[4] The influence of odors is thus deeper than is indicated by their nervous effects; they act directly on nutrition. We are led, as Passy remarks, to regard odors as very intimately related to the physiological properties of organic substances, and the sense of smell as a detached fragment of general sensibility, reacting to the same stimuli as general sensibility, but highly specialized in view of its protective function.

The reality and subtlety of the influence of odors is further shown by the cases in which very intense effects are produced even by the temporary inhalation of flowers or perfumes or other odors. Such cases of idiosyncrasy in which a person—frequently of somewhat neurotic temperament—becomes acutely sensitive to some odor or odors have been recorded in medical literature for many centuries. In these cases the obnoxious odor produces congestion of the respiratory passages, sneezing, headache, fainting, etc., but occasionally, it has been recorded, even death. (Dr. J. N. Mackenzie, in his interesting and learned paper on "The Production of the so-called 'Rose Cold,' etc.," *American Journal of Medical Sciences*, January, 1886, quotes many cases, and gives a number of references to ancient medical authors; see also Layet, art. "Odeur," *Dictionnaire Encyclopédique des Sciences Médicales*.)

---

[1] It is perhaps significant that many colors are especially liable to produce skin disorders, especially urticaria; a number of cases have been recorded by Joal, *Journal de Médecine*, July 10, 1899.

[2] Layet, art. "Vanillisme," *Dictionnaire Encyclopédique des Sciences Médicales; cf.* Audeoud, *Revue Médicale de la Suisse Romande*, October 20, 1899, summarized in the *British Medical Journal*, 1899.

[3] E. Tardif, *Les Odeurs et Parfums*, Chapter III.

[4] Féré, *Société de Biologie*, March 28, 1896.

An interesting phenomenon of the group—though it is almost too common to be described as an idiosyncrasy—is the tendency of the odor of certain flowers to affect the voice and sometimes even to produce complete loss of voice. The mechanism of the process is not fully understood, but it would appear that congestion and paresis of the larynx is produced and spasm of the bronchial tube. Botallus in 1565 recorded cases in which the scent of flowers brought on difficulty of breathing, and the danger of flowers from this point of view is well recognized by professional singers. Joal has studied this question in an elaborate paper (summarized in the *British Medical Journal*, March 3, 1895), and Dr. Cabanès has brought together (*Figaro*, January 20, 1894) the experiences of a number of well-known singers, teachers of singing, and laryngologists. Thus, Madame Renée Richard, of the Paris Opera, has frequently found that when her pupils have arrived with a bunch of violets fastened to the bodice or even with a violet and iris sachet beneath the corset, the voice has been marked by weakness and, on using the laryngoscope, she has found the vocal cords congested. Madame Calvé confirmed this opinion, and stated that she was specially sensitive to turberose and mimosa, and that on one occasion a bouquet of white lilac has caused her, for a time, complete loss of voice. The flowers mentioned are equally dangerous to a number of other singers; the most injurious flower of all is found to be the violet. The rose is seldom mentioned, and artificial perfumes are comparatively harmless, though some singers consider it desirable to be cautious in using them.

VI.

The Place of Smell in Human Sexual Selections—It has given Place to the Predominance of Vision largely because in Civilized Man it Fails to Act at a Distance—It still Plays a Part by Contributing to the Sympathies or the Antipathies of Intimate Contact.

WHEN we survey comprehensively the extensive field we have here rapidly traversed, it seems not impossible to gain a fairly accurate view of the special place which olfactory sensations play in human sexual selection. The special peculiarity of this group of sensations in man, and that which gives them an importance they would not otherwise possess, is due to the fact that we here witness the decadence of a sense which in man's remote ancestors was the very chiefest avenue of sexual allurement. In man, even the most primitive man,—to some degree even in the apes,—it has declined in importance to give place to the predominance of vision.[1] Yet, at that lower threshold of acuity at which it persists in man it still bathes us in a more or less constant atmosphere of odors, which perpetually move us to sympathy or to antipathy, and which in their finer manifestations we do not neglect, but even cultivate with the increase of our civilization.

It thus comes about that the grosser manifestations of sexual allurement by smell belong, so far as man is concerned, to a remote animal past which we have outgrown and which, on account of the diminished acuity of our olfactory organs, we could not completely recall even if we desired to; the sense of sight inevitably comes into play long before it is possible for close contact to bring into action the sense of smell. But the latent possibilities of sexual allurement by olfaction, which are inevitably embodied in the nervous structure we have inherited from our animal ancestors, still remain

---

[1] Moll has a passage on this subject, *Untersuchungen über die Libido Sexualis.* Bd. 1, pp. 376-381.

ready to be called into play. They emerge prominently from time to time in exceptional and abnormal persons. They tend to play an unusually larger part in the psychic lives of neurasthenic persons, with their sensitive and comparatively unbalanced nervous systems, and this is doubtless the reason why poets and men of letters have insisted on olfactory impressions so frequently and to so notable a degree; for the same reason sexual inverts are peculiarly susceptible to odors. For a different reason, warmer climates, which heighten all odors and also favor the growth of powerfully odorous plants, lead to a heightened susceptibility to the sexual and other attractions of smell even among normal persons; thus we find a general tendency to delight in odors throughout the East, notably in India, among the ancient Hebrews, and in Mohammedan lands.

Among the ordinary civilized population in Europe the sexual influences of smell play a smaller and yet not altogether negligible part. The diminished prominence of odors only enables them to come into action, as sexual influences, on close contact, when, in some persons at all events, personal odors may have a distinct influence in heightening sympathy or arousing antipathy. The range of variation among individuals is in this matter considerable. In a few persons olfactory sympathy or antipathy is so pronounced that it exerts a decisive influence in their sexual relationships; such persons are of olfactory type. In other persons smell has no part in constituting sexual relationships, but it comes into play in the intimate association of love, and acts as an additional excitant; when reinforced by association such olfactory impressions may at times prove irresistible. Other persons, again, are neutral in this respect, and remain indifferent either to the sympathetic or antipathetic working of personal odors, unless they happen to be extremely marked. It is probable that the majority of refined and educated people belong to the middle group of those persons who are not of predominantly olfactory type, but are liable from time to time to be influenced in this manner. Women are probably at least as often affected in this manner as men, probably more often.

On the whole, it may be said that in the usual life of man odors play a not inconsiderable part and raise problems which are not without interest, but that their demonstrable part in actual sexual selection—whether in preferential mating or in assortative mating—is comparatively small.

HEARING.

I.

The Physiological Basis of Rhythm—Rhythm as a Physiological Stimulus—The Intimate Relation of Rhythm to Movement—The Physiological Influence of Music on Muscular Action, Circulation, Respiration, etc.—The Place of Music in Sexual Selection among the Lower Animals—Its Comparatively Small Place in Courtship among Mammals—The Larynx and Voice in Man—The Significance of the Pubertal Changes—Ancient Beliefs Concerning the Influence of Music in Morals, Education, and Medicine—Its Therapeutic Uses—Significance of the Romantic Interest in Music at Puberty—Men Comparatively Insusceptible to the Specifically Sexual Influence of Music—Rarity of Sexual Perversions on the Basis of the Sense of Hearing—The Part of Music in Primitive Human Courtship—Women Notably Susceptible to the Specifically Sexual Influence of Music and the Voice.

THE sense of rhythm—on which it may be said that the sensory exciting effects of hearing, including music, finally rest —may probably be regarded as a fundamental quality of neuro-muscular tissue. Not only are the chief physiological functions of the body, like the circulation and the respiration, definitely rhythmical, but our senses insist on imparting a rhythmic grouping even to an absolutely uniform succession of sensations. It seems probable, although this view is still liable to be disputed, that this rhythm is the result of kinæsthetic sensations,—sensations arising from movement or tension started reflexly in the muscles by the external stimuli,—impressing themselves on the sensations that are thus grouped.[1] We may thus say, with Wilks, that music appears to have had its origin in muscular action.[2]

---

[1] This view has been more especially developed by J. B. Miner, *Motor, Visual, and Applied Rhythms*, Psychological Review Monograph Supplements, vol. v, No. 4, 1903.

[2] Sir S. Wilks, *Medical Magazine*, January, 1894; *cf.* Clifford Allbutt, "Music, Rhythm, and Muscle," *Nature*, February 8, 1894.

Whatever its exact origin may be, rhythm is certainly very deeply impressed on our organisms. The result is that, whatever lends itself to the neuro-muscular rhythmical tendency of our organisms, whatever tends still further to heighten and develop that rhythmical tendency, exerts upon us a very decidedly stimulating and exciting influence.

All muscular action being stimulated by rhthym, in its simple form or in its more developed form as music, rhythm is a stimulant to work. It has even been argued by Bücher and by Wundt[1] that human song had its chief or exclusive origin in rhythmical vocal accompaniments to systematized work. This view cannot, however, be maintained; systematized work can scarcely be said to exist, even to-day, among most very primitive races; it is much more probable that rhythmical song arose at a period antecedent to the origin of systematized work, in the primitive military, religious, and erotic dances, such as exist in a highly developed degree among the Australians and other savage races who have not evolved co-ordinated systematic labor. There can, however, be no doubt that as soon as systematic work appears the importance of vocal rhythm in stimulating its energy is at once everywhere recognized. Bücher has brought together innumerable examples of this association, and in the march music of soldiers and the heaving and hoisting songs of sailors we have instances that have universally persisted into civilization, although in civilization the rhythmical stimulation of work, physiologically sound as is its basis, tends to die out. Even in the laboratory the influence of simple rhythm in increasing the output of work may be demonstrated, and Féré found with the ergograph that a rhythmical grouping of the movements caused an increase of energy which often more than compensated the loss of time caused by the rhythm.[2]

---

[1] Bücher, *Arbeit und Rhythmus*, third edition, 1902; Wundt, *Völkerpsychologie*, 1900, Part I, p. 265.
[2] Féré deals fully with the question in his book, *Travail et Plaisir*, 1904, Chapter III, "Influence du Rhythme sur le Travail."

Rhythm is the most primitive element of music, and the most fundamental. Wallaschek, in his book on *Primitive Music*, and most other writers on the subject are agreed on this point. "Rhythm," remarks an American anthropologist,[1] "naturally precedes the development of any fine perception of differences in pitch, of time-quality, or of tonality. Almost, if not all, Indian songs," he adds, "are as strictly developed out of modified repetitions of a motive as are the movements of a Mozart or a Beethoven symphony." "In all primitive music," asserts Alice C. Fletcher,[2] "rhythm is strongly developed. The pulsations of the drum and the sharp crash of the rattles are thrown against each other and against the voice, so that it would seem that the pleasure derived by the performers lay not so much in the tonality of the song as in the measured sounds arrayed in contesting rhythm, and which by their clash start the nerves and spur the body to action, for the voice which alone carries the tone is often subordinated and treated as an additional instrument." Groos points out that a melody gives us the essential impression of a *voice that dances*[3]; it is a translation of spatial movement into sound, and, as we shall see, its physiological action on the organism is a reflection of that which, as we have elsewhere found,[4] dancing itself produces, and thus resembles that produced by the sight of movement. Dancing, music, and poetry were primitively so closely allied as to be almost identical; they were still inseparable among the early Greeks. The refrains in our English ballads indicate the dancer's part in them. The technical use of the word "foot" in metrical matters still persists to show that a poem is fundamentally a dance.

Aristotle seems to have first suggested that rhythm and melodies are motions, as actions are motions, and therefore signs of feeling.

[1] Fillmore, "Primitive Scales and Rhythms," *Proceedings of the International Congress of Anthropology*, Chicago, 1893.
[2] "Love Songs among the Omaha Indians," in *Proceedings* of same congress.
[3] Groos, *Spiele der Menschen*, p. 33.
[4] "Analysis of the Sexual Impulse," *Studies in the Psychology of Sex*, vol. iii.

"All melodies are motions," says Helmholtz. "Graceful rapidity, grave procession, quiet advance, wild leaping, all these different characters of motion and a thousand others can be represented by successions of tones. And as music expresses these motions it gives an expresion also to those mental conditions which naturally evoke similar motions, whether of the body and the voice, or of the thinking and feeling principle itself." (Helmholtz, *On the Sensations of Tone*, translated by A. J. Ellis, 1885, p. 250.)

From another point of view the motor stimulus of music has been emphasized by Cyples: "Music connects with the only sense that can be perfectly manipulated. Its emotional charm has struck men as a great mystery. There appears to be no doubt whatever that it gets all the marvelous effects it has beyond the mere pleasing of the ear, from its random, but multitudinous, summonses of the efferent activity, which at its vague challenges stirs unceasingly in faintly tumultuous irrelevancy. In this way, music arouses aimlessly, but splendidly, the sheer, as yet unfulfilled, potentiality within us." (W. Cyples, *The Process of Human Experience*, p. 743.)

The fundamental element of transformed motion in music has been well brought out in a suggestive essay by Goblot ("La Musique Descriptive," *Revue Philosophique*, July, 1901): "Sung or played, melody figures to the ear a successive design, a moving arabesque. We talk of *ascending* and *descending* the gamut, of *high* notes or *low* notes; the higher voice of woman is called *soprano*, or *above*, the deeper voice of man is called *bass*. *Grave* tones were so called by the Greeks because they seemed heavy and to incline downward. Sounds seem to be subject to the action of gravity; so that some rise and others fall. Baudelaire, speaking of the prelude to *Lohengrin*, remarks: 'I felt myself *delivered from the bonds of weight*.' And when Wagner sought to represent, in the highest regions of celestial space, the apparition of the angels bearing the Holy Grail to earth, he uses very high notes, and a kind of chorus played exclusively by the violins, divided into eight parts, in the highest notes of their register. The descent to earth of the celestial choir is rendered by lower and lower notes, the progressive disappearance of which represents the reascension to the ethereal regions.

"Sounds seem to rise and fall; that is a fact. It is difficult to explain it. Some have seen in it a habit derived from the usual notation by which the height of the note corresponds to its height in the score. But the impression is too deep and general to be explained by so superficial and recent a cause. It has been suggested also that high notes are generally produced by small and light bodies, low notes by heavy bodies. But that is not always true. It has been said, again, that high notes in nature are usually produced by highly placed objects, while low notes arise from caves and low placed regions. But the thunder is heard in the sky, and the murmur of a spring or the song of a cricket arise from the earth. In the human voice, again, it is said, the low notes seem to resound in the chest, high notes in the head. All this is unsatisfactory. We cannot explain by such coarse analogies an impression which is very precise, and more sensible (this fact has its importance) for an interval of half a tone than for an interval of an octave. It is probable that the true explanation is to be found in the still little understood connection between the elements of our nervous apparatus.

"Nearly all our emotions tend to produce movement. But education renders us economical of our acts. Most of these movements are repressed, especially in the adult and civilized man, as harmful, dangerous, or merely useless. Some are not completed, others are reduced to a faint incitation which externally is scarcely perceptible. Enough remain to constitute all that is expressive in our gestures, physiognomy, and attitudes. Melodic intervals possess in a high degree this property of provoking impulses of movement, which, even when repressed, leave behind internal sensations and motor images. It would be possible to study these facts experimentally if we had at our disposition a human being who, while retaining his sensations and their motor reactions, was by special circumstances rendered entirely spontaneous like a sensitive automaton, whose movements were neither intentionally produced nor intentionally repressed. In this way, melodic intervals in a hypnotized subject might be very instructive."

A number of experiments of the kind desired by Goblot had already been made by A. de Rochas in a book, copiously illustrated by very numerous instantaneous photographs, entitled *Les Sentiments, la Musique et le Geste*, 1900. Chapter III. De Rochas experimented on a single subject, Lina, formerly a model, who was placed in a condition of slight hypnosis, when various simple fragments of music were performed: recitatives, popular airs, and more especially national dances, often from remote parts of the world. The subject's gestures were exceedingly marked and varied in accordance with the character of the music. It was found that she often imitated with considerable precision the actual gestures of dances she could never have seen. The same music always evoked the same gestures, as was shown by instantaneous photographs. This subject, stated to be a chaste and well-behaved girl, exhibited no indications of definite sexual emotion under the influence of any kind of music. Some account is given in the same volume of other hypnotic experiments with music which were also negative as regards specific sexual phenomena.

It must be noted that, as a physiological stimulus, a single musical note is effective, even apart from rhythm, as is well shown by Féré's experiments with the dynamometer and the ergograph.[1] It is, however, the influence of music on muscular work which has been most frequently investigated, and both on brief efforts with the dynamometer and prolonged work with the ergograph it has been found to exert a stimulating influence. Thus, Scripture found that, while his own maximum thumb and finger grip with the dynamometer is 8 pounds, when the giant's motive from Wagner's *Rheingold* is played it rises to $8^3/_4$ pounds.[2] With the ergograph Tarchanoff found that lively music, in nervously sensitive persons, will temporarily cause the disappearance of fatigue, though slow music in a minor key had an opposite effect.[3] The varying influence on work with the ergograph of different musical intervals and different keys has been carefully studied by Féré with many interesting results. There was a very considerable degree of constancy in the results. Discords were depressing; most, but not all, major keys were stimulating; and most, but not all, minor keys depressing. In states of fatigue, however, the minor keys were more stimulating than the major, an interesting result in harmony with that stimulating influence of various painful emotions in states of organic fatigue which we have elsewhere encountered when investigating sadism.[4] "Our musical culture," Féré remarks, "only renders more perceptible to us the unconscious relationships which exist between musical art and our organisms. Those whom we consider more endowed in this respect have a deeper penetration of the phenomena accomplished within them; they feel more profoundly the marvelous reactions between the organism and the principles of musical art, they experience more strongly that art is

[1] Féré, *Sensation et Mouvement*, Chapter V; *id.*, *Travail et Plaisir*, Chapter XII.

[2] Scripture, *Thinking, Feeling, Doing*, p. 85.

[3] Tarchanoff, "Influence de la Musique sur l'Homme et sur les Animaux," *Atti dell' XI Congresso Medico Internazionale*, Rome, 1894, vol. ii, p. 153; also in *Archives Italiennes de Biologie*, 1894.

[4] "Love and Pain," *Studies in the Psychology of Sex*, vol. iii.

within them."[1] Both the higher and the lower muscular processes, the voluntary and the involuntary, are stimulated by music. Darlington and Talbot, in Titchener's laboratory at Cor-
nell University, found that the estimation of relative weights
was aided by music.[2] Lombard found, when investigating the
normal variations in the knee-jerk, that involuntary reflex
processes are always reinforced by music; a military band playing a lively march caused the knee-jerk to increase at the loud
passages and to diminish at the soft passages, while remaining
always above the normal level.[3]

With this stimulating influence of rhythm and music on
the neuro-muscular system—which may or may not be direct—
there is a concomitant influence on the circulatory and breathing apparatus. During recent years a great many experiments
have been made on man and animals bearing on the effects of
music on the heart and respiration. Perhaps the earliest of
these were carried out by the Russian physiologist Dogiel in
1880.[4] His methods were perhaps defective and his results, at
all events as regards man, uncertain, but in animals the force
and rapidity of the heart were markedly increased. Subsequent
investigations have shown very clearly the influence of music on
the circulatory and respiratory systems in man as well as in animals. That music has an apparently direct influence on the
circulation of the brain is shown by the observations of Patrizi
on a youth who had received a severe wound of the head which
had removed a large portion of the skull wall. The stimulus of

[1] Féré, *Travail et Plaisir*, Chapter XII, "Action Physiologique des
Sens Musicaux." "A practical treatise on harmony," Goblot remarks
(*Revue Philosophique*, July, 1901, p. 61), "ought to tell us in what way
such an interval, or such a succession of intervals, affects us. A the-
oretical treatise on harmony ought to tell us the explanation of these
impressions. In a word, musical harmony is a psychological science."
He adds that this science is very far from being constituted yet; we
have hardly even obtained a glimpse of it.
[2] *American Journal of Psychology*, April, 1898.
[3] *American Journal of Psychology*, November, 1887. The influence
of rhythm on the involuntary muscular system is indicated by the occasional effect of music in producing a tendency to contraction of the
bladder.
[4] *Archiv für Anatomie und Physiologie* (Physiologisches Ab-
theilung), 1880, p. 420.

melody produced an immediate increase in the afflux of blood to the brain.[1]

In Germany the question was investigated at about the same time by Mentz.[2] Observing the pulse with a sphygmograph and Marey tambour he found distinct evidence of an effect on the heart; when attention was given to the music the pulse was quickened, in the absence of attention it was slowed; Mentz also found that pleasurable sensations tended to slow the pulse and disagreeable ones to quicken it.

Binet and Courtier made an elaborate series of experiments on the action of music on the respiration (with the double pneumograph), the heart, and the capillary circulation (with the plethysmograph of Hallion and Comte) on a single subject, a man very sensitive to music and himself a cultured musician. Simple musical sounds with no emotional content accelerated the respiration without changing its regularity or amplitude. Musical fragments, mostly sung, usually well known to the subject, and having an emotional effect on him, produced respiratory irregularity either in amplitude or rapidity of breathing, in two-thirds of the trials. Exciting music, such as military marches, accelerated the breathing more than sad melodies, but the intensity of the excitation had an effect at least as great as its quality, for intense excitations always produced both quickened and deeper breathing. The heart was quickened in harmony with the quickened breathing. Neither breathing nor heart was ever slowed. As regards the capillary pulsation, an influence was exerted chiefly, if not exclusively, by gay and exciting melodies, which produced a shrinking. Throughout the experiments it was found that the most profound physiological effects were exerted by those pieces which the subject found to be most emotional in their influence on him.[3]

[1] M. L. Patrizi, "Primi esperimenti intorno all' influenza della musica sulla circolozione del sangue nel cervello umano," *International Congress für Psychologie*, Munich, 1897, p. 176.

[2] *Philosophische Studien*, vol. xi.

[3] Binet and Courtier, "La Vie Emotionelle," *Année Psychologique*, Third Year, 1897, pp. 104-125.

Guibaud studied the question on a number of subjects, confirming and extending the conclusions of Binet and Courtier. He found that the reactions of different individuals varied, but that for the same individual reactions were constant. Circulatory reaction was more often manifest than respiratory reaction. The latter might be either a simultaneous modification of depth and of rapidity or of either of these. The circulatory reaction was a peripheral vasoconstriction with diminished fullness of pulse and slight acceleration of cardiac rhythm; there was never any distinct slowing of heart under the influence of music. Guibaud remarks that when people say they feel a shudder at some passage of music, this sensation of cold finds its explanation in the production of a peripheral vasoconstriction which may be registered by the plethysmograph.[1]

Since music thus directly and powerfully affects the chief vital processes, it is not surprising that it should indirectly influence various viscera and functions. As Tarchanoff and others have demonstrated, it affects the skin, increasing the perspiration; it may produce a tendency to tears; it sometimes produces desire to urinate, or even actual urination, as in Scaliger's case of the Gascon gentleman who was always thus affected on hearing the bagpipes. In dogs it has been shown by Tarchanoff and Wartanoff that auditory stimulation increases the consumption of oxygen 20 per cent., and the elimination of carbonic acid 17 per cent.

In addition to the effects of musical sound already mentioned, it may be added that, as Epstein, of Berne, has shown,[2] the other senses are stimulated under the influence of sound, and notably there is an increase in acuteness of vision which may be experimentally demonstrated. It is probable that this effect of music in heightening the impressions received by the other senses is of considerable significance from our present point of view.

---

[1] Guibaud, *Contribution à l'étude expérimentale de l'influence de la musique sur la circulation et la respiration.* Thèse de Bordeaux, 1898, summarized in *Année Psychologique*, Fifth Year, 1899, pp. 645-649.

[2] *International Congress of Physiology*, Berne, 1895.

Why are musical tones in a certain order and rhythm pleasurable? asked Darwin in *The Descent of Man*, and he concluded that the question was insoluble. We see that, in reality, whatever the ultimate answer may be, the immediate reason is quite simple. Pleasure is a condition of slight and diffused stimulation, in which the heart and breathing are faintly excited, the neuro-muscular system receives additional tone, the viscera gently stirred, the skin activity increased; and certain combinations of musical notes and intervals act as a physiological stimulus in producing these effects.[1]

Among animals of all kinds, from insects upward, this physiological action appears to exist, for among nearly all of them certain sounds are agreeable and attractive, and other sounds indifferent and disagreeable. It appears that insects of quite different genera show much appreciation of the song of the Cicada.[2] Birds show intense interest in the singing of good performers even of other species. Experiments among a variety of animals in the Zoölogical Gardens with performances on various instruments showed that with the exception of seals none were indifferent, and all felt a discord as offensive. Many animals showed marked likes and dislikes; thus, a tiger, who was obviously soothed by the violin, was infuriated by the piccolo; the violin and the flute were preferred by most animals.[3]

Most persons have probably had occasion to observe the susceptibility of dogs to music. It may here suffice to give one personal observation. A dog (of mixed breed, partly collie), very well known to me, on hearing a nocturne of Chopin, whined and howled, especially at the more pathetic passages, once or twice catching and drawing out the actual note played; he panted, walked about anxiously, and now and then placed his head on the player's lap. When the player pro-

---

[1] The influence of association plays no necessary part in these pleasurable influences, for Féré's experiments show that an unmusical subject responds physiologically, with much precision, to musical intervals he is unable to recognize. R. MacDougall also finds that the effective quality of rhythmical sequences does not appear to be dependent on secondary associations (*Psychological Review*, January, 1903).

[2] R. T. Lewis, in *Nature Notes*, August, 1891.

[3] Cornish, "Orpheus at the Zoo," in *Life at the Zoo*, pp. 115-138.

ceeded to a more cheerful piece by Grieg, the dog at once became indifferent, sat down, yawned, and scratched himself; but as soon as the player returned once more to the nocturne the dog at once repeated his accompaniment.

There can be no doubt that among a very large number of animals of most various classes, more especially among insects and birds, the attraction of music is supported and developed on the basis of sexual attraction, the musical notes emitted serving as a sexual lure to the other sex. The evidence on this point was carefully investigated by Darwin on a very wide basis.[1] It has been questioned, some writers preferring to adopt the view of Herbert Spencer,[2] that the singing of birds is due to "overflow of energy," the relation between courtship and singing being merely "a relation of concomitance." This view is no longer tenable; whatever the precise origin of the musical notes of animals may be,—and it is not necessary to suppose that sexual attraction had a large part in their first rudimentary beginnings,—there can now be little doubt that musical sounds, and, among birds, singing, play a very large part indeed in bringing the male and the female together.[3] Usually, it would appear, it is the performance of the male that attracts the female; it is only among very simple and primitive musicians, like some insects, that the female thus attracts the male.[4] The fact that it is nearly always one sex only that is thus musically gifted should alone have sufficed to throw suspicion on any but a sexual solution of this problem of animal song.

It is, however, an exceedingly remarkable fact that, although among insects and lower vertebrates the sexual influ-

---

[1] *Descent of Man*, Chapters XIII and XIX.

[2] "The Origin of Music" (1857), *Essays*, vol. ii.

[3] Anyone who is in doubt on this point, as regards bird song, may consult the little book in which the evidence has been well summarized by Häcker, *Der Gesang der Vogel*, or the discussion in Groos's *Spiele der Thiere*, pp. 274 *et seq*.

[4] Thus, mosquitoes are irresistibly attracted by music, and especially by those musical tones which resemble the buzzing of the female; the males alone are thus attracted. (Nuttall and Shipley, and Sir Hiram Maxim, quoted in *Nature*, October 31, 1901, p. 655, and in *Lancet*, February 22, 1902.)

ence of music is so large, and although among mammals and predominantly in man the emotional and æsthetic influence of music is so great, yet neither in man nor any of the higher mammals has music been found to exert a predominant sexual influence, or even in most cases any influence at all. Darwin, while calling attention to the fact that the males of most species of mammals use their vocal powers chiefly, and sometimes exclusively, during the breeding-season, adds that "it is a surprising fact that we have not as yet any good evidence that these organs are used by male mammals to charm the female.[1] From a very different standpoint, Féré, in studying the pathology of the human sexual instinct in the light of a very full knowledge of the available evidence, states that he knows of no detailed observations showing the existence of any morbid sexual perversions based on the sense of hearing, either in reference to the human voice or to instrumental music.[2]

When, however, we consider that not only in the animals most nearly related to man, but in man himself, the larynx and the voice undergo a marked sexual differentiation at puberty, it is difficult not to believe that this change has an influence on sexual selection and sexual psychology. At puberty there is a slight hyperæmia of the larynx, accompanied by rapid development alike of the larynx itself and of the vocal cords, which become larger and thicker, while there is an associated change in the voice, which deepens. All these changes are very slight in girls, but very pronounced in boys, whose voices are said to "break" and then become lower by at least an octave. The feminine larynx at puberty only increases in the proportion of 5 to 7, but the masculine larynx in the proportion of 5 to 10. The direct dependence of this change on the general sexual development is shown not merely by its occurrence at puberty, but by the fact that in eunuchs in whom

---

[1] *Descent of Man*, second edition, p. 567. Groos, in his discussion of music, also expresses doubt whether hearing plays a considerable part in the courtship of mammals, *Spiele der Menschen*, p. 22.
[2] Féré, *L'Instinct Sexuel*, second edition, p. 137.

the testicles have been removed before puberty the voice retains its childlike qualities.[1]

As a matter of fact, I believe that we may attach a considerable degree of importance to the voice and to music generally as a method of sexual appeal. On this point I agree with Moll, who remarks that "the sense of hearing here plays a considerable part, and the stimulation received through the ears is much larger than is usually believed.[2] I am not, however, inclined to think that this influence is considerable in its action on men, although Mantegazza remarks, doubtless with a certain truth, that "some women's voices cannot be heard with impunity." It is true that the ancients deprecated the sexual or at all events the effeminating influence of some kinds of music, but they seem to have regarded it as sedative rather than stimulating; the kind of music they approved of as martial and stimulating was the kind most likely to have sexual effects in predisposed persons.

The Chinese and the Greeks have more especially insisted on the ethical qualities of music and on its moralizing and demoralizing effects. Some three thousand years ago, it is stated, a Chinese emperor, believing that only they who understood music are capable of governing, distributed administrative functions in accordance with this belief. He acted entirely in accordance with Chinese morality. The texts of Confucianism (see translations in the "Sacred Books of the East Series") show clearly that music and ceremony (or social ritual in a wide sense) are regarded as the two main guiding influences of life—music as the internal guide, ceremony as the external guide, the former being looked upon as the more important.

Among the Greeks Menander said that to many people music is a powerful stimulant to love. Plato, in the third book of the *Republic*, discusses what kinds of music should be encouraged in his ideal state. He does not clearly state that music is ever a sexual stimulant, but he appears to associate plaintive music (mixed Lydian and Hypolydian)

---

[1] See Biérent, *La Puberté*, Chapter IV; also Havelock Ellis, *Man and Woman*, fourth edition, pp. 270-272. Endriss (*Die Bishcrigen Beobachtungen von Physiologischen und Pathologischen Beziehungen der oberen Luftwege zu den Sexualorganen*, Teil III) brings together various observations on the normal and abnormal relations of the larynx to the sexual sphere.

[2] Moll, *Untersuchungen über die Libido Sexualis*, 1, p. 133.

with drunkenness, effeminacy, and idleness, and considers that such music is "useless even to women that are to be virtuously given, not to say to men." He only admits two kinds of music: one violent and suited to war, the other tranquil and suited to prayer or to persuasion. He sets out the ethical qualities of music with a thoroughness which almost approaches the great Chinese philosopher: "On these accounts we attach such importance to a musical education, because rhythm and harmony sink most deeply into the recesses of the soul, and take most powerful hold of it, bringing gracefulness in their train, and making a man graceful if he be rightly nurtured, . . . leading him to commend beautiful objects, and gladly receive them into his soul, and feed upon them, and grow to be noble and good." Plato is, however, by no means so consistent and thorough as the Chinese moralist, for having thus asserted that it is the influence of music which molds the soul into virtue, he proceeds to destroy his position with the statement that "we shall never become truly musical until we know the essential forms of temperance and courage and liberality and munificence," thus moving in a circle. It must be added that the Greek conception of music was very comprehensive and included poetry.

Aristotle took a wider view of music than Plato and admitted a greater variety of uses for it. He was less anxious to exclude those uses which were not strictly ethical. He disapproved, indeed, of the Phrygian harmony as the expression of Bacchic excitement. He accepts, however, the function of music as a κάθαρσις of emotion, a notion which is said to have originated with the Pythagoreans. (For a discussion of Aristotle's views on music, see W. L. Newman, *The Politics of Aristotle*, vol. i, pp. 359-369.)

Athenæus, in his frequent allusions to music, attributes to it many intellectual and emotional properties (*e. g.*, Book XIV, Chapter XXV) and in one place refers to "melodies inciting to lawless indulgence" (Book XIII, Chapter LXXV).

We may gather from the *Priapeia* (XXVI) that cymbals and castanets were the special accompaniment in antiquity of wanton songs and dances: "*cymbala cum crotalis, pruriginis arma.*"

The ancient belief in the moralizing influence of music has survived into modern times mainly in a somewhat more scientific form as a belief in its therapeutic effects in disordered nervous and mental conditions. (This also is an ancient belief as witnessed by the well-known example of David playing to Saul to dispel his melancholia.) In 1729 an apothecary of Oakham, Richard Broune, published a work entitled *Medicina Musica*, in which he argued that music was beneficial in many maladies. In more recent days there have been various experiments and cases brought forward showing its efficacy in special conditions.

An American physician (W. F. Hutchinson) has shown that anæsthesia may be produced with accurately made tuning forks at certain rates of vibration (summarized in the *British Medical Journal*, June 4, 1898). Ferrand in a paper read before the Paris Academy of Medicine in September, 1895, gives reasons for classing some kinds of music as powerful antispasmodics with beneficial therapeutic action. The case was subsequently reported of a child in whom night-terrors were eased by calming music in a minor key. The value of music in lunatic asylums is well recognized; see *e.g.*, Näcke, *Revue de Psychiatrie*, October, 1897. Vaschide and Vurpas (*Comptes Rendus de la Société de Biologic*, December 13, 1902) have recorded the case of a girl of 20, suffering from mental confusion with excitation and central motor disequilibrium, whose muscular equilibrium was restored and movements rendered more co-ordinated and adaptive under the influence of music.

While there has been much extravagance in the ancient doctrine concerning the effects of music, the real effects are still considerable. Not only is this demonstrated by the experiments already referred to (p. 118), indicating the efficacy of musical sounds as physiological stimulants, but also by anatomical considerations. The roots of the auditory nerves, McKendrick has pointed out, are probably more widely distributed and have more extensive connections than those of any other nerve. The intricate connections of these nerves are still only being unraveled. This points to an explanation of how music penetrates to the very roots of our being, influencing by associational paths reflex mechanisms both cerebral and somatic, so that there is scarcely a function of the body that may not be affected by the rhythmical pulsations, melodic progressions, and harmonic combinations of musical tones. (*Nature*, June 15, 1899, p. 164.)

Just as we are not entitled from the ancient belief in the influence of music on morals or the modern beliefs in its therapeutic influence—even though this has sometimes gone to the length of advocating its use in impotence[1]—to argue that music has a marked influence in exciting the specifically sexual instincts, neither are we entitled to find any similar argument in the fact that music is frequently associated with the love-feelings of youth. Men are often able to associate many of their earliest ideas of love in boyhood with women singing or playing; but in these cases it will always be found that the fascination was romantic and sentimental, and not specifically

---

[1] J. L. Roger, *Traité des Effets de la Musique*, 1803, pp. 234 and 342.

erotic.[1] In adult life the music which often seems to us to be most definitely sexual in its appeal (such as much of Wagner's *Tristan*) really produces this effect in part from the association with the story, and in part from the intellectual realization of the composer's effort to translate passion into æsthetic terms; the actual effect of the music is not sexual, and it can well be believed that the results of experiments as regards the sexual influence of the *Tristan* music on men under the influence of hypnotism have been, as reported, negative. Helmholtz goes so far as to state that the expression of sexual longing in music is identical with that of religious longing. It is quite true, again, that a soft and gentle voice seems to every normal man as to Lear "an excellent thing in woman," and that a harsh or shrill voice may seem to deaden or even destroy altogether the attraction of a beautiful face. But the voice is not usually in itself an adequate or powerful method of evoking sexual emotion in a man. Even in its supreme vocal manifestations the sexual fascination exerted by a great singer, though certainly considerable, cannot be compared with that commonly exerted by the actress. Cases have, indeed, been recorded—chiefly occurring, it is probable, in men of somewhat morbid nervous disposition—in which sexual attraction was exerted chiefly through the ear, or in which there was a special sexual sensibility to particular inflections or accents.[2] Féré mentions the case of a young man in hospital with acute arthritis who complained of painful erections whenever he heard through the door the very agreeable voice of the young woman (invisible to him) who superintended the linen.[3] But these phenomena do not appear to be common, or, at all events, very pronounced. So far as my own inquiries

---

[1] A typical example occurs in the early life of History I in Appendix B to vol. iii of these *Studies*.

[2] Vaschide and Vurpas state (*Archives de Neurologie*, May, 1904) that in their experience music may facilitate sexual approaches in some cases of satiety, and that in certain pathological cases the sexual act can only be accomplished under the influence of music.

[3] Féré, *L'Instinct Sexuel*, p. 137. Bloch (*Beiträge*, etc., vol. ii, p. 355) quotes some remarks of Kistemaecker's concerning the sound of women's garments and the way in which savages and sometimes civilized

go, only a small proportion of men would appear to experience definite sexual feelings on listening to music. And the fact that in woman the voice is so slightly differentiated from that of the child, as well as the very significant fact that among man's immediate or even remote ancestors the female's voice can seldom have served to attract the male, sufficiently account for the small part played by the voice and by music as a sexual allurement working on men.[1]

It is otherwise with women. It may, indeed, be said at the outset that the reasons which make it antecedently improbable that men should be sexually attracted through hearing render it probable that women should be so attracted. The change in the voice at puberty makes the deeper masculine voice a characteristic secondary sexual attribute of man, while the fact that among mammals generally it is the male that is most vocal—and that chiefly, or even sometimes exclusively, at the rutting season—renders it antecedently likely that among mammals generally, including the human species, there is in the female an actual or latent susceptibility to the sexual significance of the male voice,[2] a susceptibility which, under the conditions of human civilization, may be transferred

women cultivate this rustling and clinking. Gutzkow, in his *Autobiography*, said that the *frou-frou* of a woman's dress was the music of the spheres to him.

[1] The voice is doubtless a factor of the first importance in sexual attraction among the blind. On this point I have no data. The expressiveness of the voice to the blind, and the extent to which their likes and dislikes are founded on vocal qualities, is well shown by an interesting paper written by an American physician, blind from early infancy, James Cocke, "The Voice as an Index to the Soul," *Arena*, January, 1894.

[2] Long before Darwin had set forth his theory of sexual selection Laycock had pointed out the influence which the voice of the male, among man and other animals, exerts on the female (*Nervous Diseases of Women*, p. 74). And a few years later the writer of a suggestive article on "Woman in her Psychological Relations" (*Journal of Psychological Medicine*, 1851) remarked: "The sonorous voice of the male man is exactly analogous in its effect on woman to the neigh and bellow of other animals. This voice will have its effect on an amorous or susceptible organization much in the same way as color and the other visual ovarian stimuli." The writer adds that it exercises a still more important influence when modulated to music: "in this respect man has something in common with insects as well as birds."

to music generally. It is noteworthy that in novels written by women there is a very frequent attentiveness to the qualities of the hero's voice and to its emotional effects on the heroine.[1] We may also note the special and peculiar personal enthusiasm aroused in women by popular musicians, a more pronounced enthusiasm than is evoked in them by popular actors.

As an interesting example of the importance attached by women novelists to the effects of the male voice 1 may refer to George Eliot's *Mill on the Floss*, probably the most intimate and personal of George Eliot's works. In Book VI of this novel the influence of Stephen Guest (a somewhat commonplace young man) over Maggie Tulliver is ascribed almost exclusively to the effect of his bass voice in singing. We are definitely told of Maggie Tulliver's "sensibility to the supreme excitement of music." Thus, on one occasion, "all her intentions were lost in the vague state of emotion produced by the inspiring duet—emotion that seemed to make her at once strong and weak: strong for all enjoyment, weak for all resistance. Poor Maggie! She looked very beautiful when her soul was being played on in this way by the inexorable power of sound. You might have seen the slightest perceptible quivering through her whole frame as she leaned a little forward, clasping her hands as if to steady herself; while her eyes dilated and brightened into that wideopen, childish expression of wondering delight, which always came back in her happiest moments." George Eliot's novels contain many allusions to the powerful emotional effects of music.

It is unnecessary to refer to Tolstoy's *Kreutzer Sonata*, in which music is regarded as the Galeotto to bring lovers together—"the connecting bond of music, the most refined lust of the senses."

In primitive human courtship music very frequently plays a considerable part, though not usually the sole part, being generally found as the accompaniment of the song and the dance at erotic festivals.[2] The Gilas, of New Mexico, among whom courtship consists in a prolonged serenade day after day with the flute, furnish a somewhat exceptional case. Savage women

[1] Groos refers more than once to the important part played in German novels written by women by what one of them terms the "bearded male voice."

[2] Various instances are quoted in the third volume of these *Studies* when discussing the general phenomena of courtship and tumescence, "An Analysis of the Sexual Impulse."

are evidently very attentive to music; Backhouse (as quoted by Ling Roth[1]) mentions how a woman belonging to the very primitive and now extinct Tasmanian race, when shown a musical box, listened "with intensity; her ears moved like those of a dog or horse, to catch the sound."

I have found little evidence to show that music, except in occasional cases, exerts even the slightest specifically sexual effect on men, whether musical or unmusical. But I have ample evidence that it very frequently exerts to a slight but definite extent such an influence on women, even when quite normal. Judging from my own inquiries it would, indeed, seem likely that the majority of normal educated women are liable to experience some degree of definite sexual excitement from music; one states that orchestral music generally tends to produce this effect; another finds it chiefly from Wagner's music; another from military music, etc. Others simply state —what, indeed, probably expresses the experience of most persons of either sex—that it heightens one's mood. One lady mentions that some of her friends, whose erotic feelings are aroused by music, are especially affected in this way by the choral singing in Roman Catholic churches.[2]

In the typical cases just mentioned, all fairly normal and healthy women, the sexual effects of music though definite were usually quite slight. In neuropathic subjects they may occasionally be more pronounced. Thus, a medical correspondent has communicated to me the case of a married lady with one child, a refined, very beautiful, but highly neurotic, woman, married to a man with whom she has nothing in common. Her tastes lie in the direction of music; she is a splendid pianist, and her highly trained voice would have made a fortune. She confesses to strong sexual feelings and does not understand

---

[1] *The Tasmanians*, p. 20.

[2] An early reference to the sexual influence of music on women may perhaps be found in a playful passage in Swift's *Martinus Scriblerus* (possibly due to his medical collaborator, Arbuthnot): "Does not Ælian tell how the Libyan mares were excited to horsing by music? (which ought to be a caution to modest women against frequenting operas)." *Memoirs of Martinus Scriblerus*, Book I, Chapter 6. (The reference is to Ælian, *Hist. Animal*, lib. XI, cap. 18, and lib. XII, cap. 44.)

why intercourse never affords what she knows she wants. But the hearing of beautiful music, or at times the excitement of her own singing, will sometimes cause intense orgasm.

Vaschide and Vurpas, who emphasize the sexually stimulating effects of music, only bring forward one case in any detail, and it is doubtless significant that this case is a woman. "While listening to a piece of music X changes expression, her eyes become bright, the features are accentuated, a smile begins to form, an expression of pleasure appears, the body becomes more erect, there is a general muscular hypertonicity. X tells us that as she listens to the music she experiences sensations very like those of normal intercourse. The difference chiefly concerns the local genital apparatus, for there is no flow of vaginal mucus. On the psychic side the resemblance is marked." (Vaschide and Vurpas, "Du Coefficient Sexuel de l'Impulsion Musicale," *Archives de Neurologie*, May, 1904.)

It is sometimes said, or implied, that a woman (or a man) sings better under the influence of sexual emotion. The writer of an article already quoted, on "Woman in her Psychological Relations" (*Journal of Psychological Medicine*, 1851), mentions that "a young lady remarkable for her musical and poetical talents naïvely remarked to a friend who complimented her upon her singing: 'I never sing half so well as when I've had a love-fit.'" And George Eliot says: "There is no feeling, perhaps, except the extremes of fear and grief, that does not make a man sing or play the better." While, however, it may be admitted that some degree of general emotional exaltation may exercise a favorable influence on the singing voice, it is difficult to believe that definite physical excitement at or immediately before the exercise of the voice can, as a rule, have anything but a deleterious effect on its quality. It is recognized that tenors (whose voices resemble those of women more than basses, who are not called upon to be so careful in this respect) should observe rules of sexual hygiene; and menstruation frequently has a definite influence in impairing the voice (H. Ellis, *Man and Woman*, fourth edition, p. 290). As the neighborhood of menstruation is also the period when sexual excitement is most likely to be felt, we have here a further indication that sexual emotion is not favorable to singing. I agree with the remarks of a correspondent, a musical amateur, who writes: "Sexual excitement and good singing do not appear to be correlated. A woman's emotional capacity in singing or acting may be remotely associated with hysterical neuroses, but is better evinced for art purposes in the absence of disturbing sexual influences. A woman may, indeed, fancy herself the heroine of a wanton romance and 'let herself go' a little in singing with improved results. But a memory of sexual ardors will help no woman to make the best of her voice in training. Some women can only sing their best when they think of the other women they are outsinging. One girl 'lets her soul go out into her voice' thinking of jamroll, another thinking of her lover (when she has none), and most, no doubt, when they think of nothing. But no woman is likely to 'find herself' in an artistic sense because she has lost herself in another sense—not even if she has done so quite respectably."

The reality of the association between the sexual impulse and music—and, indeed, art generally—is shown by the fact that the evolution of puberty tends to be accompanied by a very marked interest in musical and other kinds of art. Lancaster, in a study of this question among a large number of young people (without reference to difference in sex, though they were largely female), found that from 50 to 75 per cent. of young people feel an impulse to art about the period of puberty, lasting a few months, or at most a year or two. It appears that 464 young people showed an increased and passionate love for music, against only 102 who experienced no change in this respect. The curve culminates at the age of 15 and falls rapidly after 16. Many of these cases were really quite unmusical.[1]

---

[1] E. Lancaster, "Psychology of Adolescence," *Pedagogical Seminary,* July, 1897.

II.

Summary—Why the Influence of Music in Human Sexual Selection is Comparatively Small.

WE have seen that it is possible to set forth in a brief space the facts at present available concerning the influence on the pairing impulse of stimuli acting through the ear. They are fairly simple and uncomplicated; they suggest few obscure problems which call for analysis; they do not bring before us any remarkable perversions of feeling.

At the same time, the stimuli to sexual excitement received through the sense of hearing, although very seldom of exclusive or preponderant influence, are yet somewhat more important than is usually believed. Primarily the voice, and secondarily instrumental music, exert a distinct effect in this direction, an effect representing a specialization of a generally stimulating physiological influence which all musical sounds exercise upon the organism. There is, however, in this respect, a definite difference between the sexes. It is comparatively rare to find that the voice or instrumental music, however powerful its generally emotional influence, has any specifically sexual effect on men. On the other hand, it seems probable that the majority of women, at all events among the educated classes, are liable to show some degree of sexual sensibility to the male voice or to instrumental music.

It is not surprising to find that music should have some share in arousing sexual emotion when we bear in mind that in the majority of persons the development of sexual life is accompanied by a period of special interest in music. It is not unexpected that the specifically sexual effects of the voice and music should be chiefly experienced by women when we remember that not only in the human species is it the male in whom the larynx and voice are chiefly modified at puberty, but that among mammals generally it is the male who is chiefly or exclusively vocal at the period of sexual activity; so that any sexual sensibility to vocal manifestations must be chiefly or exclusively manifested in female mammals.

At the best, however, although æsthetic sensibility to sound is highly developed and emotional sensibility to it profound and widespread, although women may be thrilled by the masculine voice and men charmed by the feminine voice, it cannot be claimed that in the human species hearing is a powerful factor in mating. This sense has here suffered between the lower senses of touch and smell, on the one hand, with their vague and massive appeal, and the higher sense, vision, on the other hand, with its exceedingly specialized appeal. The position of touch as the primary and fundamental sense is assured. Smell, though in normal persons it has no decisive influence on sexual attraction, acts by virtue of its emotional sympathies and antipathies, while, by virtue of the fact that among man's ancestors it was the fundamental channel of sexual sensibility, it furnishes a latent reservoir of impressions to which nervously abnormal persons, and even normal persons under the influence of excitement or of fatigue, are always liable to become sensitive. Hearing, as a sense for receiving distant perceptions has a wider field than is in man possessed by either touch or smell. But here it comes into competition with vision, and vision is, in man, the supreme and dominant sense.[1] We are always more affected by what we see than by what we hear. Men and women seldom hear each other without speedily seeing each other, and then the chief focus of interest is at once transferred to the visual centre.[2] In human sexual selection, therefore, hearing plays a part which is nearly always subordinated to that of vision.

---

[1] Nietzsche has even suggested that among primitive men delicacy of hearing and the evolution of music can only have been produced under conditions which made it difficult for vision to come into play: "The ear, the organ of fear, could only have developed, as it has, in the night and in the twilight of dark woods and caves. . . . In the brightness the ear is less necessary. Hence the character of music as an art of night and twilight." (*Morgenröthe*, p. 230.)

[2] At a concert most people are instinctively anxious to *see* the performers, thus distracting the purely musical impression, and the reasonable suggestion of Goethe that the performers should be invisible is still seldom carried into practice.

VISION.

I.

Primacy of Vision in Man—Beauty as a Sexual Allurement—The Objective Element in Beauty—Ideals of Feminine Beauty in Various Parts of the World—Savage Women sometimes Beautiful from European Point of View—Savages often Admire European Beauty—The Appeal of Beauty to some Extent Common even to Animals and Man.

VISION is the main channel by which man receives his impressions. To a large extent it has slowly superseded all the other senses. Its range is practically infinite; it brings before us remote worlds, it enables us to understand the minute details of our own structure. While apt for the most abstract or the most intimate uses, its intermediate range is of universal service. It furnishes the basis on which a number of arts make their appeal to us, and, while thus the most æsthetic of the senses, it is the sense on which we chiefly rely in exercising the animal function of nutrition. It is not surprising, therefore, that from the point of view of sexual selection vision should be the supreme sense, and that the love-thoughts of men have always been a perpetual meditation of beauty.

It would be out of place here to discuss comparatively the origins of our ideas of beauty. That is a question which belongs to æsthetics, not to sexual psychology, and it is a question on which æstheticians are not altogether in agreement. We need not even be concerned to make any definite assertion on the question whether our ideals of sexual beauty have developed under the influence of more general and fundamental laws, or whether sexual ideals themselves underlie our more general conceptions of beauty. Practically, so far as man and his immediate ancestors are concerned, the sexual and the extra-sexual factors of beauty have been interwoven from the first. The sexually beautiful object must have appealed to fundamental physiological aptitudes of reaction; the generally beautiful object must have shared in the thrill which the specifically sexual object imparted. There has been an inevitable action and reaction throughout. Just as we found that the sexual and the nonsexual influences of agreeable odors throughout nature are inextricably mingled, so it is with the motives that make an object beautiful to our eyes.[1]

The sexual element in the constitution of beauty is well recognized even by those writers who concern themselves exclusively with the æsthetic conception of beauty or with its relation to culture. It is enough to quote two or three testimonies on this point. "The whole sentimental side of our æsthetic sensibility," remarks Santayana, "—without which it would be perceptive and mathematical rather than æsthetic,—is due to our sexual organization remotely stirred. . . . If anyone were desirous to produce a being with a great susceptibility to beauty, he could not invent an instrument better designed for that object than sex. Individuals that need not unite for the birth and rearing of each generation might retain a savage independence. For them it would not be necessary that any vision should fascinate, or that any languor should soften, the prying cruelty of the eye. But sex endows the individual with a dumb and powerful instinct, which carries his body and soul continually toward another; makes it one of the dearest enjoyments of his life to select and pursue a companion, and joins to possession the keenest pleasure, to rivalry the fiercest rage, and to solitude an eternal melancholy. What more could be needed to suffuse the world with the deepest meaning and beauty? The attention is fixed upon a well-defined object, and all the effects it produces in the mind are easily regarded as powers or qualities of that object. . . . To a certain extent this kind of interest will center in the proper object of sexual passion, and in the special characteristics of the opposite sex[1]; and we find, accordingly, that woman is the most lovely object to man, and man, if female modesty would confess it, the most interesting to woman. But the effects of so fundamental and primitive a reaction are much more general. Sex is not the only object of sexual passion. When love lacks its specific object, when it does not yet understand itself, or has been sacrificed to some other interest, we see the stifled fire bursting out in various directions. . . . Passion then overflows

---

[1] "It is likely that all visible parts of the organism, even those with a definite physiological meaning, appeal to the æsthetic sense of the opposite sex," Poulton remarks, speaking primarily of insects, in words that apply still more accurately to the human species. E. Poulton, *The Colors of Animals*, 1890, p. 304.

and visibly floods those neighboring regions which it had always se-secretly watered. For the same nervous organization which sex involves, with its necessarily wide branchings and associations in the brain, must be partially stimulated by other objects than its specific or ultimate one; especially in man, who, unlike some of the lower animals, has not his instincts clearly distinct and intermittent, but always partially active, and never active in isolation. We may say, then, that for man all nature is a secondary object of sexual passion, and that to this fact the beauty of nature is largely due." (G. Santayana, *The Sense of Beauty*, pp. 59-62.)

Not only is the general fact of sexual attraction an essential element of æsthetic contemplation, as Santayana remarks, but we have to recognize also that specific sexual emotion properly comes within the æsthetic field. It is quite erroneous, as Groos well points out, to assert that sexual emotion has no æsthetic value. On the contrary, it has quite as much value as the emotion of terror or of pity. Such emotion must, however, be duly subordinated to the total æsthetic effect. (K. Groos, *Der Æsthetische Genuss*, p. 151.)

"The idea of beauty," Remy de Gourmont says, "is not an unmixed idea; it is intimately united with the idea of carnal pleasure. Stendhal obscurely perceived this when he defined beauty as 'a promise of happiness.' Beauty is a woman, and women themselves have carried docility to men so far as to accept this aphorism which they can only understand in extreme sexual perversion. . . . Beauty is so sexual that the only uncontested works of art are those that simply show the human body in its nudity. By its perseverance in remaining purely sexual Greek statuary has placed itself forever above all discussion. It is beautiful because it is a beautiful human body, such a one as every man or every woman would desire to unite with in the perpetuation of the race. . . . That which inclines to love seems beautiful; that which seems beautiful inclines to love. This intimate union of art and of love is, indeed, the only explanation of art. Without this genital echo art would never have been born and never have been perpetuated. There is nothing useless in these deep human depths; everything which has endured is necessary. Art is the accomplice of love. When love is taken away there is no art; when art is taken away love is nothing but a physiological need." (Remy de Gourmont, *Culture des Idées*, 1900, p. 103, and *Mercure de France*, August, 1901, pp. 298 *et seq.*)

Beauty as incarnated in the feminine body has to some extent become the symbol of love even for women. Colin Scott finds that it is common among women who are not inverted for female beauty whether on the stage or in art to arouse sexual emotion to a greater extent than male beauty, and this is confirmed by some of the histories I have recorded in the Appendix to the third volume of these *Studies*. Scott considers that female beauty has come to be regarded as typical of ideal beauty, and thus tends to produce an emotional effect on both sexes alike. It is certainly rare to find any æsthetic admiration of men among women, except in the case of women who have had some training in art. In this matter it would seem that woman passively accepts the ideals of man. "Objects which excite a man's desire," Colin Scott remarks, "are often, if not generally, the same as those affecting woman. The female body has a sexually stimulating effect upon both sexes. Statutes of female forms are more liable than those of male form to have a stimulating effect upon women as well as men. The evidence of numerous literary expressions seems to show that under the influence of sexual excitement a woman regards her body as made for man's gratification, and that it is this complex emotion which forms the initial stage, at least, of her own pleasure. Her body is the symbol for her partner, and indirectly for her, through his admiration of it, of their mutual joy and satisfaction." (Colin Scott, "Sex and Art," *American Journal of Pscyhology*, vol. vii, No. 2, p. 206; also private letter.)

At the same time it must be remembered that beauty and the conception of beauty have developed on a wider basis than that of the sexual impulse only, and also that our conceptions of the beautiful, even as concerns the human form, are to some extent objective, and may thus be in part reduced to law. Stratz, in his books on feminine beauty, and notably in *Die Schönheit des Weiblichen Körpers*, insists on the objective element in beauty. Papillault, again, when discussing the laws of growth and the beauty of the face, argues that beauty of line in the face is objective, and not a creation of fancy, since it is associated with the highest human functions, moral and social. He remarks on the contrast between the prehistoric man of Chancelade,—delicately made, with elegant face and high forehead,—who created the great Magdalenian civilization, and his seemingly much more powerful, but less beautiful, predecessor, the man of Spy, with enormous muscles and powerful jaws. (*Bulletin de la Société d'Anthropologie*, 1899, p. 220.)

The largely objective character of beauty is further indicated by the fact that to a considerable extent beauty is the expression of health. A well and harmoniously developed body, tense muscles, an elastic and finely toned skin, bright eyes, grace and animation of carriage—all these things which are essential to beauty are the conditions of health. It has not been demonstrated that there is any correlation between beauty and longevity, and the proof would not be easy to give, but it is quite probable that such a correlation may exist, and various indications point in this direction. One of the most delightful of Opie's pictures is the portrait of Pleasance Reeve (afterward Lady Smith) at the age of 17. This singularly beautiful and animated brunette lived to the age of 104. Most people are probably acquainted with similar, if less marked, cases of the same tendency.

The extreme sexual importance of beauty, so far, at all events, as conscious experience is concerned, is well illustrated by the fact that, although three other senses may and often do play a not inconsiderable part in the constitution of a person's sexual attractiveness,—the tactile element being, indeed, fundamental,—yet in nearly all the most elaborate descriptions of attractive individuals it is the visible elements that are in most cases chiefly emphasized. Whether among the lowest savages or in the highest civilization, the poet and story-teller who seeks to describe an ideally lovely and desirable woman always insists mainly, and often exclusively, on those characters which appeal to the eye. The richly laden word *beauty* is a synthesis of complex impressions obtained through a single sense, and so simple, comparatively, and vague are the impressions derived from the other senses that none of them can furnish us with any corresponding word.

Before attempting to analyze the conception of beauty, regarded in its sexual appeal to the human mind, it may be well to bring together a few fairly typical descriptions of a beautiful woman as she appears to the men of various nations.

In an Australian folklore story taken down from the lips of a native some sixty years ago by W. Dunlop (but evidently not in the native's exact words) we find this description of an Australian beauty: "A man took as his wife a beautiful girl who had long, glossy hair hanging around her face and down her shoulders, which were plump and round. Her face was adorned with red clay and her person wrapped in a fine large opossum rug fastened by a pin formed from the small bone of the kangaroo's leg, and also by a string attached to a wallet made of rushes neatly plaited of small strips skinned from their outside after they had been for some time exposed to the heat of the fire; which being thrown on her back, the string passing under one arm and across her breast, held the soft rug in a fanciful position of considerable elegance; and she knew well how to show to advantage her queenlike figure when she walked with her polished yam stick held in one of her small hands and her little feet appearing below the edge of the rug" (W. Dunlop, "Australian Folklore Stories," *Journal of the Anthropological Institute*, August and November, 1898, p. 27).

A Malay description of female beauty is furnished by Skeat. "The brow (of the Malay Helen for whose sake a thousand desperate battles are fought in Malay romances) is like the one-day-old moon; her eyebrows resemble 'pictured clouds,' and are 'arched like the fighting-cock's (artificial) spur'; her cheek resembles the 'sliced-off cheek of a mango'; her nose, 'an opening jasmine bud'; her hair, the 'wavy blossom shoots of the areca-palm'; slender is her neck, 'with a triple row of dimples'; her bosom ripening, her waist 'lissom as the stalk of a flower,' her head 'of a perfect oval' (literally, bird's-egg shaped), her fingers like the leafy 'spears of lemon-grass' or the 'quills of the porcupine,' her eyes 'like the splendor of the planet Venus,' and her lips 'like the fissure of a pomegranate.'" (W. W. Skeat, *Malay Magic*, 1900, p. 363.)

In Mitford's *Tales of Old Japan* (vol. i, p. 215) a "peerlessly beautiful girl of 16" is thus described: "She was neither too fat nor too thin, neither too tall nor too short; her face was oval, like a melon-seed, and her complexion fair and white; her eyes were narrow and bright, her teeth small and even; her nose was aquiline, and her mouth delicately formed, with lovely red lips; her eyebrows were long and fine; she had a profusion of long black hair; she spoke modestly, with a soft, sweet voice, and when she smiled, two lovely dimples appeared in her cheeks; in all her movements she was gentle and refined." The Japanese belle of ancient times, Dr. Nagayo Sensai remarks (*Lancet*, February 15, 1890) had a white face, a long, slender throat and neck, a narrow chest, small thighs, and small feet and hands. Bälz, also, has emphasized the ethereal character of the Japanese ideal of feminine beauty, delicate, pale and slender, almost uncanny; and Stratz, in his interesting book, *Die Körperformen in Kunst und Leben der Japaner* (second edition, 1904), has dealt fully with the subject of Japanese beauty.

The Singalese are great connoisseurs of beauty, and a Kandyan deeply learned in the matter gave Dr. Davy the following enumeration of a woman's points of beauty: "Her hair should be voluminous, like the tail of the peacock, long, reaching to the knees, and terminating in graceful curls; her eyebrows should resemble the rainbow, her eyes, the blue sapphire and the petals of the blue manilla-flower. Her nose should be like the bill of the hawk; her lips should be bright and red, like coral or the young leaf of the iron-tree. Her teeth should be small, regular, and closely set, and like jessamine buds. Her neck should be large and round, resembling the berrigodea. Her chest should be capacious; her breasts, firm and conical, like the yellow cocoa-nut, and her waist small—almost small enough to be clasped by the hand. Her hips should be wide; her limbs tapering; the soles of her feet, without any hollow, and the surface of her body in general soft, delicate, smooth, and rounded, without the asperities of projecting bones and sinews." (J. Davy, *An Account of the Interior of Ceylon*, 1821, p. 110.)

The "Padmini," or lotus-woman, is described by Hindu writers as the type of most perfect feminine beauty. "She in whom the following signs and symptoms appear is called a *Padmini:* Her face is pleasing as the full moon; her body, well clothed with flesh, is as soft as the Shiras or mustard flower; her skin is fine, tender, and fair as the yellow lotus, never dark colored. Her eyes are bright and beautiful as the orbs of the fawn, well cut, and with reddish corners. Her bosom is hard, full, and high; she has a good neck; her nose is straight and lovely; and three folds or wrinkles cross her middle—about the umbilical region. Her *yoni* [vulva] resembles the opening lotus bud, and her love-seed is perfumed like the lily that has newly burst. She walks with swanlike [more exactly, flamingolike] gait, and her voice is low and musical as the note of the Kokila bird [the Indian cuckoo]; she delights in white raiment, in fine jewels, and in rich dresses. She eats little, sleeps lightly, and being as respectful and religious as she is clever and courteous, she is ever anxious to worship the gods and to enjoy the conversation of Brahmans. Such, then, is the Padmini, or lotus-woman." (*The Kama Sutra of Vatsyayana*, 1883, p. 11.)

The Hebrew ideal of feminine beauty is set forth in various passages of the *Song of Songs*. The poem is familiar, and it will suffice to quote one passage:—

"How beautiful are thy feet in sandals, O prince's daughter!
Thy rounded thighs are like jewels,
The work of the hands of a cunning workman.
Thy navel is like a rounded goblet
Wherein no mingled wine is wanting;
Thy belly is like a heap of wheat
Set about with lilies.
Thy two breasts are like two fawns
That are twins of a roe.
Thy neck is like the tower of ivory;
Thine eyes as the pools in Heshbon, by the gate of Bathrabbim;
Thy nose is like the tower of Lebanon
That looketh toward Damascus.
Thine head upon thee is like Carmel
And the hair of thine head like purple;
The king is held captive in the tresses thereof.
This thy stature is like to a palm-tree,
And thy breasts to clusters of grapes,
And the smell of thy breath like apples,
And thy mouth like the best wine."

And the man is thus described in the same poem:—

"My beloved is fair and ruddy,
  The chiefest among ten thousand.
  His head as the most fine gold,
  His locks are bushy (or curling), and black as a raven.
  His eyes are like doves beside the water-brooks,
  Washed with milk and fitly set.
  His cheeks are as a bed of spices, as banks of sweet herbs;
  His lips are as lilies, dropping liquid myrrh.
  His hands are as rings of gold, set with beryl;
  His body is as ivory work, overlaid with sapphires.
  His legs are as pillars of marble, set upon sockets of fine gold.
  His aspect is like Lebanon, excellent as the cedars.
  His mouth is most sweet; yea, he is altogether lovely."

"The maiden whose loveliness inspires the most impassioned expressions in Arabic poetry," Lane states, "is celebrated for her slender figure: She is like the cane among plants, and is elegant as a twig of the oriental willow. Her face is like the full moon, presenting the strongest contrast to the color of her hair, which is of the deepest hue of night, and falls to the middle of her back (Arab ladies are extremely fond of full and long hair). A rosy blush overspreads the center of each cheek; and a mole is considered an additional charm. The Arabs, indeed, are particularly extravagant in their admiration of this natural beauty spot, which, according to its place, is compared to a drop of ambergris upon a dish of alabaster or upon the surface of a ruby. The eyes of the Arab beauty are intensely black,[1] large, and long, of the form of an almond: they are full of brilliancy; but this is softened by long silken lashes, giving a tender and languid expression that is full of enchantment and scarcely to be improved by the adventitious aid of the black border of kohl; for this the lovely maiden adds rather for the sake of fashion than necessity, having what the Arabs term natural kohl. The eyebrows are thin and arched; the forehead is wide and fair as ivory; the nose straight; the mouth, small; the lips of a brilliant red; and the teeth, like pearls set in coral. The forms of the bosom are compared to two pomegranates; the waist is slender; the hips are wide and large; the feet and hands, small; the fingers, tapering, and their extremities dyed with the deep orange tint imparted by the leaves of the henna."

Lane adds a more minute analysis from an unknown author quoted by El-Ishâkee: "Four things in a woman should be *black*—the

---

[1] "The Arabs in general," Lane remarks, "entertain a prejudice against blue eyes—a prejudice said to have arisen from the great number of blue-eyed persons among certain of their northern enemies."

hair of the head, the eyebrows, the eyelashes, and the dark part
of the eyes; four *white*—the complexion of the skin, the white of
the eyes, the teeth, and the legs; four *red*—the tongue, the lips, the
middle of the cheeks, and the gums; four *round*—the head, the neck,
the forearms, and tne ankles; four *long*—the back, the fingers, the
arms, and the legs; four *wide*—the forehead, the eyes, the bosom, and
the hips; four *fine*—the eyebrows, the nose, the lips, and the fingers;
four *thick*—the lower part of the back, the thighs, the calves of the
legs, and the knees; four *small*—the ears, the breasts, the hands, and
the feet." (E. W. Lane, *Arabian Society in the Middle Ages*, 1883,
pp. 214-216.)

A Persian treatise on the figurative terms relating to beauty
shows that the hair should be black, abundant, and wavy, the eyebrows dark and arched. The eyelashes also must be dark, and like
arrows from the bow of the eyebrows. There is, however, no insistence on the blackness of the eyes. We hear of four varieties of
eye: the dark-gray eye (or nàrcissus eye); the narrow, elongated
eye of Turkish beauties; the languishing, or love-intoxicated, eye;
and the wine-colored eye. Much stress is laid on the quality of
brilliancy. The face is sometimes described as brown, but more especially as white and rosy. There are many references to the down on
the lips, which is described as greenish (sometimes bluish) and compared to herbage. This down and that on the cheeks and the stray
hairs near the ears were regarded as very great beauties. A beauty
spot on the chin, cheek, or elsewhere was also greatly admired, and
evoked many poetic comparisons. The mouth must be very small. In
stature a beautiful woman must be tall and erect, like the cypress or
the maritime pine. While the Arabs admired the rosiness of the legs
and thighs, the Persians insisted on white legs and compared them
to silver and crystal. (*Anîs El-Ochchâq*, by Shereef-Eddin Romi, translated by Huart, *Bibliothèque de l'École des Hautes Études*, Paris,
fasc. 25, 1875.)

In the story of Kamaralzaman in the *Arabian Nights* El-Sett
Budur is thus described: "Her hair is so brown that it is blacker
than the separation of friends. And when it is arrayed in three
tresses that reach to her feet I seem to see three nights at once.

"Her face is as white as the day on which friends meet again.
If I look on it at the time of the full moon I see two moons at once.

"Her cheeks are formed of an anemone divided into two corollas;
they have the purple tinge of wine, and her nose is straighter and
more delicate than the finest sword-blade.

"Her lips are colored agate and coral; her tongue secretes
eloquence; her saliva is more desirable than the juice of grapes.

"But her bosom, blessed be the Creator, is a living seduction. It bears twin breasts of the purest ivory, rounded. and that may be held within the five fingers of one hand.

"Her belly has dimples full of shade and arranged with the harmony of the Arabic characters on the seal of a Coptic scribe in Egypt. And the belly gives origin to her finely modeled and elastic waist.

"At the thought of her flanks I shudder, for thence depends a mass so weighty that it obliges its owner to sit down when she has risen and to rise when she lies.

"Such are her flanks; and from them descend, like white marble, her glorious thighs, solid and straight, united above beneath their crown. Then come the legs and the slender feet, so small that I am astounded they can bear so great a weight."

An Egyptian stela in the Louvre sings the praise of a beautiful woman, a queen who died about 700 B.C., as follows: "The beloved before all women, the king's daughter who is sweet in love, the fairest among women, a maid whose like none has seen. Blacker is her hair than the darkness of night, blacker than the berries of the blackberry bush (?). Harder are her teeth (?) than the flints on the sickle. A wreath of flowers is each of her breasts, close nestling on her arms." Wiedemann, who quotes this, adds: "During the whole classic period of Egyptian history with few exceptions (such, for example, as the reign of that great innovator, Amenophis IV) the ideal alike for the male and the female body was a slender and but slightly developed form. Under the Ethiopian rule and during the Ptolemaic period in Egypt itself we find, for the first time, that the goddesses are represented with plump and well-developed outlines. Examination of the mummies shows that the earlier ideal was based upon actual facts, and that in ancient Egypt slender, sinewy forms distinguished both men and women. Intermariage with other races and harem life may have combined in later times to alter the physical type, and with it to change also the ideal of beauty." (A. Wiedemann, *Popular Literature in Ancient Egypt*, p. 7.)

Commenting on Plato's ideas of beauty in the *Banquet* Eméric-David gives references from Greek literature showing that the typical Greek beautiful woman must be tall, her body supple, her fingers long, her foot small and light, the eyes clear and moderately large, the eyebrows slightly arched and almost meeting, the nose straight and firm, nearly—but not quite—aquiline, the breath sweet as honey. (Eméric-David, *Recherches sur l'Art Statuaire*, new edition, 1863, p. 42.)

At the end of classic antiquity, probably in the fifth century, Aristænetus in his first Epistle thus described his mistress Lais: "Her cheeks are white, but mixed in imitation of the splendor of the rose; her lips are thin, by a narrow space separated from the cheeks, but more red; her eyebrows are black and divided in the middle; the nose straight and proportioned to the thin lips; the eyes large and bright, with very black pupils, surrounded by the clearest white, each color more brilliant by contrast. Her hair is naturally curled, and, as Homer's saying is, like the hyacinth. The neck is white and proportioned to the face, and though unadorned more conspicuous by its delicacy; but a necklace of gems encircles it, on which her name is written in jewels. She is tall and elegantly dressed in garments fitted to her body and limbs. When dressed her appearance is beautiful; when undressed she is all beauty. Her walk is composed and slow; she looks like a cypress or a palm stirred by the wind. I cannot describe how the swelling, symmetrical breasts raise the constraining vest, nor how delicate and supple her limbs are. And when she speaks, what sweetness in her discourse!"

Renier has studied the feminine ideal of the Provençal poets, the troubadours who used the "langue d'oc." "They avoid any description of the feminine type. The indications refer in great part to the slender, erect, fresh appearance of the body, and to the white and rosy coloring. After the person generally, the eyes receive most praise; they are sweet, amorous, clear, smiling, and bright. The color is never mentioned. The mouth is laughing, and vermilion, and, smiling sweetly, it reveals the white teeth and calls for the delights of the kiss. The face is clear and fresh, the hand white and the hair constantly blonde. The troubadours seldom speak of the rest of the body. Peire Vidal is an exception, and his reference to the well-raised breasts may be placed beside a reference by Bertran de Born. The general impression conveyed by the love lyrics of the langue d'oc is one of great convention. There seemed to be no salvation outside certain phrases and epithets. The woman of Provence, sung by hundreds of poets, seems to have been composed all of milk and roses, a blonde Nuremburg doll." (R. Renier, *Il Tipo Estetico della Donna nel Mediævo*, 1885, pp. 1-24.)

The conventional ideal of the troubadours is, again, thus described: "She is a lady whose skin is white as milk, whiter than the driven snow, of peculiar purity in whiteness. Her cheeks, on which vermilion hues alone appear, are like the rosebud in spring, when it has not yet opened to the full. Her hair, which is nearly always bedecked and adorned with flowers, is invariably of the color of flax, as soft as silk, and shimmering with a sheen of the finest gold." (J. F. Rowbotham, *The Troubadours and Courts of Love*, p. 228.)

In the most ancient Spanish romances, Renier remarks, the definite indications of physical beauty are slight. The hair is "of pure gold," or simply fair (*rubios*, which is equal to *blondos*, a word of later introduction), the face white and rosy, the hand soft, white, and fragrant;

in one place we find a reference to the uncovered breasts, whiter than crystal. But usually the ancient Castilian romances do not deal with these details. The poet contents himself with the statement that a lady is the sweetest woman in the world, *la mas linda mujer del mundo*." (R. Renier, *Il Tipo Estetico della Donna nel Mediœvo*, pp. 68 *et seq.*)

In a detailed and well-documented thesis, Alwin Schultz describes the characteristics of the beautiful woman as she appealed to the German authors of the twelfth and thirteenth centuries. She must be of medium height and slender. Her hair must be fair, like gold; long, bright, and curly; a man's must only reach to his shoulders. Dark hair is seldom mentioned and was not admired. The parting of the hair must be white, but not too broad. The forehead must be white and bright and rounded, without wrinkles. The eyebrows must be darker than the hair, arched, and not too broad, as though drawn with a pencil, the space betwen them not too broad. The eyes must be bright, clear, and sparkling, not too large or too small; nothing definite was said of the color, but they were evidently usually blue. The nose must be of medium size, straight, and not curved. The cheeks must be white, tinged with red; if the red was absent by nature women used rouge. The mouth must be small; the lips full and red. The teeth must be small, white, and even. The chin must be white, rounded, lovable, dimpled; the ears small and beautiful; the neck of medium size, soft, white, and spotless; the arm small; the hands and fingers long; the joints small, the nails white and bright and well cared for. The bosom must be white and large; the breasts high and rounded, like apples or pears, small and soft. The body generally must be slender and active. The lower parts of the body are very seldom mentioned, and many poets are even too modest to mention the breasts. The buttocks must be rounded, one poet, indeed, mentions, and the thighs soft and white, the *meinel* (mons) brown. The legs must be straight and narrow, the calves full, the feet small and narrow, with high instep. The color of the skin generally must be clear and of a tempered rosiness. (A. Schultz, *Quid de Perfecta Corporis Humani Pulchritudine Germani Sæculi XII et XIII Senserint*, 1866.) A somewhat similar, but shorter, account is given by K. Weinhold (*Die Deutschen Frauen im Mittelalter*, 1882, bd. 1, pp. 219 *et seq*). Weinhold considers that, like the French, the Germans admired the mixed eye, *vair* or gray.

Adam de la Halle, the Artois *trouvère* of the thirteenth century, in a piece ("Li Jus Adan ou de la feuillie") in which he brings himself forward, thus describes his mistress: "Her hair had the brilliance of gold, and was twisted into rebellious curls. Her forehead was very regular, white, and smooth; her eyebrows, delicate and even, were two brown arches, which seemed traced with a brush. Her eyes, bright and well cut, seemed to me *vairs* and full of caresses; they were large beneath, and their lids like little sickles, adorned by twin folds, veiled or revealed at her will her loving gaze. Between her eyes descended the pipe of her nose, straight and beautiful, mobile when she was gay; on either side were her rounded, white cheeks, on which laughter impressed two dimples, and which one could see blushing beneath her veil. Beneath the nose opened a mouth with blossoming lips; this mouth, fresh and vermilion as a rose, revealed the white teeth, in regular array; beneath the chin sprang the white neck, descending full and round to the shoulder. The powerful nape, white and without any little wandering hairs, protruded a little over the dress. To her sloping shoulders were attached long arms, large or slender where they so should be. What shall I say of her white hands, with their long fingers, and knuckles without knots, delicately ending in rosy nails attached to the flesh by a clear and single line? I come to her bosom with its firm breasts, but short and high pointed, revealing the valley of love between them, to her round belly, her arched flanks. Her hips were flat, her legs round, her calf large; she had a slender ankle, a lean and arched foot. Such she was as I saw her, and that which her chemise hid was not of less worth." (Houdoy, *La Beauté des Femmes*, p. 125, who quotes the original of this passage, considers it the ideal model of the mediæval woman.)

In the twelfth century story of *Aucassin et Nicolette*, "Nicolette had fair hair, delicate and curling; her eyes were gray (*vairs*) and smiling; her face admirably modeled. Her nose was high and well placed; her lips small and more vermilion than the cherry or the rose in summer; her teeth were small and white; her firm little breasts raised her dress as would two walnuts. Her figure was so slender that you could inclose it with your two hands, and the flowers of the marguerite, which her toes broke as she walked with naked feet, seemed black in comparison with her feet and legs, so white was she."

"Her hair was divided into a double tress," says Alain of Lille in the twelfth century, "which was long enough to kiss the ground; the parting, white as the lily and obliquely traced, separated the hair, and this want of symmetry, far from hurting her face, was one of the elements of her beauty. A golden comb maintained that abundant hair whose brilliance rivaled it, so that the fascinated eye could scarce distinguish the gold of the hair from the gold of the comb. The expanded forehead had the whiteness of milk, and rivaled the lily; her bright eyebrows shone like gold, not standing up in a brush, and, without being too scanty, orderly arranged. The eyes, serene and brilliant in their friendly light, seemed twin stars, her nostrils embalsamed with the odor of honey, neither too depressed in shape nor too prominent, were of distinguished form; the nard of her mouth offered to the smell a treat of sweet odors, and her half-open lips invited a kiss. The teeth seemed cut in ivory; her cheeks, like the carnation of the rose, gently illuminated her face and were tempered by the transparent whiteness of her veil. Her chin, more polished than crystal, showed silver reflections, and her slender neck fitly separated her head from the shoulders. The firm rotundity of her breasts attested the full expansion of youth; her charming arms, advancing toward you, seemed to call for caresses; the regular curve of her flanks, justly proportioned, completed her beauty. All the visible traits of her face and form thus sufficiently told what those charms must be that the bed alone knew." (The Latin text is given by Houdoy, *La Beauté des Femmes du XIIe au XVIe Siècle*, p. 119. Robert de Flagy's portrait of Blanchefleur in *Sarin-le-Loherain*, written in same century, reveals very similar traits.)

"The young woman appeared with twenty brightly polished daggers and swords," we read in the Irish *Tain Bo Cuailgne* of the Badhbh or Banshee who appeared to Meidhbh, "together with seven braids for the dead, of bright gold, in her right hand; a speckled garment of green ground, fastened by a bodkin at the breast under her fair, ruddy countenance, enveloped her form; her teeth were so new and bright that they appeared like pearls artistically set in her gums; like the ripe berry of the mountain ash were her lips; sweeter was her voice than the notes of the gentle harp-strings when touched by the most skillful finger, and emitting the most enchanting melody; whiter than the snow of one night was her skin, and beautiful to behold were her garments, which reached to her well molded, bright-nailed feet; copious tresses of her tendriled, glossy, golden hair hung before, while others dangled behind and reached the calf of her leg." (*Ossianic Transactions*, vol. ii, p. 107.)

An ancient Irish hero is thus described: "They saw a great hero approaching them; fairest of the heroes of the world; larger and taller than any man; bluer than ice his eye; redder than the fresh rowan berries his lips; whiter than showers of pearl his teeth; fairer than the snow of one night his skin; a protecting shield with a golden border was upon him, two battle-lances in his hands; a sword with knobs of ivory [teeth of the sea-horse], and ornamented with gold, at his side; he had no other accoutrements of a hero besides these; he had golden hair on his head, and had a fair, ruddy countenance." (*The Banquet of Dun na n-gedh*, translated by O'Donovan, *Irish Archæological Society*, 1842.)

The feminine ideal of the Italian poets closely resembles that of those north of the Alps. Petrarch's Laura, as described in the *Canzoniere*, is white as snow; her eyes, indeed, are black, but the fairness of her hair is constantly emphasized; her lips are rosy; her teeth

white; her cheeks rosy; her breast youthful; her hands white and
slender. Other poets insist on the tall, white, delicate body; the
golden or blonde hair; the bright or starry eyes (without mention of
color), the brown or black arched eyebrows, the straight nose, the
small mouth, the thin vermilion lips, the small and firm breasts.
(Renier, *Il Tipo Estetico*, pp. 87 *et seq.*)

Marie de France, a French mediæval writer of the twelfth century,
who spent a large part of her life in England, in the *Lai of Lanval*
thus describes a beautiful woman: "Her body was beautiful, her hips
low, the neck whiter than snow, the eyes gray *(vairs)*, the face white,
the mouth beautiful, the nose well placed, the eyebrows brown, the
forehead beautiful, the head curly and blonde; the gleam of gold
thread was less bright than her hair beneath the sun."

The traits of Boccaccio's ideal of feminine beauty, a voluptuous
ideal as compared with the ascetic mediæval ideal which had previously prevailed, together with the characteristics of the very beautiful
and almost classic garments in which he arrayed women, have been
brought together by Hortis (*Studi sulle opere Latine del Boccaccio*,
1879, pp. 70 *et seq.*). Boccaccio admired fair and abundant wavy hair,
dark and delicate eyebrows, and brown or even black eyes. It was
not until some centuries later, as Hortis remarks, that Boccaccio's
ideal woman was embodied by the painter in the canvases of Titian.

The first precise description of a famous beautiful woman was
written by Niphus in the sixteenth century in his *De Pulchro et
Amore*, which is regarded as the first modern treatise on æsthetics.
The lady described is Joan of Aragon, the greatest beauty of her
time, whose portrait by Raphael (or more probably Giulio Romano)
is in the Louvre. Niphus, who was the philosopher of the pontifical
court and the friend of Leo X, thus describes this princess, whom,
as a physician, he had opportunities of observing accurately: "She is
of medium stature, straight, and elegant, and possesses the grace
which can only be imparted by an assemblage of characteristics which
are individually faultless. She is neither fat nor bony, but succulent;
her complexion is not pale, but white tinged with rose; her long
hair is golden; her ears are small and in proportion with the size
of her mouth. Her brown eyebrows are semicircular, not too bushy,
and the individual hairs short. Her eyes are blue *(cæsius)*, brighter
than stars, radiant with grace and gaiety beneath the dark-brown
eyelashes, which are well spaced and not too long. The nose, symmetrical and of medium size, descends perpendicularly from between
the eyebrows. The little valley separating the nose from the upper
lip is divinely proportioned. The mouth, inclined to be rather small,
is always stirred by a sweet smile; the rather thick lips are made of
honey and coral. The teeth are small, polished as ivory, and sym-

metrically ranged, and the breath has the odor of the sweetest per-fumes. Her voice is that of a goddess. The chin is divided by a dim-ple; the whole face approximates to a virile rotundity. The straight long neck, white and full, rises gracefully from the shoulders. On the ample bosom, revealing no indication of the bones, arise the rounded breasts, of equal and fitting size, and exhaling the perfume of the peaches they resemble. The rather plump hands, on the back like snow, on the palm like ivory, are exactly the length of the face; the full and rounded fingers are long and terminating in round, curved nails of soft color. The chest as a whole has the form of a pear, re-versed, but a little compressed, and the base attached to the neck in a delightfully well-proportioned manner. The belly, the flanks, and the secret parts are worthy of the chest; the hips are large and rounded; the thighs, the legs, and the arms are in just proportion. The breadth of the shoulders is also in the most perfect relation to the dimensions of the other parts of the body; the feet, of medium length, terminate in beautifully arranged toes." (Houdoy reproduces this passage in *La Beauté des Femmes; cf.* also Stratz, *Die Schönheit des Weiblichen Körpers*, Chapter III.)

Gabriel de Minut, who published in 1587 a treatise of no very great importance, *De la Beauté*, also wrote under the title of *La Paulegraphie* a very elaborate description, covering sixty pages, of Paule de Viguier, a Gascon lady of good family and virtuous life living at Toulouse. Minut was her devoted admirer and addressed an affectionate poem to her just before his death. She was seventy years of age when he wrote the elaborate account of her beauty. She had blue eyes and fair hair, though belonging to one of the darkest parts of France.

Ploss and Bartels (*Das Weib*, bd. 1, sec. 3) have independently brought together a number of passages from the writers of many coun-tries describing their ideals of beauty. On this collection I have not drawn.

When we survey broadly the ideals of feminine beauty set down by the peoples of many lands, it is interesting to note that they all contain many features which appeal to the æsthetic taste of the modern European, and many of them, indeed, contain no features which obviously clash with his canons of taste. It may even be said that the ideals of some savages affect us more sympathetically than some of the ideals of our own mediæval ancestors. As a matter of fact, European travelers in all parts of the world have met with women who were gracious and pleasant to look on, and not seldom even in the strict sense beautiful, from the standpoint of European standards. Such individuals have been found even among those races with the greatest notoriety for ugliness.

Even among so primitive and remote a people as the Australians beauty in the European sense is sometimes found. "I have on two occasions," Lumholtz states, "seen what might be called beauties among the women of western Queensland. Their hands were small, their feet neat and well shaped, with so high an instep that one asked oneself involuntarily where in the world they had acquired this aristocratic mark of beauty. Their figure was above criticism, and their skin, as is usually the case among the young women, was as soft as velvet. When these black daughters of Eve smiled and showed their beautiful white teeth, and when their eyes peeped coquettishly from beneath the curly hair which hung in quite the modern fashion down their foreheads," Lumholtz realized that even here women could exert the influence ascribed by Goethe to women generally. (C. Lumholtz, *Among Cannibals*, p. 132.) Much has, again, been written about the beauty of the American Indians. See, *e.g.*, an article by Dr. Shufeldt, "Beauty from an Indian's Point of View," *Cosmopolitan Magazine*, April, 1895. Among the Seminole Indians, especially, it is said that types of handsome and comely women are not uncommon. (Clay MacCauley, "Seminole Indians of Florida," *Fifth Annual Report of the Bureau of Ethnology*, 1883-1884, pp. 493 *et seq.*)

There is much even in the negress which appeals to the European as beautiful. "I have met many negresses," remarks Castellani (*Les Femmes au Congo*, p. 2), "who could say proudly in the words of the Song of Songs, 'I am black, but comely.' Many of our peasant women have neither the same grace nor the same delicate skin as some natives of Cassai or Songha. As to color, I have seen on the African continent creatures of pale gold or even red copper whose fine and satiny skin rivals the most delicate white skins; one may, indeed, find beauties among women of the darkest ebony." He adds that, on the whole, there is no comparison with white women, and that the negress soon becomes hideous.

The very numerous quotations from travelers concerning the women of all lands quoted by Ploss and Bartels (*Das Weib*, seventh edition, bd. i, pp. 88-106) amply suffice to show how frequently some degree of beauty is found even among the lowest human races. *Cf.*, also, Mantegazza's survey of the women of different races from this point of view, *Fisiologia della Donna*, Cap. IV.

The fact that the modern European, whose culture may be supposed to have made him especially sensitive to æsthetic beauty, is yet able to find beauty among even the women of savage races serves to illustrate the statement already made that, whatever modifying influences may have to be admitted, beauty is to a large extent an objective matter. The existence of this objective element in beauty is confirmed by the fact that it is sometimes found that the men of the lower races admire European women more than women of their own race. There is reason to believe that it is among the more intelligent men of lower race—that is to say those whose æsthetic feelings are more developed—that the admiration for white women is most likely to be found.

"Mr. Winwood Reade," stated Darwin, "who has had ample opportunities for observation, not only with the negroes of the West Coast of Africa, but with those of the interior who have never associated with Europeans, is convinced that their ideas of beauty are, *on the whole*, the same as ours; and Dr. Rohlfs writes to me to the same effect with respect to Bornu and the countries inhabited by the Pullo tribes. Mr. Reade found that he agreed with the negroes in their estimation of the beauty of the native girls; and that their appreciation of the beauty of European women corresponded with ours. . . . The Fuegians, as I have been informed by a missionary who long resided with them, considered European women as extremely beautiful . . . I should add that a most experienced observer, Captain [Sir R.] Burton, believes that a woman whom we consider beautiful is admired throughout the world." (Darwin, *Descent of Man*, Chapter XIX.)

Mantegazza quotes a conversation between a South American chief and an Argentine who had asked him which he preferred, the women of his own people or Christian women; the chief replied that he admired Christian women most, and when asked the reason said that they were whiter and taller, had finer hair and smoother skin. (Mantegazza, *Fisiologia della Donna*, Appendix to Cap. VIII.)

Nordenskjöld, as quoted by Ploss and Bartels, states that the Eskimo regard their own type as more ugly than that produced by crossing with white persons, and, according to Kropf, the Nosa Kaffers admire and seek the fairer half-castes in preference to their own women of pure race (Ploss and Bartels, *Das Weib*, seventh edition, b¹. 1, p. 78). There is a widespread admiration for fairness, it may be added, among dark peoples. Fair men are admired by the Papuans at Torres Straits (*Reports of the Cambridge Anthropological Expedition*, vol. v, p. 327). The common use of powder among the women of dark-skinned peoples bears witness to the existence of the same ideal.

Stratz, in his books *Die Schönheit des Weiblichen Körpers* and *Die Rassenschönheit des Weibes*, argues that the ideal of beauty is fundamentally the same throughout the world, and that the finest persons among the lower races admire and struggle to attain the type which is only found commonly and in perfection among the white peoples of Europe. When in Japan he found that among the numerous photographs of Japanese beauties everywhere to be seen, his dragoman, a Japanese of low birth, selected as the most beautiful those which displayed markedly the Japanese type with narrow-slitted eyes and broad nose. When he sought the opinion of a Japanese photographer, who called himself an artist and had some claim to be so considered, the latter selected as most beautiful three Japanese girls who in Europe also would have been considered pretty. In Java, also, when selecting from a large number of Javanese girls a few suitable for photographing, Stratz was surprised to find that a Javanese doctor pointed out as most beautiful those which most closely corresponded to the European type. (Stratz, *Die Rassenschönheit des Weibes*, fourth edition, 1903, p. 3; *id.*, *Die Körperformen der Japaner*, 1904, p. 78.)

Stratz reproduces (Rassenschonheit, pp. 36 *et seq.*) a representation of Kwan-yin, the Chinese goddess of divine love, and quotes some remarks of Borel's concerning the wide deviation of the representations of the goddess, a type of gracious beauty, from the Chinese racial type. Stratz further reproduces the figure of a Buddhistic goddess from Java (now in the Archæological Museum of Leyden) which represents a type of loveliness corresponding to the most refined and classic European ideal.

Not only is there a fundamentally objective element in beauty throughout the human species, but it is probably a significant fact that we may find a similar element throughout the whole animated world. The things that to man are most beautiful throughout Nature are those that are intimately associated with, or dependent upon, the sexual process and the sexual instinct. This is the case in the plant world. It is so throughout most of the animal world, and, as Professor Poulton, in referring to this often unexplained and indeed unnoticed fact, remarks, "the song or plume which excites the mating impulse in the hen is also in a high proportion of cases most pleasing to man himself. And not only this, but in their past history, so far as it has been traced (*e.g.*, in the development of the characteristic markings of the male peacock and argus pheasant), such features have gradually become more and more pleasing to us as they have acted as stronger and stronger stimuli to the hen."[1]

---

[1] *Nature*, April 14, 1898, p. 55.

II.

Beauty to Some Extent Consists Primitively in an Exaggeration of the Sexual Characters—The Sexual Organs—Mutilations, Adornments, and Garments—Sexual Allurement the Original Object of Such Devices—The Religious Element—Unæsthetic Character of the Sexual Organs—Importance of the Secondary Sexual Characters—The Pelvis and Hips—Steatopygia—Obesity—Gait—The Pregnant Woman as a Mediæval Type of Beauty—The Ideals of the Renaissance—The Breasts—The Corset—Its Object—Its History—Hair—The Beard—The Element of National or Racial Type in Beauty—The Relative Beauty of Blondes and Brunettes—The General European Admiration for Blondes—The Individual Factors in the Constitution of the Idea of Beauty—The Love of the Exotic.

In the constitution of our ideals of masculine and feminine beauty it was inevitable that the sexual characters should from a very early period in the history of man form an important element. From a primitive point of view a sexually desirable and attractive person is one whose sexual characters are either naturally prominent or artificially rendered so. The beautiful woman is one endowed, as Chaucer expresses it,

"With buttokes brode and brestës rounde and hye";

that is to say, she is the woman obviously best fitted to bear children and to suckle them. These two physical characters, indeed, since they represent aptitude for the two essential acts of motherhood, must necessarily tend to be regarded as beautiful among all peoples and in all stages of culture, even in high stages of civilization when more refined and perverse ideals tend to find favor, and at Pompeii as a decoration on the east side of the Purgatorium of the Temple of Isis we find a representation of Perseus rescuing Andromeda, who is shown as a woman with a very small head, small hands and feet, but with a fully developed body, large breasts, and large projecting nates.[1]

---

[1] Figured in Mau's *Pompeii,* p. 174.

(156)

To a certain extent—and, as we shall see, to a certain extent only—the primary sexual characters are objects of admiration among primitive peoples. In the primitive dances of many peoples, often of sexual significance, the display of the sexual organs on the part of both men and women is frequently a prominent feature. Even down to mediæval times in Europe the garments of men sometimes permitted the sexual organs to be visible. In some parts of the world, also, the artificial enlargement of the female sexual organs is practiced, and thus enlarged they are considered an important and attractive feature of beauty.

Sir Andrew Smith informed Darwin that the elongated nymphæ (or "Hottentot apron") found among the women of some South African tribes was formerly greatly admired by the men (*Descent of Man*, Chapter XIX). This formation is probably a natural peculiarity of the women of these races which is very much exaggerated by intentional manipulation due to the admiration it arouses. The missionary Merensky reported the prevalence of the practice of artificial elongation among the Basuto and other peoples, and the anatomical evidence is in favor of its partly artificial character. (The Hottentot apron is fully discussed by Ploss and Bartels, *Das Weib*, bd. 1, sec. vi.)

In the Jaboo country on the Bight of Benin in West Africa, Daniell stated, it was considered ornamental to elongate the labia and the clitoris artificially; small weights were appended to the clitoris and gradually increased. (W. F. Daniell, *Topography of Gulf of Guinea*, 1849, pp. 24, 53.)

Among the Bawenda of the northern Transvaal, the missionary Wessmann states, it is customary for young girls from the age of 8 to spend a certain amount of time every day in pulling the *labia majora* in order to elongate them; in selecting a wife the young men attach much importance to this elongation, and the girl whose labia stand out most is most attractive. (*Zeitschrift für Ethnologie*, 1894, ht. 4, p. 363.)

It may be added that in various parts of the world mutilations of the sexual organs of men and women, or operations upon them, are practiced, for reasons which are imperfectly known, since it usually happens that the people who practice them are unable to give the reason for the practice, or they assign a reason which is manifestly not that which originally prompted the practice. Thus, the excision of the clitoris, practiced in many parts of East Africa and frequently supposed to be for the sake of dulling sexual feeling (J. S. King, *Journal of the Anthropological Society*, Bombay, 1890, p. 2), seems very doubtfully accounted for thus, for the women have it done of their own accord; "all Sobo women [Niger coast] have their clitoris cut off; unless they have this done they are looked down upon, as slave women who do not get cut; as soon, therefore, as a Sobo woman has collected enough money, she goes to an operating woman and pays her to do the cutting." (*Journal of the Anthropological Institute*, August-November, 1898, p. 117.) The Comte de Cardi investigated this matter in the Niger Delta: "I have questioned both native men and women," he states, "to try and get the natives' reason for this rite, but the almost universal answer to my queries was, 'it is our country's fashion.'" One old man told him it was practiced because favorable to continence, and several old women said that once the women of the land used to suffer from a peculiar kind of madness which this rite reduced. (*Journal of the Anthropological Institute*, August-November, 1899, p. 59.) In the same way the subincision of the urethra (mika operation of Australia) is frequently supposed to be for the purpose of preventing conception (See, *e.g.*, the description of the operation by J. G. Garson, *Medical Press*, February 21, 1894), but this is very doubtful, and E. C. Stirling found that subincised natives often had large families. (*Intercolonial Quarterly Journal of Medicine and Surgery*, 1894.)

A passage in the *Mainz Chronicle* for 1367 (as quoted by Schultz, *Das Hofische Leben*, p. 297) shows that at that time the tunics of the men were so made that it was always possible for the sexual organs to be seen in walking or sitting.

This insistence on the naked sexual organs as objects of attraction is, however, comparatively rare, and confined to peoples in a low state of culture. Very much more widespread is the attempt to beautify and call attention to the sexual organs by tattooing,[1] by adornment and by striking peculiarities of clothing. The tendency for beauty of clothing to be accepted as a substitute for beauty of body appears early in the history of mankind, and, as we know, tends to be absolutely accepted in civilization.[2] "We exclaim," as Goethe remarks, "'What a

---

[1] As a native of Lukunor said to the traveler Mertens, "It has the same object as your clothes, to please the women."

[2] "The greatest provocations of lust are from our apparel," as Burton states (*Anatomy of Melancholy*, Part III, Sec. II, Mem. II, Subs. III), illustrating this proposition with immense learning. Stanley Hall (*American Journal of Psychology*, vol. ix, Part III, pp. 365 *et seq.*) has some interesting observations on the various psychic influences of clothing; *cf.* Bloch, *Beiträge zur Ætiologie der Psychopathia Sexualis*, Teil II, pp. 330 *et seq.*

beautiful little foot!' when we have merely seen a pretty shoe; we admire the lovely waist when nothing has met our eyes but an elegant girdle." Our realities and our traditional ideals are hopelessly at variance; the Greeks represented their statues without pubic hair because in real life they had adopted the oriental custom of removing the hairs; we compel our sculptors and painters to make similar representations, though they no longer correspond either to realities or to our own ideas of what is beautiful and fitting in real life. Our artists are themselves equally ignorant and confused, and, as Stratz has repeatedly shown, they constantly reproduce in all innocence the deformations and pathological characters of defective models. If we were honest, we should say—like the little boy before a picture of the Judgment of Paris, in answer to his mother's question as to which of the three goddesses he thought most beautiful— "I can't tell, because they haven't their clothes on."

The concealment actually attained was not, however, it would appear, originally sought. Various authors have brought together evidence to show that the main primitive purpose of adornment and clothing among savages is not to conceal the body, but to draw attention to it and to render it more attractive. Westermarck, especially, brings forward numerous examples of savage adornments which serve to attract attention to the sexual regions of man and woman.[1] He further argues that the primitive object of various savage peoples in practicing circumcision, as other similar mutilations, is really to secure sexual attractiveness, whatever religious significance they may sometimes have developed subsequently. A more recent view

---

[1] *History of Human Marriage*, Chapter IX, especially p. 201. We have a striking and comparatively modern European example of an article of clothing designed to draw attention to the sexual sphere in the codpiece (the French *braguette*), familiar to us through fifteenth and sixteenth century pictures and numerous allusions in Rabelais and in Elizabethan literature. This was originally a metal box for the protection of the sexual organs in war, but subsequently gave place to a leather case only worn by the lower classes, and became finally an elegant article of fashionable apparel, often made of silk and adorned with ribbons, even with gold and jewels. (See, *e.g.*, Bloch, *Beiträge zur Ätiologie der Psychopathia Sexualis*, Teil I, p. 159.)

represents the magical influence of both adornment and mutilation as primary, as a method of guarding and insulating dangerous bodily functions. Frazer, in *The Golden Bough*, is the most able and brilliant champion of this view, which undoubtedly embodies a large element of truth, although it must not be accepted to the absolute exclusion of the influence of sexual attractiveness. The two are largely woven in together.[1]

There is, indeed, a general tendency for the sexual functions to take on a religious character and for the sexual organs to become sacred at a very early period in culture. Generation, the reproductive force in man, animals, and plants, was realized by primitive man to be a fact of the first magnitude, and he symbolized it in the sexual organs of man and woman, which thus attained to a solemnity which was entirely independent of purposes of sexual allurement. Phallus worship may almost be said to be a universal phenomenon; it is found even among races of high culture, among the Romans of the Empire and the Japanese to-day; it has, indeed, been thought by some that one of the origins of the cross is to be found in the phallus.

"Hardly any other object," remarks Dr. Richard Andree, "has been with such great unanimity represented by nearly all peoples as the phallus, the symbol of procreative force in the religions of the East and an object of veneration at public festivals. In the Moabitic Baal Peor, in the cult of Dionysos, everywhere, indeed, except in Persia, we meet with Priapic representations and the veneration accorded to the generative organ. It is needless to refer to the great significance of the *Linga puja*, the procreative organ of the god Siva, in India, a god to whom more temples were erected than to any other Indian deity. Our museums amply show how common phallic representations are in Africa, East Asia, the Pacific, frequently in connection with religious worship." (R. Andree, "Amerikansche Phallus-Darstellungen," *Zeitschrift für Ethnologie*, 1895, ht. 6, p. 678.)

Women have no external generative organ like the phallus to play a large part in life as a sacred symbol. There is, however, some

---

[1] A correspondent in Ceylon has pointed out to me that in the Indian statues of Buddha, Vishnu, goddesses, etc., the necklace always covers the nipples, a sexually attractive adornment being thus at the same time the guardian of the orifices of the body. Crawley (*The Mystic Rose*, p. 135) regards mutilations as in the nature of permanent amulets or charms.

reason to believe that the triangle is to some extent such a symbol. Lejeune ("La Representation Sexuelle en Religion, Art, et Pédagogie," *Bulletin de la Société d'Anthropologie*, Paris, October 3, 1901) brings forward reasons in favor of the view that the triangular hair-covered region of the mons veneris has had considerable significance in this respect, and he presents various primitive figures in illustration.

Apart from the religious and magical properties so widely accorded to the primary sexual characters, there are other reasons why they should not often have gained or long retained any great importance as objects of sexual allurement. They are unnecessary and inconvenient for this purpose. The erect attitude of man gives them here, indeed, an advantage possessed by very few animals, among whom it happens with extreme rarity that the primary sexual characters are rendered attractive to the eye of the opposite sex, though they often are to the sense of smell. The sexual regions constitute a peculiarly vulnerable spot, and remain so even in man, and the need for their protection which thus exists conflicts with the prominent display required for a sexual allurement. This end is far more effectively attained, with greater advantage and less disadvantage, by concentrating the chief ensigns of sexual attractiveness on the upper and more conspicuous parts of the body. This method is well-nigh universal among animals as well as in man.

There is another reason why the sexual organs should be discarded as objects of sexual allurement, a reason which always proves finally decisive as a people advances in culture. They are not æsthetically beautiful. It is fundamentally necessary that the intromittent organ of the male and the receptive canal of the female should retain their primitive characteristics; they cannot, therefore, be greatly modified by sexual or natural selection, and the exceedingly primitive character they are thus compelled to retain, however sexually desirable and attractive they may become to the opposite sex under the influence of emotion, can rarely be regarded as beautiful from the point of view of æsthetic contemplation. Under the influence of art there is a tendency for the sexual organs to be diminished in size, and in no civilized country has the artist ever chosen to give an erect organ to his representations of ideal masculine beauty. It is mainly because the unæsthetic character of a woman's sexual region is almost imperceptible in any ordinary and normal position of the nude body that the feminine form is a more æsthetically beautiful object of contemplation than the masculine. Apart from this character we are probably bound, from a strictly æsthetic point of view, to regard the male form as more æsthetically beautiful.[1] The female form, moreover, usually overpasses very swiftly the period of the climax of its beauty, often only retaining it during a few weeks.

The following communication from a correspondent well brings out the divergences of feeling in this matter:

"You write that the sex organs, in an excited condition, cannot be called æsthetic. But I believe that they are a source, not only of curiosity and wonder to many persons, but also objects of admiration. I happen to know of one man, extremely intellectual and refined, who delights in lying between his mistress's thighs and gazing long at the dilated vagina. Also another man, married, and not intellectual, who always tenderly gazes at his wife's organs, in a strong light, before intercourse, and kisses her there and upon the abdomen. The wife, though amative, confessed to another woman that she could not understand the attraction. On the other hand, two married men have told me that the sight of their wives' genital parts would disgust them, and that they have never seen them.

"If the sexual parts cannot be called æsthetic, they have still a strong charm for many passionate lovers, of both sexes, though not often, I believe, among the unimaginative and the uneducated, who are apt to ridicule the organs or to be repelled by them. Many women confess that they are revolted by the sight of even a husband's complete nudity, though they have no indifference for sexual embraces. I think that the stupid bungle of Nature in making the generative organs serve as means of relieving the bladder has much to do with this revulsion. But some women of erotic temperament find pleasure in looking at the penis of a husband or lover, in handling it, and in kissing it. Prostitutes do this in the way of business; some chaste, passionate wives act thus voluntarily. This is scarcely morbid, as the mammalia

---

[1] Mantegazza, in his discussion of this point, although an ardent admirer of feminine beauty, decides that woman's form is not, on the whole, more beautiful than man's. See Appendix to Cap. IV of *Fisiologia della Donna*.

of most species smell and lick each others' genitals. Probably primitive man did the same."

Brantôme (*Vie des Dames Galantes*, Discours II) has some remarks to much the same effect concerning the difference between men, some of whom take no pleasure in seeing the private parts of their wives or mistresses, while others admire them and delight to kiss them.

I must add that, however natural or legitimate the attraction of the sexual parts may be to either sex, the question of their purely æsthetic beauty remains unaffected.

Remy de Gourmont, in a discussion of the æsthetic element in sexual beauty, considers that the invisibility of the sexual organs is the decisive fact in rendering women more beautiful than men. "Sex, which is sometimes an advantage, is always a burden and always a flaw; it exists for the race and not for the individual. In the human male, and precisely because of his erect attitude, sex is the predominantly striking and visible fact, the point of attack in a struggle at close quarters, the point aimed at from a distance, an obstacle for the eye, whether regarded as a rugosity on the surface or as breaking the middle of a line. The harmony of the feminine body is thus geometrically much more perfect, especially when we consider the male and the female at the moment of desire when they present the most intense and natural expression of life. Then the woman, whose movements are all interior, or only visible by the undulation of her curves, preserves her full æsthetic value, while the man, as it were, all at once receding toward the primitive state of animality, seems to throw off all beauty and become reduced to the simple and naked conditon of a genital organism." (Remy de Gourmont, *Physique de l'Amour*, p. 69.) Remy de Gourmont proceeds, however, to point out that man has his revenge after a woman has become pregnant, and that, moreover, the proportions of the masculine body are more beautiful than those of the feminine body.

The primary sexual characters of man and woman have thus never at any time played a very large part in sexual allurement. With the growth of culture, indeed, the very methods which had been adopted to call attention to the sexual organs were by a further development retained for the purpose of concealing them. From the first the secondary sexual characters have been a far more widespread method of sexual allurement than the primary sexual characters, and in the most civilized countries to-day they still constitute the most attractive of such methods to the majority of the population.

The main secondary sexual characters in woman and the type which they present in beautiful and well-developed persons are summarized as follows by Stratz, who in his book on the beauty of the body in woman sets forth the reasons for the characteristics here given:—

Delicate bony structure.
Rounded forms and breasts.
Broad pelvis.
Long and abundant hair.
Low and narrow boundary of pubic hair.
Sparse hair in armpit.
No hair on body.
Delicate skin.
Rounded skull.
Small face.
Large orbits.
High and slender eyebrows.
Low and small lower jaw.
Soft transition from cheek to neck.
Rounded neck.
Slender wrist.

Small hand, with long index finger.
Rounded shoulders.
Straight, small clavicle.
Small and long thorax.
Slender waist.
Hollow sacrum.
Prominent and domed nates.
Sacral dimples.
Rounded and thick thighs.
Low and obtuse pubic arch.
Soft contour of knee.
Rounded calves.
Slender ankle.
Small toes.
Long second and short fifth toe.
Broad middle incisor teeth.

(Stratz, *Die Schönheit des Weiblichen Körpers*, fourteenth edition, 1903, p. 200. This statement agrees at most points with my own exposition of the secondary sexual characters: *Man and Woman*, fourth edition, revised and enlarged, 1904.)

Thus we find, among most of the peoples of Europe, Asia, and Africa, the chief continents of the world, that the large hips and buttocks of women are commonly regarded as an important feature of beauty. This secondary sexual character represents the most decided structural deviation of the feminine type from the masculine, a deviation demanded by the reproductive function of women, and in the admiration it arouses sexual selection is thus working in a line with natural selection. It cannot be said that, except in a very moderate degree, it has always been regarded as at the same time in a line with the claims of purely æsthetic beauty. The European artist frequently seeks to attenuate rather than accentuate the protuberant lines of the feminine hips, and it is noteworthy that the Japanese also regard small hips as beautiful. Nearly everywhere else large hips and buttocks are regarded as a mark of beauty, and the average man is of this opinion even in the most æsthetic countries. The contrast of this exuberance with the more closely knit male form, the force of association, and the unquestionable fact that such development is the condition needed for healthy motherhood, have served as a basis for an ideal of sexual attractiveness which appeals to nearly all people more strongly than a more narrowly æsthetic ideal, which must inevitably be somewhat hermaphroditic in character.

Broad hips, which involve a large pelvis, are necessarily a characteristic of the highest human races, because the races with the largest heads must be endowed also with the largest pelves to enable their large heads to enter the world. The white race, according to Bacarisse, has the broadest sacrum, the yellow race coming next, the black race last. The white race is also stated to show the greatest curvature of the sacrum, the yellow race next, while the black race has the flattest sacrum.[1] The black race thus possesses the least developed pelvis, the narrowest, and the flattest. It is certainly not an accidental coincidence that it is precisely among people of black race that we find a simulation of the large pelvis of the higher races admired and cultivated in the form of steatopygia. This is an enormously exaggerated development of the subcutaneous layer of fat which normally covers the buttocks and upper parts of the thighs in woman, and in this extreme form constitutes a kind of natural fatty tumor. Steatopygia cannot be said to exist, according to Deniker, unless the projection of the buttocks exceeds 4 per cent. of the individual's height; it frequently equals 10 per cent. True steatopygia only exists among Bushman and Hottentot women, and among the peoples who are by blood connected with them. An unusual development of the buttocks is, however, found among the Woloffs and many other African peoples.[2] There can be no doubt that among the

---

[1] For a discussion of the anthropology of the feminine pelvis, see Ploss and Bartels, *Das Weib*, bd. 1. Sec. VI.

[2] Ploss and Bartels, *loc. cit.*; Deniker, *Revue d'Anthropologie*, January 15, 1889, and *Races of Man*, p. 93.

black peoples of Africa generally, whether true steatopygia exists among them or not, extreme gluteal development is regarded as a very important, if not the most important, mark of beauty, and Burton stated that a Somali man was supposed to choose his wife by ranging women in a row and selecting her who projected farthest *a tergo*.[1] In Europe, it must be added, clothing enables this feature of beauty to be simulated. Even by some African peoples the posterior development has been made to appear still larger by the use of cushions, and in England in the sixteenth century we find the same practice well recognized, and the Elizabethan dramatists refer to the "bumroll," which in more recent times has become the bustle, devices which bear witness to what Watts, the painter, called "the persistent tendency to suggest that the most beautiful half of humanity is furnished with tails."[2] In reality, as we see, it is simply a tendency, not to simulate an animal character, but to emphasize the most human and the most feminine of the secondary sexual characters, and therefore, from the sexual point of view, a beautiful feature.[3]

Sometimes admiration for this characteristic is associated with admiration for marked obesity generally, and it may be noted that a somewhat greater degree of fatness may also be regarded as a feminine secondary sexual character. This admiration is specially marked among several of the black peoples of Africa, and here to become a beauty a woman must, by drinking enormous quantities of milk, seek to become very fat. Sonnini noted that to some extent the same thing might be found among the Mohammedan women of Egypt. After bright eyes and a soft, polished, hairless skin, an Egyptian woman, he stated, most desired to obtain *embonpoint;* men admired fat

---

[1] Darwin,

[2] G. F. Watts, "On Taste in Dress," *Nineteenth Century*, 1883.

[3] From mediæval times onwards there has been a tendency to treat the gluteal region with contempt, a tendency well marked in speech and custom among the lowest classes in Europe to-day, but not easily traceable in classic times. Dühren (*Das Geschlechtsleben in England*, bd. II, pp. 359 *et seq.*) brings forward quotations from æsthetic writers and others dealing with the beauty of this part of the body.

women and women sought to become fat. "The idea of a very fat woman," Sonnini adds, "is nearly always accompanied in Europe by that of softness of flesh, effacement of form, and defect of elasticity in the outlines. It would be a mistake thus to represent the women of Turkey in general, where all seek to become fat. It is certain that the women of the East, more favored by Nature, preserve longer than others the firmness of the flesh, and this precious property, joined to the freshness and whiteness of their skin, renders them very agreeable. It must be added that in no part of the world is cleanliness carried so far as by the women of the East."[1]

The special characteristics of the feminine hips and buttocks become conspicuous in walking and may be further emphasized by the special method of walking or carriage. The women of some southern countries are famous for the beauty of their way of walk; "the goddess is revealed by her walk," as Virgil said. In Spain, especially, among European countries, the walk very notably gives expression to the hips and buttocks. The spine is in Spain very curved, producing what is termed *ensellure,* or saddle-back—a characteristic which gives great flexibility to the back and prominence to the gluteal regions, sometimes slightly simulating steatopygia. The vibratory movement naturally produced by walking and sometimes artificially heightened thus becomes a trait of sexual beauty. Outside of Europe such vibration of the flanks and buttocks is more frankly displayed and cultivated as a sexual allurement. The Papuans are said to admire this vibratory movement of the buttocks in their women. Young girls are practiced in it by their mothers for hours at a time as soon as they have reached the age of 7 or 8, and the Papuan maiden walks thus whenever she is in the presence of men, subsiding into a simpler gait when no men are present. In some parts of tropical Africa the women walk in this fashion. It is also known to the Egyptians, and by the Arabs is called *ghung*.[2] As Mantegazza remarks, the

---

[1] Sonnini, *Voyage, etc.,* vol. i, p. 308.
[2] Ploss and Bartels, *Das Weib,* bd. 1, Sec. III; Mantegazza, *Fisiologia della Donna,* Chapter III.

essentially feminine character of this gait makes it a method of sexual allurement. It should be observed that it rests on feminine anatomical characteristics, and that the natural walk of a femininely developed woman is inevitably different from that of a man.

In an elaborate discussion of beauty of movement Stratz summarizes the special characters of the gait in woman as follows: "A woman's walk is chiefly distinguished from a man's by shorter steps, the more marked forward movement of the hips, the greater length of the phase of rest in relation to the phase of motion, and by the fact that the compensatory movements of the upper parts of the body are less powerfully supported by the action of the arms and more by the revolution of the flanks. A man's walk has a more pushing and active character, a woman's a more rolling and passive character; while a man seems to seek to catch his fleeing equilibrium, a woman seems to seek to preserve the equilibrium she has reached . . . . A woman's walk is beautiful when it shows the definitely feminine and rolling character, with the greatest predominance of the moment of extension over that of flexion." (Stratz, *Die Schönheit des Weiblichen Körpers*, fourteenth edition, p. 275.)

An occasional development of the idea of sexual beauty as associated with developed hips is found in the tendency to regard the pregnant woman as the most beautiful type. Stratz observes that a woman artist once remarked to him that since motherhood is the final aim of woman, and a woman reaches her full flowering period in pregnancy, she ought to be most beautiful when pregnant. This is so, Stratz replied, if the period of her full physical bloom chances to correspond with the early months of pregnancy, for with the onset of pregnancy metabolism is heightened, the tissues become active, the tone of the skin softer and brighter, the breasts firmer, so that the charm of fullest bloom is increased until the moment when the expansion of the womb begins to destroy the harmony of the form. At one period of European culture, however,— at a moment and among a people not very sensitive to the most exquisite æsthetic sensations,—the ideal of beauty has even involved the character of advanced pregnancy. In northern Europe during the centuries immediately preceding the Renaissance the ideal of beauty, as we may see by the pictures of the time, was a pregnant woman, with protuberant abdomen and body more or less extended backward. This is notably apparent in the work of the Van Eycks: in the Eve in the Brussels Gallery; in the wife of Arnolfini in the highly finished portrait group in the National Gallery; even the virgins in the great masterpiece of the Van Eycks in the Cathedral at Ghent assume the type of the pregnant woman.

"Through all the middle ages down to Dürer and Cranach," quite truly remarks Laura Marholm (as quoted by I. Bloch, *Beiträge zur Ætiologie der Psychopathia Sexualis*, Teil I, p. 154), "we find a very peculiar type which has falsely been regarded as one of merely ascetic character. It represents quiet, peaceful, and cheerful faces, full of innocence; tall, slender, young figures; the shoulders still scanty; the breasts small, with slender legs beneath their garments; and round the upper part of the body clothing that is tight almost to the point of constriction. The waist comes just under the bosom, and from this point the broad skirts in folds give to the most feminine part of the feminine body full and absolutely unhampered power of movement and expansion. The womanly belly even in saints and virgins is very pronounced in the carriage of the body and clearly protuberant beneath the clothing. It is the maternal function, in sacred and profane figures alike, which marks the whole type—indeed, the whole conception—of women." For a brief period this fashion reappeared in the eighteenth century, and women wore pads and other devices to increase the size of the abdomen.

With the Renaissance this ideal of beauty disappeared from art. But in real life we still seem to trace its survival in the fashion for that class of garments which involved an immense amount of expansion below the waist and secured such expansion by the use of whalebone hoops and similar devices. The Elizabethan farthingale was such a garment. This was originally a Spanish invention, as indicated by the name (from *verdugardo*, provided with hoops), and reached England through France. We find the fashion at its most extreme point in the fashionable dress of Spain in the seventeenth century, such as it has been immortalized by Velasquez. In England hoops died out during the reign of George III but were revived for a time, half a century later, in the Victorian crinoline.[1]

Only second to the pelvis and its integuments as a secondary sexual character in woman we must place the breasts.[2] Among barbarous and civilized peoples the beauty of the breast is usually highly esteemed. Among Europeans, indeed, the importance of this region is so highly esteemed that the general rule against the exposure of the body is in its favor abrogated, and the breasts are the only portion of the body, in the narrow sense, which a European lady in full dress is allowed more or less to uncover. Moreover, at various periods and notably in the eighteenth century, women naturally deficient in this respect have sometimes worn artificial busts made of wax. Savages, also, sometimes show admiration for this part of the body, and in the Papuan folk-tales, for instance, the sole distinguishing mark of a beautiful woman is breasts that stand up.[3] On the other hand, various savage peoples even appear to regard the development of the breasts as ugly and adopt devices for flattening this part of the body.[4] The feeling that prompts this practice is not unknown in modern Europe, for the Bulgarians are said to regard developed breasts as ugly; in mediæval Europe, indeed, the general ideal of feminine slenderness was opposed to developed breasts, and the garments tended to compress them. But in a very high degree of civilization this feeling is unknown, as, indeed, it is unknown to most barbarians, and the beauty of a woman's breasts, and of

---

[1] Bloch brings together various interesting quotations concerning the farthingale and the crinoline. (*Beiträge zur Ætiologie der Psychopathia Sexualis*, Teil I, p. 156.) He states that, like most other feminine fashions in dress, it was certainly invented by prostitutes.

[2] The racial variations in the form and character of the breasts are great, and there are considerable variations even among Europeans. Even as regards the latter our knowledge is, however, still very vague and incomplete; there is here a fruitful field for the medical anthropologist. Ploss and Bartels have brought together the existing data (*Das Weib*, bd. 1, Sec. VIII). Stratz also discusses the subject (*Die Schönheit das Weiblichen Körpers*, Chapter X).

[3] *Cambridge Anthropological Expedition to Torres Straits*, vol. v, p. 28.

[4] These devices are dealt with and illustrations given by Ploss and Bartels, *Das Weib (loc. cit.)*.

any natural or artificial object which suggests the gracious curves of the bosom, is a universal source of pleasure.

The casual vision of a girl's breasts may, in the chastest youth, evoke a strange perturbation. *(Cf., e.g.,* a passage in an early chapter of Marcelle Tinayre's *La Maison du Péché.)* We need not regard this feeling as of purely sexual origin; and in addition even to the æsthetic element it is probably founded to some extent on a reminiscence of the earliest associations of life. This element of early association was very well set forth long ago by Erasmus Darwin:—

"When the babe, soon after it is born into this cold world, is applied to its mother's bosom, its sense of perceiving warmth is first agreeably affected; next its sense of smell is delighted with the odor of her milk; then its taste is gratified by the flavor of it; afterward the appetites of hunger and of thirst afford pleasure by the possession of their object, and by the subsequent digestion of the aliment; and, last, the sense of touch is delighted by the softness and smoothness of the milky fountain, the source of such variety of happiness.

"All these various kinds of pleasure at length become associated with the form of the mother's breast, which the infant embraces with its hands, presses with its lips, and watches with its eyes; and thus acquires more accurate ideas of the form of its mother's bosom than of the odor, flavor, and warmth which it perceives by its other senses. And hence at our maturer years, when any object of vision is presented to us which by its wavy or spiral lines bears any similitude to the form of the female bosom, whether it be found in a landscape with soft gradations of raising and descending surface, or in the forms of some antique vases, or in other works of the pencil or the chisel, we feel a general glow of delight which seems to influence all our senses; and if the object be not too large we experience an attraction to embrace it with our lips as we did in our early infancy the bosom of our mother." (E. Darwin, *Zoönomia*, 1800, vol. i, p. 174.)

The general admiration accorded alike to developed breasts and a developed pelvis is evidenced by a practice which, as embodied in the corset, is all but universal in many European countries, as well as the extra-European countries inhabited by the white race, and in one form or another is by no means unknown to peoples of other than the white race.

The tightening of the waist girth was little known to the Greeks of the best period, but it was practiced by the Greeks of the decadence and by them transmitted to the Romans;

there are many references in Latin literature to this practice, and the ancient physician wrote against it in the same sense as modern doctors. So far as Christian Europe is concerned it would appear that the corset arose to gratify an ideal of asceticism rather than of sexual allurement. The bodice in early mediæval days bound and compressed the breasts and thus tended to efface the specifically feminine character of a woman's body. Gradually, however, the bodice was displaced downward, and its effect, ultimately, was to render the breasts more prominent instead of effacing them. Not only does the corset render the breasts more prominent; it has the further effect of displacing the breathing activity of the lungs in an upward direction, the advantage from the point of sexual allurement thus gained being that additional attention is drawn to the bosom from the respiratory movement thus imparted to it. So marked and so constant is this artificial respiratory effect, under the influence of the waist compression habitual among civilized women, that until recent years it was commonly supposed that there is a real and fundamental difference in breathing between men and women, that women's breathing is thoracic and men's abdominal. It is now known that under natural and healthy conditions there is no such difference, but that men and women breathe in a precisely identical manner. The corset may thus be regarded as the chief instrument of sexual allurement which the armory of costume supplies to a woman, for it furnishes her with a method of heightening at once her two chief sexual secondary characters, the bosom above, the hips and buttocks below. We cannot be surprised that all the scientific evidence in the world of the evil of the corset is powerless not merely to cause its abolition, but even to secure the general adoption of its comparatively harmless modifications.

Several books have been written on the history of the corset. Léoty (*Le Corset à travers les Ages*, 1893) accepts Bouvier's division of the phases through which the corset has passed: (1) the bands, or fasciæ, of Greek and Roman ladies; (2) period of transition during greater part of middle ages, classic traditons still subsisting; (3) end of middle ages and beginning of Renaissance, when tight bodices were worn; (4) the period of whalebone bodices, from middle of sixteenth to end of eighteenth centuries; (5) the period of the modern corset. We hear of embroidered girdles in Homer. Even in Rome, however, the fasciæ were not in general use, and were chiefly employed either to support the breasts or to compress their excessive development, and then called *mamillare*. The *zona* was a girdle, worn usually round the hips, especially by young girls. The modern corset is a combination of the *fascia* and the *zona*. It was at the end of the fourteenth century that Isabeau of Bavaria introduced the custom of showing the breasts uncovered, and the word "corset" was then used for the first time.

Stratz, in his *Frauenkleidung* (pp. 366 *et seq.*), and in his *Schönheit des Weiblichen Körpers*, Chapters VIII, X, and XVI, also deals with the corset, and illustrates the results of compression on the body. For a summary of the evidence concerning the difference of respiration in man and woman, its causes and results, see Havelock Ellis, *Man and Woman*, fourth edition, 1904, pp. 228-244. With reference to the probable influence of the corset and unsuitable clothing generally during early life in impeding the development of the mammary glands, causing inability to suckle properly, and thus increasing infant mortality, see especially a paper by Professor Bollinger (*Correspondenz-blatt Deutsch. Gesell. Anthropologie*, October, 1899).

The compression caused by the corset, it must be added, is not usually realized or known by those who wear it. Thus, Rushton Parker and Hugh Smith found, in two independent series of measurements, that the waist measurement was, on the average, two inches less over the corset than round the naked waist; "the great majority seemed quite unaware of the fact." In one case the difference was as much as five inches. (*British Medical Journal*, September 15 and 22, 1900.)

The breasts and the developed hips are characteristics of women and are indications of functional effectiveness as well as sexual allurement. Another prominent sexual character which belongs to man, and is not obviously an index of function, is furnished by the hair on the face. The beard may be regarded as purely a sexual adornment, and thus comparable to the somewhat similar growth on the heads of many male animals. From this point of view its history is interesting, for it illustrates the tendency with increase of civilization not merely to dispense with sexual allurement in the primary sexual organs, but even to disregard those growths which would appear to have been developed solely to act as sexual allurements. The cultivation of the beard belongs peculiarly to barbarous races. Among these races it is frequently regarded as the most sacred and beautiful part of the person, as an object to swear by, an object to which the slightest insult must be treated as deadly. Holding such a position, it must doubtless act as a sexual allurement. "Allah has specially created an angel in Heaven," it is said in the *Arabian Nights*, "who has no other occupation than to sing the praises of the Creator for giving a beard to men and long hair to women." The sexual character of the beard and the other hirsute appendage is significantly indicated by the fact that the ascetic spirit in Christianity has always sought to minimize or to hide the hair. Altogether apart, however, from this religious influence, civilization tends to be opposed to the growth of hair on the masculine face and especially to the beard. It is part of the well-marked tendency with civilization to the abolition of sexual differences. We find this general tendency among the Greeks and Romans, and, on the whole, with certain variations and fluctuations of fashion, in modern Europe also. Schopenhauer frequently referred to this disappearance of the beard as a mark of civilization, "a barometer of culture."[1] The absence of facial hair heightens æsthetic beauty of form, and is not felt to remove any substantial sexual attraction.

That even the Egyptians regarded the beard as a mark of beauty and an object of veneration is shown by the fact that the priests wore it long and cut it off in grief (Herodotus, *Euterpe*, Chapter XXXVI). The respect with which the beard was regarded among the ancient Hebrews is indicated in the narrative (II Samuel, Chapter X) which tells how, when David sent his servants to King Hanun the latter shaved off half their beards; they were too ashamed to return in this condition, and remained at Jericho until their beards had grown again. A passage in Ordericus Vitalis (*Ecclesiastical History*, Book VIII, Chapter X) is interesting both as regards the fashions of the twelfth century in England and Normandy and the feeling that prompted Ordericus. Speaking of the men of his time, he wrote: "The forepart of their head is

---

[1] See, *e.g.*, *Parerga und Paralipomena*, bd. 1, p. 189, and bd. 2, p. 482. Moll has also discussed this point (*Untersuchungen über die Libido Sexualis*, bd. I, pp. 384 *et seq.*).

bare after the manner of thieves, while at the back they nourish long hair like harlots. In former times penitents, captives and pilgrims usually went unshaved and wore long beards, as an outward mark of their penace or captivity or pilgrimage. Now almost all the world wear crisped hair and beards, carrying on their faces the token of their filthy lust like stinking goats. Their locks are curled with hot irons, and instead of wearing caps they bind their heads with fillets. A knight seldom appears in public with his head uncovered, and properly shaved, according to the apostolic precept (I Corinthians, Chapter XI, verses 7 and 14)."

We have seen that there is good reason for assuming a certain fundamental tendency whereby the most various peoples of the world, at all events in the person of their most intelligent members, recognize and accept a common ideal of feminine beauty, so that to a certain extent beauty may be said to have an objectively æsthetic basis. We have further found that this æsthetic human ideal is modified, and very variously modified in different countries and even in the same country at different periods, by a tendency, prompted by a sexual impulse which is not necessarily in harmony with æsthetic canons, to emphasize, or even to repress, one or other of the prominent secondary sexual characters of the body. We now come to another tendency which is apt to an even greater extent to limit the cultivation of the purely æsthetic ideal of beauty: the influences of national or racial type.

To the average man of every race the woman who most completely embodies the type of his race is usually the most beautiful, and even mutilations and deformations often have their origin, as Humboldt long since pointed out, in the effort to accentuate the racial type.[1] Eastern women possess by

---

[1] Speaking of some South American tribes, he remarks (*Travels*, English translations, 1814, vol. iii, p. 236) that they "have as great an antipathy to the beard as the Eastern nations hold it in reverence. This antipathy is derived from the same source as the predilection for flat foreheads, which is seen in so singular a manner in the statues of the Aztec heroes and divinities. Nations attach the idea of beauty to everything which particularly characterizes their own physical conformation, their natural physiognomy." See also Westermarck, *History of Marriage*, p. 261. Ripley (*Races of Europe*, pp. 49, 202) attaches much importance to the sexual selection founded on a tendency of this kind.

nature large and conspicuous eyes, and this characteristic they seek still further to heighten by art. The Ainu are the hairiest of races, and there is nothing which they consider so beautiful as hair. It is difficult to be sexually attracted to persons who are fundamentally unlike ourselves in racial constitution.[1]

It frequently happens that this admiration for racial characteristics leads to the idealization of features which are far removed from æsthetic beauty. The firm and rounded breast is certainly a feature of beauty, but among many of the black peoples of Africa the breasts fall at a very early period, and here we sometimes find that the hanging breast is admired as beautiful.

The African Baganda, the Rev. J. Roscoe states (*Journal of the Anthropological Institute*, January-June, 1902, p. 72), admire hanging breasts to such an extent that their young women tie them down in order to hasten the arrival of this condition.

"The most remarkable trait of beauty in the East," wrote Sonnini, "is to have large black eyes, and nature has made this a characteristic sign of the women of these countries. But, not content with this, the women of Egypt wish their eyes to be still larger and blacker. To attain this Mussulmans, Jewesses, and Christians, rich and poor, all tint their eyelids with galena. They also blacken the lashes (as Juvenal tells us the Roman ladies did) and mark the angles of the eye so that the fissure appears larger." (Sonnini, *Voyage dans la Haute et Basse Egypte*, 1799, vol. i, p. 290.) Kohl is thus only used by the women who have what the Arabs call "natural kohl." As Flinders Petrie has found, the women of the so-called "New Race," between the sixth and tenth dynasties of ancient Egypt, used galena and malachite for painting their faces. Jewish women in the days of the prophets painted their eyes with kohl as do some Hindu women to-day.

"The Ainu have a great affection for their beards. They regard them as a sign of manhood and strength and consider them as especially handsome. They look upon them, indeed, as a great and highly prized treasure." (J. Batchelor, *The Ainu and their Folklore*, p. 162.)

A great many theories have been put forward to explain the Chinese fashion of compressing and deforming the foot. The Chinese are

[1] "Differences of race are irreducible," Abel Hermant remarks (*Confession d'un Enfant d'Hier*, p. 209), "and between two beings who love each other they cannot fail to produce exceptional and instructive reactions. In the first superficial ebullition of love, indeed, nothing notable may be manifested, but in a fairly short time the two lovers, in-

great admirers of the feminine foot, and show extreme sexual sensitiveness in regard to it. Chinese women naturally possess very small feet, and the main reason for binding them is probably to be found in the desire to make them still smaller. (See, *e.g.*, Stratz, *Die Frauenkleidung*, 1904, p. 101.)

An interesting question, which in part finds its explanation here and is of considerable significance from the point of view of sexual selection, concerns the relative admiration bestowed on blondes and brunettes. The question is not, indeed, one which is entirely settled by racial characteristics. There is something to be said on the matter from the objective standpoint of æsthetic considerations. Stratz, in a chapter on beauty of coloring in woman, points out that fair hair is more beautiful because it harmonizes better with the soft outlines of woman, and, one may add, it is more brilliantly conspicuous; a golden object looks larger than a black object. The hair of the armpit, also, Stratz considers should be light. On the other hand, the pubic hair should be dark in order to emphasize the breadth of the pelvis and the obtusity of the angle between the mons veneris and the thighs. The eyebrows and eyelashes should also be dark in order to increase the apparent size of the orbits. Stratz adds that among many thousand women he has only seen one who, together with an otherwise perfect form, has also possessed these excellencies in the highest measure. With an equable and matt complexion she had blonde, very long, smooth hair, with sparse, blonde, and curly axillary hair; but, although her eyes were blue, the eyebrows and eyelashes were black, as also was the not overdeveloped pubic hair.[1]

We may accept it as fairly certain that, so far as any objective standard of æsthetic beauty is recognizable, that standard involves the supremacy of the fair type of woman. Such supremacy in beauty has doubtless been further supported by

nately hostile, in striving to approach each other strike against an invisible partition which separates them. Their sensibilities are divergent; everything in each shocks the other; even their anatomical conformation, even the language of their gestures; all is foreign."

[1] C. H. Stratz, *Die Schönheit des Weiblichen Körpers*, fourteenth edition, Chapter XII.

the fact that in most European countries the ruling caste, the aristocratic class, whose superior energy has brought it to the top, is somewhat blonder than the average population.

The main cause, however, in determining the relative amount of admiration accorded in Europe to blondes and to brunettes is the fact that the population of Europe must be regarded as predominantly fair, and that our conception of beauty in feminine coloring is influenced by an instinctive desire to seek this type in its finest forms. In the north of Europe there can, of course, be no question concerning the predominant fairness of the population, but in portions of the centre and especially in the south it may be considered a question. It must, however, be remembered that the white population occupying all the shores of the Mediterranean have the black peoples of Africa immediately to the south of them. They have been liable to come in contact with the black peoples and in contrast with them they have tended not only to be more impressed with their own whiteness, but to appraise still more highly its blondest manifestations as representing a type the farthest removed from the negro. It must be added that the northerner who comes into the south is apt to overestimate the darkness of the southerner because of the extreme fairness of his own people. The differences are, however, less extreme than we are apt to suppose; there are more dark people in the north than we commonly assume, and more fair people in the south. Thus, if we take Italy, we find in its fairest part, Venetia, according to Raseri, that there are 8 per cent. communes in which fair hair predominates, 81 per cent. in which brown predominates, and only 11 per cent. in which black predominates; as we go farther south black hair becomes more prevalent, but there are in most provinces a few communes in which fair hair is not only frequent, but even predominant. It is somewhat the same with light eyes, which are also most abundant in Venetia and decrease to a slighter extent as we go south. It is possible that in former days the blondes prevailed to a greater degree than to-day in the south of Europe. Among the Berbers of the Atlas Mountains, who are probably allied to the South Europeans, there appears to be a fairly considerable proportion of blondes,[1] while on the other hand there is some reason to believe that blondes die out under the influence of civilization as well as of a hot climate.

However this may be, the European admiration for blondes dates back to early classic times. Gods and men in Homer would appear to be frequently described as fair.[2] Venus is nearly always blonde, as was Milton's Eve. Lucian refers to women who dye their hair. The Greek sculptors gilded the hair of their statues, and the figurines in many cases show very fair hair.[3] The Roman custom of dyeing the hair light, as Renier has shown, was not due to the desire to be like the fair Germans, and when Rome fell it would appear that the custom of dyeing the hair persisted, and never died out; it is mentioned by Anselm, who died at the beginning of the twelfth century.[4]

In the poetry of the people in Italy brunettes, as we should expect, receive much commendation, though even here the blondes are preferred. When we turn to the painters and poets of Italy, and the æsthetic writers on beauty from the Renaissance onward, the admiration for fair hair is unqualified, though there is no correspondingly unanimous admiration for blue eyes. Angelico and most of the pre-Raphaelite artists usually painted their women with flaxen and light-golden hair, which often became brown with the artists of the Renaissance period. Firenzuola, in his admirable dialogue on feminine beauty, says that a woman's hair should be like gold or honey

---

[1] See, *e.g.*, Sergi, *The Mediterranean Race*, pp. 59-75.

[2] Sergi (*The Mediterranean Race*, Chapter I), by an analysis of Homer's color epithets, argues that in very few cases do they involve fairness; but his attempt scarcely seems successful, although most of these epithets are undoubtedly vague and involve a certain range of possible color.

[3] Léchat's study of the numerous realistic colored statues recently discovered in Greece (summarized in *Zentralblatt für Anthropologie*, 1904, ht. 1, p. 22) shows that with few exceptions the hair is fair.

[4] Renier, *Il Tipo Estetico*, pp. 127 *et seq.* In another book, *Les Femmes Blondes selon les Peintres de l'École de Venise*, par deux Venitiens (one of these "Venetians" being Armand Baschet), is brought together much information concerning the preference for blondes in literature, together with a great many of the recipes anciently used for making the hair fair.

or the rays of the sun. Luigini also, in his *Libro della bella Donna*, says that hair must be golden. So also thought Petrarch and Ariosto. There is, however, no corresponding predilection among these writers for blue eyes. Firenzuola said that the eyes must be dark, though not black. Luigini said that they must be bright and black. Niphus had previously said that the eyes should be "black like those of Venus" and the skin ivory, even a little brown. He mentions that Avicenna had praised the mixed, or gray, eye.

In France and other northern countries the admiration for very fair hair is just as marked as in Italy, and dates back to the earliest ages of which we have a record. "Even before the thirteenth century," remarks Houdoy, in his very interesting study of feminine beauty in northern France during mediæval times, "and for men as well as for women, fair hair was an essential condition of beauty; gold is the term of comparison almost exclusively used."[1] He mentions that in the *Acta Sanctorum* it is stated that Saint Godelive of Bruges, though otherwise beautiful, had black hair and eyebrows and was hence contemptuously called a crow. In the *Chanson de Roland* and all the French mediæval poems the eyes are invariably *vairs*. This epithet is somewhat vague. It comes from *varius*, and signifies mixed, which Houdoy regards as showing various irradiations, the same quality which later gave rise to the term *iris* to describe the pupillary membrane.[2] *Vair* would thus describe not so much the color of the eye as its brilliant and sparkling quality. While Houdoy may have been correct, it still seems probable that the eye described as *vair* was usually assumed to be "various" in color also, of the kind we commonly call gray, which is usually applied to blue eyes encircled with a ring of faintly sprinkled brown pigment. Such eyes are fairly typical of northern France and frequently beautiful. That this was the case seems to be clearly indicated by the fact that, as Houdoy himself points out, a few centuries later the *vair* eye

---

[1] J. Houdoy, *La Beauté des Femmes dans la Littérature et dans l'Art du XIIe au XVIe Siècle*, 1876, pp. 32 *et seq.*

[2] Houdoy, *op. cit.*, pp. 41 *et seq.*

was regarded as *vert,* and green eyes were celebrated as the most beautiful.[1] The etymology was false, but a false etymology will hardly suffice to change an ideal. At the Renaissance Jehan Lemaire, when describing Venus as the type of beauty, speaks of her green eyes, and Ronsard, a little later, sang:—

> "Noir je veux l'œil et brun le teint,
> Bien que l'œil verd toute la France adore."

Early in the sixteenth century Brantôme quotes some lines current in France, Spain, and Italy according to which a woman should have a white skin, but black eyes and eyebrows, and adds that personally he agrees with the Spaniard that "a brunette is sometimes equal to a blonde,"[2] but there is also a marked admiration for green eyes in Spanish literature; not only in the typical description of a Spanish beauty in the *Celestina* (Act I) are the eyes green, but Cervantes, for example, when referring to the beautiful eyes of a woman, frequently speaks of them as green.

It would thus appear that in Continental Europe generally, from south to north, there is a fair uniformity of opinion as regards the pigmentary type of feminine beauty. Such variation as exists seemingly involves a somewhat greater degree of darkness for the southern beauty in harmony with the greater racial darkness of the southerner, but the variations fluctuate within a narrow range; the extremely dark type is always excluded, and so it would seem probable is the extremely fair type, for blue eyes have not, on the whole, been considered to form part of the admired type.

If we turn to England no serious modification of this conclusion is called for. Beauty is still fair. Indeed, the very word "fair" in England itself means beautiful. That in the seventeenth century it was generally held essential that beauty should be blonde is indicated by a passage in the *Anatomy of Melancholy,* where Burton argues that "golden hair was ever

---

[1] Houdoy, *op. cit.,* p. 83.
[2] Brantôme, *Vie des Dames Galantes,* Discours II.

in great account," and quotes many examples from classic and more modern literature.[1]   That this remains the case is sufficiently evidenced by the fact that the ballet and chorus on the English stage wear yellow wigs, and the heroine of the stage is blonde, while the female villain of melodrama is a brunette.

While, however, this admiration of fairness as a mark of beauty unquestionably prevails in England, I do not think it can be said—as it probably can be said of the neighboring and closely allied country of France—that the most beautiful women belong to the fairest group of the community.   In most parts of Europe the coarse and unbeautiful plebeian type tends to be very dark; in England it tends to be very fair.   England is, however, somewhat fairer generally than most parts of Europe; so that, while it may be said that a very beautiful woman in France or in Spain may belong to the blondest section of the community, a very beautiful woman in England, even though of the same degree of blondeness as her Continental sister, will not belong to the extremely blonde section of the English community.   It thus comes about that when we are in northern France we find that gray eyes, a very fair but yet unfreckled complexion, brown hair, finely molded features, and highly sensitive facial expression combine to constitute a type which is more beautiful than any other we meet in France, and it belongs to the fairest section of the French population. When we cross over to England, however, unless we go to a so-called "Celtic" district, it is hopeless to seek among the blondest section of the community for any such beautiful and refined type.   The English beautiful woman, though she may still be fair, is by no means very fair, and from the English standpoint she may even sometimes appear somewhat dark[2]: In determining what I call the index of pigmentation—or degree of darkness of the eyes and hair—of different groups in the National Portrait Gallery I found that the "famous beau-

---

[1] *Anatomy of Melancholy*, Part III, Sec. II, Mem. II, Subs. II.
[2] It is significant that Burton (*Anatomy of Melancholy, loc cit.*), while praising golden hair, also argues that "of all eyes black are most amiable," quoting many examples to this effect from classic and later literature.

ties" (my own personal criterion of beauty not being taken into account) was somewhat nearer to the dark than to the light end of the scale.[1] If we consider, at random, individual instances of famous English beauties they are not extremely fair. Lady Venetia Stanley, in the early seventeenth century, who became the wife of Sir Kenelm Digby, was somewhat dark, with brown hair and eyebrows. Mrs. Overall, a little later in the same century, a Lancashire woman, the wife of the Dean of St. Paul's, was, says Aubrey, "the greatest beauty in her time in England," though very wanton, with "the loveliest eyes that were ever seen"; if we may trust a ballad given by Aubrey she was dark with black hair. The Gunnings, the famous beauties of the eighteenth century, were not extremely fair, and Lady Hamilton, the most characteristic type of English beauty, had blue, brown-flecked eyes and dark chestnut hair. Coloration is only one of the elements of beauty, though an important one. Other things being equal, the most blonde is most beautiful; but it so happens that among the races of Great Britain the other things are very frequently not equal, and that, notwithstanding a conviction ingrained in the language, with us the fairest of women is not always the "fairest." So magical, however, is the effect of brilliant coloring that it serves to keep alive in popular opinion an unqualified belief in the universal European creed of the beauty of blondeness.

We have seen that underlying the conception of beauty, more especially as it manifests itself in woman to man, are to be found at least three fundamental elements: First there is the general beauty of the species as it tends to culminate in the white peoples of European origin; then there is the beauty due to the full development or even exaggeration of the sexual and more especially the secondary sexual characters; and last there is the beauty due to the complete embodiment of the particular racial or national type. To make the analysis fairly complete must be added at least one other factor: the influence of individual taste. Every individual, at all events in

---

[1] "Relative Abilities of the Fair and the Dark," *Monthly Review*, August, 1901; *cf.* H. Ellis, *A Study of British Genius*, p. 215.

civilization, within certain narrow limits, builds up a feminine ideal of his own, in part on the basis of his own special organization and its demands, in part on the actual accidental attractions he has experienced. It is unnecessary to emphasize the existence of this factor, which has always to be taken into account in every consideration of sexual selection in civilized man. But its variations are numerous and in impassioned lovers it may even lead to the idealization of features which are in reality the reverse of beautiful. It may be said of many a man, as d'Annunzio says of the hero of his *Trionfo della Morte* in relation to the woman he loved, that "he felt himself bound to her by the real qualities of her body, and not only by those which were most beautiful, but specially by *those which were least beautiful*" (the novelist italicizes these words), so that his attention was fixed upon her defects, and emphasized them, thus arousing within himself an impetuous state of desire. Without invoking defects, however, there are endless personal variations which may all be said to come within the limits of possible beauty or charm. "There are no two women," as Stratz remarks, "who in exactly the same way stroke back a rebellious lock from their brows, no two who hold the hand in greeting in exactly the same way, no two who gather up their skirts as they walk with exactly the same movement."[1] Among the multitude of minute differences—which yet can be seen and felt—the beholder is variously attracted or repelled according to his own individual idiosyncrasy, and the operations of sexual selection are effected accordingly.

Another factor in the constitution of the ideal of beauty, but one perhaps exclusively found under civilized conditions, is the love of the unusual, the remote, the exotic. It is commonly stated that rarity is admired in beauty. This is not strictly true, except as regards combinations and characters which vary only in a very slight degree from the generally admired type. "*Jucundum nihil est quod non reficit variatas*," according to the saying of Publilius Syrus. The greater nervous restlessness

---

[1] Stratz, *Die Schönheit des Weiblichen Körpers*, p. 217.

and sensibility of civilization heightens this tendency, which is not infrequently found also among men of artistic genius. One may refer, for instance, to Baudelaire's profound admiration for the mulatto type of beauty.[1] In every great centre of civilization the national ideal of beauty tends to be somewhat modified in exotic directions, and foreign ideals, as well as foreign fashions, become preferred to those that are native. It is significant of this tendency that when, a few years since, an enterprising Parisian journal hung in its *salle* the portraits of one hundred and thirty-one actresses, etc., and invited the votes of the public by ballot as to the most beautiful of them, not one of the three women who came out at the head of the poll was French. A dancer of Belgian origin (Cléo de Merode) was by far at the head with over 3000 votes, followed by an American from San Francisco (Sybil Sanderson), and then a Polish woman.

---

[1] Bloch *(Beiträge zur Ätiologie der Psychopathia Sexualis*, Teil II, pp. 261, *et seq.)* brings together some facts bearing on the admiration for negresses in Paris and elsewhere.

III.

Beauty not the Sole Element in the Sexual Appeal of Vision—Movement—The Mirror—Narcissism—Pygmalionism—Mixoscopy—The Indifference of Women to Male Beauty—The Significance of Woman's Admiration of Strength—The Spectacle of Strength is a Tactile Quality made Visible.

OUR discussion of the sensory element of vision in human sexual selection has been mainly an attempt to disentangle the chief elements of beauty in so far as beauty is a stimulus to the sexual instinct. Beauty by no means comprehends the whole of the influences which make for sexual allurement through vision, but it is the point at which all the most powerful and subtle of these are focused; it represents a fairly definite complexus, appealing at once to the sexual and to the æsthetic impulses, to which no other sense can furnish anything in any degree analogous. It is because this conception of beauty has arisen upon it that vision properly occupies the supreme position in man from the point of view which we here occupy.

Beauty is thus the chief, but it is not the sole, element in the sexual appeal of vision. In all parts of the world this has always been well understood, and in courtship, in the effort to arouse tumescence, the appeals to vision have been multiplied and at the same time aided by appeals to the other senses. Movement, especially in the form of dancing, is the most important of the secondary appeals to vision. This is so well recognized that it is scarcely necessary to insist upon it here; it may suffice to refer to a single typical example. The most decent of Polynesian dances, according to William Ellis, was the *hura*, which was danced by the daughters of chiefs in the presence of young men of rank with the hope of gaining a future husband. "The daughters of the chiefs, who were the dancers on these occasions, at times amounted to five or six, though occasionally only one exhibited her symmetry of figure and gracefulness of action. Their dress was singular, but elegant. The head was ornamented with a fine and beautiful braid of human hair, wound round the head in the form of a turban. A triple wreath of scarlet, white, and yellow flowers adorned the head-dress. A lose vest of spotted cloth covered the lower part of the bosom. The tihi, of fine white stiffened cloth frequently edged with a scarlet border, gathered like a large frill, passed under the arms and reached below the waist; while a handsome fine cloth, fastened round the waist with a band or sash, covered the feet. The breasts were ornamented with rainbow-colored mother-of-pearl shells, and a covering of curiously wrought network and feathers. The music of the hura was the large and small drum and occasionally the flute. The movements were generally slow, but always easy and natural, and no exertion on the part of the performers was wanting to render them graceful and attractive."[1] We see here, in this very typical example, how the extraneous visual aids of movement, color, and brilliancy are invoked in conjunction with music to make the appeal of beauty more convincing in the process of sexual selection.

It may be in place here to mention, in passing, the considerable place which vision occupies in normal and abnormal methods of heightening tumescence under circumstances which exclude definite selection by beauty. The action of mirrors belongs to this group of phenomena. Mirrors are present in profusion in high-class brothels—on the walls and also above the beds. Innocent youths and girls are also often impelled to contemplate themselves in mirrors and sometimes thus produce the first traces of sexual excitement. I have referred to the developed forms of this kind of self-contemplation in the Study of Auto-erotism, and in this connection have alluded to the fable of Narcissus, whence Näcke has since devised the term Narcissism for this group of phenomena. It is only necessary to mention the enormous production of photographs, representing normal and abnormal sexual actions, specially prepared for the purpose of exciting or of gratifying sexual appetites, and the frequency with which even normal photographs of the nude appeal to the same lust of the eyes.

---

[1] William Ellis, *Polynesian Researches,* second edition, 1832, vol. 1, p. 215.

Pygmalionism, or falling in love with statues, is a rare form of erotomania founded on the sense of vision and closely related to the allurement of beauty. (I here use "pygmalionism" as a general term for the sexual love of statues; it is sometimes restricted to cases in which a man requires of a prostitute that she shall assume the part of a statue which gradually comes to life, and finds sexual gratification in this performance alone; Eulenburg quotes examples, *Sexuale Neuropathie*, p. 107.) An emotional interest in statues is by no means uncommon among young men during adolescence. Heine, in *Florentine Nights*, records the experiences of a boy who conceived a sentimental love for a statue, and, as this book appears to be largely autobiographical, the incident may have been founded on fact. Youths have sometimes masturbated before statues, and even before the image of the Virgin; such cases are known to priests and mentioned in manuals for confessors. Pygmalionism appears to have been not uncommon among the ancient Greeks, and this has been ascribed to their æsthetic sense; but the manifestation is due rather to the absence than to the presence of æsthetic feeling, and we may observe among ourselves that it is the ignorant and uncultured who feel the indecency of statues and thus betray their sense of the sexual appeal of such objects. We have to remember that in Greece statues played a very prominent part in life, and also that they were tinted, and thus more lifelike than with us. Lucian, Athenæus, Ælian, and others refer to cases of men who fell in love with statues. Tarnowsky (*Sexual Instinct*, English edition, p. 85) mentions the case of a young man who was arrested in St. Petersburg for paying moonlight visits to the statue of a nymph on the terrace of a country house, and Krafft-Ebing quotes from a French newspaper the case which occurred in Paris during the spring of 1877 of a gardener who fell in love with a Venus in one of the parks. (I. Bloch, *Beiträge zur Ætiologie der Psychopathia Sexualis*, Teil II, pp. 297-305, brings together various facts bearing on this group of manifestations.)

Necrophily, or a sexual attraction for corpses, is sometimes regarded as related to pygmalionism. It is, however, a more profoundly morbid manifestation, and may perhaps be regarded as a kind of perverted sadism.

Founded on the sense of vision also we find a phenomenon, bordering on the abnormal, which is by Moll termed mixoscopy. This means the sexual pleasure derived from the spectacle of other persons engaged in natural or perverse sexual actions. (Moll, *Konträre Sexualempfindung*, third edition, p. 308. Moll considers that in some cases mixoscopy is related to masochism. There is, however, no necessary connection between the two phenomena.) Brothels are prepared to accommodate visitors who merely desire to look on, and for their convenience carefully contrived peepholes are provided; such visitors are in

Paris termed *"voyeurs."* It is said by Coffignon that persons hide at night in the bushes in the Champs Elysées in the hope of witnessing such scenes between servant girls and their lovers. In England during a country walk I have come across an elderly man carefully ensconced behind a bush and intently watching through his field-glass a couple of lovers reclining on a bank, though the actions of the latter were not apparently marked by any excess of indecorum. Such impulses are only slightly abnormal, whatever may be said of them from the point of view of good taste. They are not very far removed from the legitimate curiosity of the young woman who, believing herself unobserved, turns her glass on to a group of young men bathing naked. They only become truly perverse when the gratification thus derived is sought in preference to natural sexual gratification. They are also not normal when they involve, for instance, a man desiring to witness his wife in the act of coitus with another man. I have been told of the case of a scientific man who encouraged his wife to promote the advances of a young friend of his own, in his own drawing-room, he himself remaining present and apparently taking no notice; the younger man was astonished, but accepted the situation. In such a case, when the motives that led up to the episode are obscure, we must not too hastily assume that masochism or even mixoscopy is involved. For information on some of the points mentioned above see, *e.g.*, I. Bloch, *Beiträge zur Ætiologie der Psychopathia Sexualis*, Teil I, pp. 200 *et seq.*; Teil II, pp. 195 *et seq.*)

Wide, however, as is the appeal of beauty in sexual selection, it cannot be said to cover by any means the whole of the visual field in its sexual relationship. Beauty in the human species is, above all, a feminine attribute, making its appeal to men. Even for women, as has already been noted, beauty is still a feminine quality, which they usually admire, and in cases of inversion worship with an ardor which equals, if it does not surpass, that experienced by normal men. But the normal woman experiences no corresponding cult for the beauty of man. The perfection of the body of man is not behind that of woman in beauty, but the study of it only appeals to the artist or the æsthetician; it arouses sexual enthusiasm almost exclusively in the male sexual invert. Whatever may be the case among animals or even among savages, in civilization the man who is most successful with women is not the most handsome man, and may be the reverse of handsome.[1] The maiden, according to the old saying, who has to choose between Adonis and Hercules, will turn to Hercules.

A correspondent writes: "Men are generally attracted in the first instance by a woman's beauty, either of face or figure. Frequently this is the highest form of love they are capable of. Personally, my own love is always prompted by this. In the case of my wife there was certainly a leaven of friendship and moral sympathies but these alone would never have been translated into love had she not been young and good-looking. Moreover, I have felt intense passion for other women in my relations with whom the elements of moral or mental sympathy have not entered. And always, as youth and beauty went, I believe I should transfer my love to some one else.

"Now, in woman I fancy this element of beauty and youth does not enter so much. I have questioned a large number of women—some married, some unmarried, young and old ladies, shopgirls, servants, prostitutes, women whom I have known only as friends, others with whom I have had sexual relations—and I cannot recollect one instance when a woman said she had fallen in love with a man for his looks. The nearest approach to any sign of this was in the instance of one, who noticed a handsome man sitting near us in a hotel, and said to me: 'I should like him to kiss me.'

"I have also noticed that women do not like looking at my body, when naked, as I like looking at theirs. My wife has, on a few occasions, put her hand over my body, and expressed pleasure at the feeling of my skin. (I have very fair, soft skin.) But I have never seen women exhibit the excitement that is caused in me by the sight of their bodies, which I love to look at, to stroke, to kiss all over."

It is interesting to point out, in this connection, that the admiration of strength is not confined to the human female. It is by the spectacle of his force that the male among many of the lower animals sexually affects the female. Darwin duly allows for this fact, while some evolutionists, and notably Wallace, consider that it covers the whole field of sexual selection. When choice exists, Wallace states, "all the facts appear to be consistent with the choice depending on a variety of male characteristics, with some of which color is often correlated. Thus, it is the opinion of some of the best observers that vigor and liveliness are most attractive, and these are, no doubt, usually associated with some intensity of color. . . . There is reason to be-

---

[1] Stendhal (*De l'Amour*, Chapter XVIII) has some remarks on this point, and refers to the influence over women possessed by Lekain, the famous actor, who was singularly ugly. "It is *passion*," he remarks, "which we demand; beauty only furnishes *probabilities*."

lieve that it is his [the male bird's] presistency and energy rather than his beauty which wins the day." (A. R. Wallace, *Tropical Nature*, 1898, p. 199.) In his later book, *Darwinism* (p. 295), Wallace reaffirms his position that sexual selection means that in the rivalry of males for the female the most vigorous secures the advantage; "ornament," he adds, "is the natural product and direct outcome of superabundant health and vigor." As regards woman's love of strength, see Westermarck, *History of Marriage*, p. 255.

Women admire a man's strength rather than his beauty. This statement is commonly made, and with truth, but, so far as I am aware, its meaning is never analyzed. When we look into it, I think, we shall find that it leads us into a special division of the visual sphere of sexual allurement. The spectacle of force, while it remains strictly within the field of vision, really brings to us, although unconsciously, impressions that are correlated with another sense—that of touch. We instinctively and unconsciously translate visible energy into energy of pressure. In admiring strength we are really admiring a tactile quality which has been made visible. It may therefore be said that, while through vision men are sexually affected mainly by the more purely visual quality of beauty, women are more strongly affected by visual impressions which express qualities belonging to the more fundamentally sexual sense of touch.

The distinction between the man's view and the woman's view, here pointed out, is not, it must be added, absolute. Even for a man, beauty, with all these components which we have already analyzed in it, is not the sole sexual allurement of vision. A woman is not necessarily sexually attractive in the ratio of her beauty, and with even a high degree of beauty may have a low degree of attraction. The addition of vivacity or the addition of languor may each furnish a sexual allurement, and each of these is a translated tactile quality which possesses an obscure potency from vague sexual implications.[1] But while

---

[1] The charm of a woman's garments to a man is often due in part to their expressiveness in rendering impressions of energy, vivacity, or languor. This has often been realized by the poets, and notably by Herrick, who was singularly sensitive to these qualities in a woman's garments.

in the man the demand for these translated pressure qualities in the visible attractiveness of a woman are not usually quite clearly realized, in a woman the corresponding craving for the visual expression of pressure energy is much more pronounced and predominant. It is not difficult to see why this should be so, even without falling back on the usual explanation that natural selection implies that the female shall choose the male who will be the most likely father of strong children and the best protector of his family. The more energetic part in physical love belongs to the man, the more passive part to the woman; so that, while energy in a woman is no index to effectiveness in love, energy in a man furnishes a seeming index to the existence of the primary quality of sexual energy which a woman demands of a man in the sexual embrace. It may be a fallacious index, for muscular strength is not necessarily correlated with sexual vigor, and in its extreme degrees appears to be more correlated with its absence. But it furnishes, in Stendhal's phrase, a probability of passion, and in any case it still remains a symbol which cannot be without its effect. We must not, of course, suppose that these considerations are always or often present to the consciousness of the maiden who "blushingly turns from Adonis to Hercules," but the emotional attitude is rooted in more or less unerring instincts. In this way it happens that even in the field of visual attraction sexual selection influences women on the underlying basis of the more primitive sense of touch, the fundamentally sexual sense.

Women are very sensitive to the quality of a man's touch, and appear to seek and enjoy contact and pressure to a greater extent than do men, although in early adolescence this impulse seems to be marked in both sexes. "There is something strangely winning to most women," remarks George Eliot, in *The Mill on the Floss*, "in that offer of the firm arm; the help is not wanted physically at that moment, but the sense of help—the presence of strength that is outside them and yet theirs—meets a continual want of the imagination."

Women are often very critical concerning a man's touch and his method of shaking hands. Stanley Hall (*Adolescence*, vol. ii, p. 8) quotes a gifted lady as remarking: "I used to say that, however much I liked a man, I could never marry him if I did not like the touch of his hand, and I feel so yet."

Among the elements of sexual attractiveness which make a special appeal to women, extreme personal cleanliness would appear to take higher rank than it takes in the eyes of a man, some men, indeed, seeming to make surprisingly small demands of a woman in this respect. If this is so we may connect it with the fact that beauty in a woman's eye is to a much greater extent than in a man's a picture of energy, in other words, a translation of pressure contacts, with which the question of physical purity is necessarily more intimately associated than it is with the picture of purely visual beauty. It is noteworthy that Ovid (*Ars Amandi*, lib. I) urges men who desire to please women to leave the arts of adornment and effeminacy to those whose loves are homosexual, and to practice a scrupulous attention to extreme neatness and cleanliness of body and garments in every detail, a sun-browned skin, and the absence of all odor. Some two thousand years later Brummell in an age when extravagance and effeminacy often marked the fashions of men, introduced a new ideal of unobtrusive simplicity, extreme cleanliness (with avoidance of perfumes), and exquisite good taste; he abhorred all eccentricity, and may be said to have constituted a tradition which Englishmen have ever since sought, more or less successfully to follow; he was idolized by women.

It may be added that the attentiveness of women to tactile contacts is indicated by the frequency with which in them it takes on morbid forms, as the *délire du contact*, the horror of contamination, the exaggerated fear of touching dirt. (See, *e.g.*, Raymond and Janet, *Les Obsessions et la Psychasthénie.*)

IV.

The Alleged Charm of Disparity in Sexual Attraction—The Admiration for High Stature—The Admiration for Dark Pigmentation—The Charm of Parity—Conjugal Mating—The Statistical Results of Observation as Regards General Appearance, Stature, and Pigmentation of Married Couples—Preferential Mating and Assortative Mating—The Nature of the Advantage Attained by the Fair in Sexual Selection—The Abhorrence of Incest and the Theories of its Cause—The Explanation in Reality Simple—The Abhorrence of Incest in Relation to Sexual Selection—The Limits to the Charm of Parity in Conjugal Mating—The Charm of Disparity in Secondary Sexual Characters.

WHEN we are dealing with the senses of touch, smell, and hearing it is impossible at present, and must always remain somewhat difficult, to investigate precisely the degree and direction of their influence in sexual selection. We can marshal in order—as has here been attempted—the main facts and considerations which clearly indicate that there is and must be such an influence, but we cannot even attempt to estimate its definite direction and still less to measure it precisely. With regard to vision, we are in a somewhat better position. It is possible to estimate the direction of the influence which certain visible characters exert on sexual selection, and it is even possible to attempt their actual measurement, although there must frequently be doubt as to the interpretation of such measurements.

Two facts render it thus possible to deal more exactly with the influence of vision on sexual selection than with the influence of the other senses. In the first place, men and women consciously seek for certain visible characters in the persons to whom they are attracted; in other words, their "ideals" of a fitting mate are visual rather than tactile, olfactory, or auditory. In the second place, whether such "ideals" are potent in actual mating, or whether they are modified or even inhibited by more potent psychological or general biological influences, it is in either case possible to measure and compare the visible characters of mated persons.

The two visible characters which are at once most frequently sought in a mate and most easily measurable are degree of stature and degree of pigmentation. Every youth or maiden pictures the person he or she would like for a lover as tall or short, fair or dark, and such characters are measurable and have on a large scale been measured. It is of interest in illustration of the problem of sexual selection in man to consider briefly what results are at present obtainable regarding the influence of these two characters.

It has long been a widespread belief that short people are sexually attracted to tall people, and tall people to short; that in the matter of stature men and women are affected by what Bain called the "charm of disparity." It has not always prevailed. Many centuries ago Leonardo da Vinci, whose insight at so many points anticipated our most modern discoveries, affirmed clearly and repeatedly the charm of parity. After remarking that painters tend to delineate the figures that resemble themselves he adds that men also fall in love with and marry those who resemble themselves; *"chi s'innamora voluntieri s'innamorano de cose a loro simiglianti,"* he elsewhere puts it.[1] But from that day to this, it would seem Leonardo's statements have remained unknown or unnoticed. Bernardin de Saint-Pierre said that "love is the result of contrasts," and Schopenhauer affirmed the same point very decisively; various scientific and unscientific writers have repeated this statement.[2]

So far as stature is concerned, there appears to be very little reason to suppose that this "charm of disparity" plays any notable part in constituting the sexual ideals of either men or women. Indeed, it may probably be affirmed that both men and women seek tallness in the person to whom they are sexually attracted. Darwin quotes the opinion of Mayhew that

[1] L. da Vinci, *Frammenti*, selected by Solmi, pp. 177-180.
[2] Westermarck, who accepts the "charm of disparity," gives references, *History of Human Marriage*, p. 354.

among dogs the females are strongly attracted to males of large size.[1] I believe this is true, and it is probably merely a particular instance of a general psychological tendency.

It is noteworthy as an indication of the direction of the sexual ideal in this matter that the heroines of male novelists are rarely short and the heroes of female novelists almost invariably tall. A reviewer of novels addressing to lady novelists in the *Speaker* (July 26, 1890) "A Plea for Shorter Heroes," publishes statistics on this point. "Heroes," he states, "are longer this year than ever. Of the 192 of whom I have had my word to say since October of last year, 27 were merely tall, and 11 were only slightly above the middle height. No less than 85 stood exactly six feet in their stocking soles, and the remainder were considerably over the two yards. I take the average to be six feet three."

As a slight test alike of the supposed "charm of disparity" as well as of the general degree in which tall and short persons are sought as mates by those of the opposite sex I have examined a series of entries in the *Round-About*, a publication issued by a club, of which the president is Mr. W. T. Stead, having for its object the purpose of promoting correspondence, friendship, and marriage between its members. There are two classes of entries, one inserted with a view to "intellectual friendship," the other with a view to marriage. I have not thought it necessary to recognize this distinction here; if a man describes his own physical characteristics and those of the lady he would like as a friend, I assume that, from the point of view of the present inquiry, he is much on the same footing as the man who seeks a wife. In the series of entries which I have examined 35 men and women state approximately the height of the man or woman they seek to know; 30 state in additon their own height. The results are expressed in the table on the following page.

Although the cases are few, the results are, in two main respects, sufficiently clear without multiplication of data. In the first place, those who seek parity, whether men or women, are in a majority over those who seek disparity. In the second place, the existence of any disparity at all is due only to tbe universal desire to find a tall person. Not one man or woman sets down shortness as his or her ideal. The very fact that no man in these initial announcements ventures to set himself down as short (although a considerable proportion describe themselves as tall) indicates a consciousness that shortness is undesirable, as also does the fact that the women very frequently describe themselves as tall.

---

[1] *Descent of Man*, Part II, Chapter XVIII.

The same charm of disparity which has been supposed to rule in selective attraction as regards stature has also been assumed as regards pigmentation. The fair, it is said, are attracted to the dark, the dark to the fair. Again, it must be said that this common assumption is not confirmed either by introspection or by any attempt to put the matter on a statistical basis.[1]

WOMEN.		MEN.		TOTALS.
Tall women seek tall men	8	Tall men seek tall women	6	14
Short women seek short men	0	Short men seek short women,	0	0
Medium-sized women seek medium-sized men	0	Medium-sized men seek medium-sized women	3	3
Seek parity	8	Seek parity	9	17
Tall women seek short men	0	Tall men seek short women	0	0
Short women seek tall men	4	Short men seek tall women	0	4
Medium-sized woman seeks tall man	1	Medium-sized men seek tall women	8	9
Seek disparity	5	Seek disparity	8	13
		Men of unknown height seek tall women	5	5

Most people who will carefully introspect their own feelings and ideals in this matter will find that they are not attracted to persons of the opposite sex who are strikingly unlike themselves in pigmentary characters. Even when the abstract ideal

[1] Bloch (*Beiträge zur Ætiologie der Psychopathia Sexualis*, Teil II, pp. 260 *et seq.*) refers to the tendency to admixture of races and to the sexual attraction occasionally exerted by the negress and sometimes the negro on white persons as evidence in favor of such charm of disparity. In part, however, we are here concerned with vague statements concerning imperfectly known facts, in part with merely individual variations, and with that love of the exotic under the stimulation of civilized conditions to which reference has already been made (p. 184).

of a sexually desirable person is endowed with certain pigmentary characters, such as blue eyes or darkness,—either of which is liable to make a vaguely romantic appeal to the imagination, —it is usually found, on testing the feeling for particular persons, that the variation from the personal type of the subject is usually only agreeable within narrow limits, and that there is a very common tendency for persons of totally opposed pigmentary types, even though they may sometimes be considered to possess a certain æsthetic beauty, to be regarded as sexually unattractive or even repulsive. With this feeling may perhaps be associated the feeling, certainly very widely felt, that one would not like to marry a person of foreign, even though closely allied, race.

From the same number of the *Round-About* from which I have extracted the data on stature, I have obtained corresponding data on pigmentation, and have embodied them in the following table. They are likewise very scanty, but they probably furnish as good a general indication of the drift of ideals in this matter as we should obtain from more extensive data of the same character.

WOMEN.		MEN.		TOTALS.
Fair women seek fair men	2	Fair men seek fair women	2	4
Dark woman seeks dark man	1	Dark men seek dark women	7	8
Seek parity	3	Seek parity	9	12
Fair women seek dark men	4	Fair men seek dark women	3	7
Dark woman seeks fair man	1	Dark men seek fair women	4	5
Seek disparity	5	Medium-colored man seeks dark woman	1	1
		Medium-colored man seeks fair woman	1	1
		Seek disparity	9	14
		Men of unknown color seek dark women	3	3

It will be seen that in the case of pigmentation there is not as in the case of stature a decided charm of parity in the formation of sexual ideals. The phenomenon, however, remains essentially analogous. Just as in regard to stature there is without exception an abstract admiration for tall persons, so here, though to a less marked extent, there is a general admiration for dark persons. As many as 5 out of 8 women and 14 out of 21 men seek a dark partner. This tendency ranges itself with the considerations already brought forward (p. 182), leading us to believe that, in England at all events, the admiration of fairness is not efficacious to promote any sexual selection, and that if there is actually any such selection it must be put down to other causes. No doubt, even in England the abstract æsthetic admiration of fairness is justifiable and may influence the artist. Probably also it influences the poet, who is affected by a long-established convention in favor of fairness, and perhaps also by a general tendency on the part of our poets to be themselves fair and to yield to the charm of parity,—the tendency to prefer the women of one's own stock,—which we have already found to be a real force.[1] But, as a matter of fact, our famous English beauties are not very fair; probably our handsomest men are not very fair, and the abstract sexual ideals of both our men and our women thus go out toward the dark.

The formation of a sexual ideal, while it furnishes a predisposition to be attracted in a certain direction, and undoubtedly has a certain weight in sexual choice, is not by any means the whole of sexual selection. It is not even the whole of the psychic element in sexual selection. Let us take, for instance, the question of stature. There would seem to be a general tendency for both men and women, apart from and before experience, to desire sexually large persons of the opposite sex. It may even be that this is part of a wider zoölogical tendency. In the human species it shows itself also on the spiritual plane, in the desire for the infinite, in the deep and unreasoning feeling that it is impossible to have too much of a good thing. But it not

---

[1] In this connection the exceptional case of Tennyson is of interest. He was born and bred in the very fairest part of England (Lincolnshire), but he himself and the stock from which he sprang were dark to a very remarkable degree. In his work, although it reveals traces of the conventional admiration for the fair, there is a marked and unusual admiration for distinctly dark women, the women resembling the stock to which he himself belonged. See Havelock Ellis, "The Color Sense in Literature," *Contemporary Review*, May, 1896.

infrequently happens that a man in whose youthful dreams of
love the heroine has always been large, has not been able to
calculate what are the special nervous and other characteristics
most likely to be met in large women, nor how far these correlated characteristics would suit his own instinctive demands.
He may, and sometimes does, find that in these other demands, which prove to be more important and insistent than
the desire for stature, the tall women he meets are less likely to
suit him than the medium or short women.[1] It may thus happen
that a man whose ideal of woman has always been as tall may
yet throughout life never be in intimate relationship with a tall
woman because he finds that practically he has more marked
affinities in the case of shorter women. His abstract ideals are
modified or negatived by more imperative sympathies or antipathies.

In one field such sympathies have long been recognized,
especially by alienists, as leading to sexual unions of parity,
notwithstanding the belief in the generally superior attraction
of disparity. It has often been pointed out that the neuropathic, the insane and criminal, "degenerates" of all kinds, show
a notable tendency to marry each other. This tendency has not,
however, been investigated with any precision.[2]

The first attempt on a statistical basis to ascertain what
degree of parity or disparity is actually attained by sexual selection was made by Alphonse de Candolle.[3] Obtaining his facts
from Switzerland, North Germany, and Belgium, he came to
the conclusion that marriages are most commonly contracted
between persons with different eye-colors, except in the case of
brown-eyed women, who (as Schopenhauer stated, and as is

---

[1] It is noteworthy that in the *Round-About*, already referred to,
although no man expresses a desire to meet a short woman, when he
refers to announcements by women as being such as would be likely
to suit him, the persons thus pointed out are in a notable proportion
short.

[2] It has been discussed by F. J. Debret, *La Selection Naturelle
dans l'espèce humaine* (Thèse de Paris), 1901. Debret regards it as due
to natural selection.

[3] "Hérédité de la Couleur des Yeux dans l'espèce humaine," *Archives
des Sciences physiques et naturelles*, sér. iii, vol. xii, 1884, p. 109.

seen in the English data of the sexual ideal I have brought forward) are found more attractive than others.

The first series of serious observations tending to confirm the result reached by the genius of Leonardo da Vinci and to show that sexual selection results in the pairing of like rather than of unlike persons was made by Hermann Fol, the embryologist.[1] He set out with the popular notion that married people end by resembling each other, but when at Nice, which is visited by many young married couples on their honeymoons, he was struck by the resemblances already existing immediately after marriage. In order to test the matter he obtained the photographs of 251 young and old married couples not personally known to him. The results were as follows:—

COUPLES.	RESEMBLANCES (PERCENTAGE).	NONRESEMBLANCES (PERCENTAGE).	TOTAL.
Young	132, about 66.66	66, about 33.33	198
Old	38, about 71.70	15, about 28.30	53

He concluded that in the immense majority of marriages of inclination the contracting parties are attracted by similarities, and not by dissimilarities, and that, consequently, the resemblances between aged married couples are not acquired during conjugal life. Although Fol's results were not obtained by good methods, and do not cover definite points like stature and eye-color, they represented the conclusions of a highly skilled and acute observer and have since been amply confirmed.

Galton could not find that the average results from a fairly large number of cases indicated that stature, eye-color, or other personal characteristics notably influenced sexual selection, as evidenced by a comparison of married couples.[2] Karl

---

[1] *Revue Scientifique*, Jan., 1891.

[2] F. Galton, *Natural Inheritance*, p. 85. It may be remarked that while Galton's tables on page 206 show a slight excess of disparity as regards sexual selection in stature, in regard to eye color they anticipate Karl Pearson's more extensive data and in marriages of disparity show a decided deficiency of observed over chance results. In *English Men of Science* (pp. 28-33), also, Galton found that among the parents parity decidedly prevailed over disparity (78 to 31) alike as regards temperament, hair color, and eye color.

Pearson, however, in part making use of a large body of
data obtained by Galton, referring to stature and eye-color,
has reached the conclusion that sexual selection ultimately results in a marked degree of parity so far as these characters are
concerned.[1]   As regards stature, he is unable to find evidence
of what he terms "preferential mating"; that is to say, it does
not appear that any preconceived ideals concerning the desirability of tallness in sexual mates leads to any perceptibly
greater tallness of the chosen mate; husbands are not taller
than men in general, nor wives than women in general.   In
regard to eye-color, however, there appeared to be evidence of
preferential mating.   Husbands are very decidedly fairer than
men in general, and though there is no such marked difference
in women, wives are also somewhat fairer than women in general.   As regards "assortative mating," as it is termed by Pearson,—the tendency to parity or to disparity between husbands
and wives,—the results were in both cases decisive.   Tall men
marry women who are somewhat above the average in height;
short men marry women who are somewhat below the average,
so that husband and wife resemble each other in stature as
closely as uncle and niece.   As regards eye-color there is also
a tendency for like to marry like; the light-eyed men tend to
marry light-eyed women more often than dark-eyed women;
the dark-eyed men tend to marry dark-eyed women more often
than light-eyed.   There remains, however, a very considerable
difference in the eye-color of husband and wife; in the 774
couples dealt with by Pearson there are 333 dark-eyed women to
only 251 dark-eyed men, and 523 light-eyed men to only 441
light-eyed women.   The women in the English population are
darker-eyed than the men[2]; but the difference is scarcely so

---

[1] Karl Pearson, *Phil. Trans. Royal Society*, vol. clxxxvii, p. 273,
and vol. cxcv, p. 113; *Proceedings of the Royal Society*, vol. lxvi, p. 28;
Grammar of Science, second edition, 1900, pp. 425 *et seq.*; *Biometrika*,
November, 1903.   The last-named periodical also contains a study on
"Assortative Mating in Man," bringing forward evidence to show that,
apart from environmental influence, "length of life is a character which
is subject to selection"; that is to say, the long-lived tend to marry
the long-lived, and the short-lived to marry the short-lived.

[2] For a summary of the evidence on this point see Havelock Ellis,
Man and Woman, fourth edition, 1904, pp. 256-264.

great as this; so that even if wives are not so dark-eyed as women generally it would appear that the ideal admiration for the dark-eyed may still to some extent make itself felt in actual mating.

While we have to recognize that the modification and even total inhibition of sexual ideals in the process of actual mating is largely due to psychic causes, such causes do not appear to cover the whole of the phenomena. Undoubtedly they count for much, and the man or the woman who, from whatever causes, has constituted a sexual ideal with certain characters may in the actual contacts of life find that individuals with other and even opposed characters most adequately respond to his or her psychic demands. There are, however, other causes in play here which at first sight may seem to be not of a purely psychic character. One unquestionable cause of this kind comes into action in regard to pigmentary selection. Fair people, possibly as a matter of race more than from absence of pigment, are more energetic than dark people. They possess a sanguine vigor and impetuosity which, in most, though not in all, fields and especially in the competition of practical life, tend to give them some superiority over their darker brethren. The greater fairness of husbands in comparison with men in general, as found by Karl Pearson, is thus accounted for; fair men are most likely to obtain wives. Husbands are fairer than men in general for the same reason that, as I have shown elsewhere,[1] created peers are fairer than either hereditary peers or even most groups of intellectual persons; they have possessed in higher measure the qualities that insure success. It may be added that with the recognition of this fact we have not really left the field of sexual psychology, for, as has already been pointed out, that energy which thus insures success in practical life is itself a sexual allurement to women. Energy in a woman in courtship is less congenial to her sexual attitude than to a man's, and is not attractive to men; thus it is not surprising, even apart from the probably greater beauty of dark women,

---

[1] "The Comparative Abilities of the Fair and the Dark," *Monthly Review*, August, 1901.

that the preponderance of fairness among wives as compared
to women generally, indicated by Karl Pearson's data, is very
slight. It may possibly be accounted for altogether by homogamy
—the tendency of like to marry like—in the fair husbands.

The energy and vitality of fair people is not, however, it
is probable, merely an indirect cause of the greater tendency of
fair men to become husbands; that is to say, it is not merely
the result of the generally somewhat greater ability of the fair to
attain success in temporal affairs. In addition to this, fair men,
if not fair women, would appear to show a tendency to a greater
activity in their specifically sexual proclivities. This is a point
which we shall encounter in a later *Study* and it is therefore
unnecessary to discuss it here.

In dealing with the question of sexual selection in man
various writers have been puzzled by the problem presented by
that abhorrence of incest which is usually, though not always,
so clearly marked among the different races of mankind.[1] It was
once commonly stated, as by Morgan and by Maine, that this
abhorrence was the result of experience; the marriages of closely
related persons were found to be injurious to offspring and were
therefore avoided. This theory, however, is baseless because the
marriages of closely related persons are not injurious to the offspring. Consanguineous marriages, so closely as they can be
investigated on a large scale,—that is to say, marriages between
cousins,—as Huth was the first to show, develop no tendency
to the production of offspring of impaired quality provided the
parents are sound; they are only injurious in this respect in so
far as they may lead to the union of couples who are both defective in the same direction. According to another theory,
that of Westermarck, who has very fully and ably discussed the
whole question,[2] "there is an innate aversion to sexual intercourse between persons living very closely together from early
youth, and, as such persons are in most cases related, this

---

[1] The fact that even in Europe the abhorrence to incest is not
always strongly felt is brought out by Bloch, *Beiträge zur Ætiologie
der Psychopathia Sexualis*, Teil II, pp. 263 *et seq.*

[2] Westermarck, *History of Marriage*, Chapters XIV and XV.

feeling displays itself chiefly as a horror of intercourse between near kin." Westermarck points out very truly that the prohibition of incest could not be founded on experience even if (as he is himself inclined to believe) consanguineous marriages are injurious to the offspring; incest is prevented "neither by laws, nor by customs, nor by education, but by an *instinct* which under normal circumstances makes sexual love between the nearest kin a psychic impossibility." There is, however, a very radical objection to this theory. It assumes the existence of a kind of instinct which can with difficulty be accepted. An instinct is fundamentally a more or less complicated series of reflexes set in action by a definite stimulus. An innate tendency at once so specific and so merely negative, involving at the same time deliberate intellectual processes, can only with a certain force be introduced into the accepted class of instincts. It is as awkward and artificial an instinct as would be, let us say, an instinct to avoid eating the apples that grew in one's own orchard.[1]

The explanation of the abhorrence to incest is really, however, exceedingly simple. Any reader who has followed the discussion of sexual selection in the present volume and is also familiar with the "Analysis of the Sexual Impulse" set forth in the previous volume of these *Studies* will quickly perceive that the normal failure of the pairing instinct to manifest itself in the case of brothers and sisters, or of boys and girls brought up together from infancy, is a merely negative phenomenon due to the inevitable absence under those circumstances of the conditions which evoke the pairing impulse. Courtship is the process by which powerful sensory stimuli proceeding from a person of the opposite sex gradually produce the physiological state of tumescence, with its psychic concomitant of love and desire, more or less necessary for mating to be effected. But between those who have been brought up together from childhood all the sensory stimuli of vision, hearing, and touch have been dulled by

---

[1] Crawley (*The Mystic Rose*, p. 446) has pointed out that it is not legitimate to assume the possibility of an "instinct" of this character; instinct has "nothing in its character but a response of function to environment."

use, trained to the calm level of affection, and deprived of their potency to arouse the erethistic excitement which produces sexual tumescence.[1] Brothers and sisters in relation to each other have at puberty already reached that state to which old married couples by the exhaustion of youthful passion and the slow usage of daily life gradually approximate. Passion between brother and sister is, indeed, by no means so rare as is sometimes supposed, and it may be very strong, but it is usually aroused by the aid of those conditions which are normally required for the appearance of passion, more especially by the unfamiliarity caused by a long separation. In reality, therefore, the usual absence of sexual attraction between brothers and sisters requires no special explanation; it is merely due to the normal absence under these circumstances of the conditions that tend to produce sexual tumescence and the play of those sensory allurements which lead to sexual selection.[2] It is a purely negative phenomenon and it is quite unnecessary, even if it were legitimate, to invoke any instinct for its explanation. It is probable that the same tendency also operates among animals to some extent, tending to produce a stronger sexual attraction toward those of their species to whom they have not become habituated.[3] In animals, and in man also when living under primitive condi-

---

[1] Fromentin, in his largely autobiographic novel *Dominique*, makes Olivier say: "Julie is my cousin, which is perhaps a reason why she should please me less than anyone else. I have always known her. We have, as it were, slept in the same cradle. There may be people who would be attracted by this almost fraternal relationship. To me the very idea of marrying someone whom I knew as a baby is as absurd as that of coupling two dolls."

[2] It may well be, as Crawley argues (*The Mystic Rose*, Chapter XVII), that sexual taboo plays some part among primitive people in preventing incestuous union, as, undoubtedly, training and moral ideas do among civilized peoples.

[3] The remarks of the Marquis de Brisay, an authority on doves, as communicated to Giard (*L'Intermédiare des Biologistes*, November 20, 1897), are of much interest on this point, since they correspond to what we find in the human species: "Two birds from the same nest rarely couple. Birds coming from the same nest behave as though they regarded coupling as prohibited, or, rather, they know each other too well, and seem to be ignorant of their difference in sex, remaining unaffected in their relations by the changes which make them adults." Westermarck (*op. cit.*, p. 334) has some remarks on a somewhat similar tendency sometimes observed in dogs and horses.

tions, sexual attraction is not a constant phenomenon[1]; it is an occasional manifestation only called out by powerful stimulation. It is not its absence which we need to explain; it is its presence which needs explanation, and such an explanation we find in the analysis of the phenomena of courtship.

The abhorrence of incest is an interesting and significant phenomenon from our present point of view, because it instructively points out to us the limits to that charm of parity which apparently makes itself felt to some considerable extent in the constitution of the sexual ideal and still more in the actual homogamy which seems to predominate over heterogamy. This homogamy is, it will be observed, a *racial* homogamy; it relates to anthropological characters which mark stocks. Even in this racial field, it is unnecessary to remark, the homogamy attained is not, and could not be, absolute; nor would it appear that such absolute racial homogamy is even desired. A tall man who seeks a tall woman can seldom wish her to be as tall as himself; a dark man who seeks a dark woman certainly will not be displeased at the inevitably greater or less degree of pigment which he finds in her eyes as compared to his own.

But when we go outside the racial field this tendency to homogamy disappears at once. A man marries a woman who, with slight, but agreeable, variations, belongs to a like stock to himself. The abhorrence of incest indicates that even the sexual attraction to people of the same stock has its limits, for it is not strong enough to overcome the sexual indifference between persons of near kin. The desire for novelty shown in this sexual indifference to near kin and to those who have been housemates from childhood, together with the notable sexual attractiveness often possessed by a strange youth or maiden who arrives in a small town or village, indicates that slight differences in stock, if not, indeed, a positive advantage from this point of view, are certainly not a disadvantage. When we leave the consideration of racial differences to consider sexual differences, not only do we no longer find any charm of parity, but we find that there

---

[1] See Appendix to vol. iii of these *Studies*, "The Sexual Impulse among Savages."

is an actual charm of disparity. At this point it is necessary
to remember all that has been brought forward in earlier pages[1]
concerning the emphasis of the secondary sexual characters in
the ideal of beauty. All those qualities which the woman desires
to see emphasized in the man are the precise opposite of the
qualities which the man desires to see emphasized in the woman.
The man must be strong, vigorous, energetic, hairy, even rough,
to stir the primitive instincts of the woman's nature; the woman
who satisfies this man must be smooth, rounded, and gentle. It
would be hopeless to seek for any homogamy between the manly
man and the virile woman, between the feminine woman and
the effeminate man. It is not impossible that this tendency to
seek disparity in sexual characters may exert some disturbing
influences on the tendency to seek parity in anthropological
racial characters, for the sexual difference to some extent makes
itself felt in racial characters. A somewhat greater darkness of
women is a secondary (or, more precisely, tertiary) sexual character, and on this account alone, it is possible, somewhat attractive to men.[2] A difference in size and stature is a very
marked secondary sexual character. In the considerable body
of data concerning the stature of married couples reproduced
by Pearson from Galton's tables, although the tall on the average tend to marry the tall, and the short the short, it is yet
noteworthy that, while the men of 5 ft. 4 ins. have more wives
at 5 ft. 2 ins. than at any other height, men of 6 ft. show, in an
exactly similar manner, more wives at 5 ft. 2 ins. than at any
other height, although for many intermediate heights the most
numerous groups of wives are taller.[3]

In matters of carriage, habit, and especially clothing the
love of sexual disparity is instinctive, everywhere well marked,
and often carried to very great lengths. To some extent such

---

[1] See, especially, *ante*, pp. 163 *et seq.*

[2] Kistemaecker, as quoted by Bloch (*Beiträge, etc.*, ii, p. 340), al-
ludes in this connection to the dark clothes of men and to the tendency
of women to wear lighter garments, to emphasize the white underlinen,
to cultivate pallor of the face, to use powder. "I am white and you
are brown; ergo, you must love me": this affirmation, he states, may
be found in the depths of every woman's heart.

[3] K. Pearson, *Grammar of Science*, second edition, p. 430.

differences are due to the opposing demands of more fundamental differences in custom and occupation. But this cause by no means adequately accounts for them, since it may sometimes happen that what in one land is the practice of the men is in another the practice of the women, and yet the practices of the two sexes are still opposed.[1] Men instinctively desire to avoid doing things in women's ways, and women instinctively avoid doing things in men's ways, yet both sexes admire in the other sex those things which in themselves they avoid. In the matter of clothing this charm of disparity reaches its highest point, and it has constantly happened that men have even called in the aid of religion to enforce a distinction which seemed to them so urgent.[2] One of the greatest of sex allurements would be lost and the extreme importance of clothes would disappear at once if the two sexes were to dress alike; such identity of dress has, however, never come about among any people.

---

[1] In *Man and Woman* (fourth edition, p. 65) I have referred to a curious example of this tendency to opposition which is of almost world-wide extent. Among some people it is, or has been, the custom for the women to stand during urination, and in these countries it is usually the custom for the man to squat; in most countries the practices of the sexes in this matter are opposed.

[2] It is sufficient to quote one example. At the end of the six-teenth century it was a serious objection to the fashionable wife of an English Brownist pastor in Amsterdam that she had "bodies [a bodice or corset] tied to the petticoat with points [laces] as men do their doublets and their hose, contrary to I Thess., v, 22, conferred with Deut. xxii, 5; and I John ii, 16."

V.

Summary of the Conclusions at Present Attainable in Regard to the Nature of Beauty and its Relation to Sexual Selection.

THE consideration of vision has led us into a region in which, more definitely and precisely than is the case with any other sense, we can observe and even hope to measure the operation of sexual selection in man. In the conception of feminine beauty we possess an instrument of universal extension by which it seems possible to measure the nature and extent of such selection as exercised by men on women. This conception, with which we set out, is, however, by no means so precise, so easily available for the attainment of sound conclusions, as at first sight it may seem to be.

It is true that beauty is not, as some have supposed, a mere matter of caprice. It rests in part on (1) an objective basis of æsthetic character which holds all its variations together and leads to a remarkable approximation among the ideals of feminine beauty cherished by the most intelligent men of all races. But beyond this general objective basis we find that (2) the specific characters of the race or nation tend to cause divergence in the ideals of beauty, since beauty is often held to consist in the extreme development of these racial or national anthropological features; and it would, indeed, appear that the full development of racial characters indicates at the same time the full development of health and vigor. We have further to consider that (3) in most countries an important and usually essential element of beauty lies in the emphasis of the secondary and tertiary sexual characters: the special characters of the hair in woman, her breasts, her hips, and innumerable other qualities of minor saliency, but all apt to be of significance from the point of view of sexual selection. In addition we have (4) the factor of individual taste, constituted by the special organization and the peculiar experiences of the individual and inevitably affecting his ideal of beauty. Often this individual factor is merged into collective shapes, and in this way are constituted passing fashions in the matter of beauty, certain influences which normally affect only the individual having become potent enough to affect many individuals. Finally, in states of high civilization and in individuals of that restless and nervous temperament which is common in civilization, we have (5) a tendency to the appearance of an exotic element in the ideal of beauty, and in place of admiring that kind of beauty which most closely approximates to the type of their own race men begin to be agreeably affected by types which more or less deviate from that with which they are most familiar.

While we have these various and to some extent conflicting elements in a man's ideal of feminine beauty, the question is still further complicated by the fact that sexual selection in the human species is not merely the choice of the woman by the man, but also the choice of the man by the woman. And when we come to consider this we find that the standard is altogether different, that many of the elements of beauty as it exists in woman for man have here fallen away altogether, while a new and preponderant element has to be recognized in the shape of a regard for strength and vigor. This, as I have pointed out, is not a purely visual character, but a tactile pressure character translated into visual terms.

When we have stated the sexual ideal we have not yet, however, by any means stated the complete problem of human sexual selection. The ideal that is desired and sought is, in a large measure, not the outcome of experience; it is not even necessarily the expression of the individual's temperament and idiosyncrasy. It may be largely the result of fortuitous circumstances, of slight chance attractions in childhood, of accepted traditions consecrated by romance. In the actual contacts of life the individual may find that his sexual impulse is stirred by sensory stimuli which are other than those of the ideal he had cherished and may even be the reverse of them.

Beyond this, also, we have reason for believing that factors of a still more fundamentally biological character, to some extent deeper even than all these psychic elements, enter into the problem of sexual selection. Certain individuals, apart altogether from the question of whether they are either ideally or practically the most fit mates, display a greater energy and achieve a greater success than others in securing partners. These individuals possess a greater constitutional vigor, physical or mental, which conduces to their success in practical affairs generally, and probably also heightens their specifically philogamic activities.

Thus, the problem of human sexual selection is in the highest degree complicated. When we gather together such scanty data of precise nature as are at present available, we realize that, while generally according with the results which the evidence not of a quantitative nature would lead us to accept, their precise significance is not at present altogether clear. It would appear on the whole that in choosing a mate we tend to seek parity of racial and individual characters together with disparity of secondary sexual characters. But we need a much larger number of groups of evidence of varying character and obtained under varying conditions. Such evidence will doubtless accumulate now that its nature is becoming defined and the need for it recognized. In the meanwhile we are, at all events, in a position to assert, even with the evidence before us, that now that the real meaning of sexual selection is becoming clear its efficacy in human evolution can no longer be questioned.

APPENDICES.

APPENDIX A.

THE ORIGINS OF THE KISS.

MANIFESTATIONS resembling the kiss, whether with the object of expressing affection or sexual emotion, are found among various animals much lower than man. The caressing of the antennæ practiced by snails and various insects during sexual intercourse is of the nature of a kiss. Birds use their bills for a kind of caress. Thus, referring to guillemots and their practice of nibbling each other's feet, and the interest the mate always takes in this proceeding, which probably relieves irritation caused by insects, Edmund Selous remarks: "When they nibble and preen each other they may, I think, be rightly said to cosset and caress, the expression and pose of the bird receiving the benefit being often beatific."[1] Among mammals, such as the dog, we have what closely resembles a kiss, and the dog who smells, licks, and gently bites his master or a bitch, combines most of the sensory activities involved in the various forms of the human kiss.

As practiced by man, the kiss involves mainly either the sense of touch or that of smell. Occasionally it involves to some extent both sensory elements.[2]

The tactile kiss is certainly very ancient and primitive. It is common among mammals generally. The human infant exhibits, in a very marked degree, the impulse to carry everything to the mouth and to lick or attempt to taste it, possibly, as Compayre suggests,[3] from a memory of the action of the lips pro-

---

[1] E. Selous, *Bird Watching*, 1901, p. 191. This author adds: "It seems probable indeed that the conferring a practical benefit of the kind indicated may be the origin of the caress throughout nature."

[2] Tylor terms the kiss "the salute by tasting," and d'Enjoy defines it as "a bite and a suction"; there seems, however, little evidence to show that the kiss contains any gustatory element in the strict sense.

[3] Compayre, *L'Evolution intellectuelle et morale de l'enfant*, p. 9.

truded to seize the maternal nipple. The affectionate child, as Mantegazza remarks,[1] not only applies inanimate objects to its lips or tongue, but of its own impulse licks the people it likes. Stanley Hall, in the light of a large amount of information he obtained on this point, found that "some children insist on licking the cheeks, necks, and hands of those they wish to caress," or like having animals lick them.[2] This impulse in children may be associated with the maternal impulse in animals to lick the young. "The method of licking the young practiced by the mother," remarks S. S. Buckman, "would cause licking to be associated with happy feelings. And, further, there is the allaying of parasitical irritation which is afforded by the rubbing and hence results in pleasure. It may even be suggested that the desire of the mother to lick her young was prompted in the first place by a desire to bestow on her offspring a pleasure she felt herself." The licking impulse in the child may thus, it is possible, be regarded as the evanescent manifestation of a more fundamental animal impulse,[3] a manifestation which is liable to appear in adult life under the stress of strong sexual emotion. Such an association is of interest if, as there is some reason to believe, the kiss of sexual love originated as a development of the more primitive kiss bestowed by the mother on her child, for it is sometimes found that the maternal kiss is practiced where the sexual kiss is unknown.

The impulse to bite is also a part of the tactile element which lies at the origin of kissing. As Stanley Hall notes, children are fond of biting, though by no means always as a method of affection. There is, however, in biting a distinctly sexual origin to invoke, for among many animals the teeth (and among birds the bill) are used by the male to grasp the female more firmly during intercourse. This point has been discussed in the

---

[1] Mantegazza, *Physiognomy and Expression*, p. 144.
[2] G. Stanley Hall, "The Early Sense of Self," *American Journal of Psychology*, April, 1898, p. 361.
[3] In some parts of the world the impulse persists into adult life. Sir S. Baker (*Ismailia*, p. 472) mentions licking the eyes as a sign of affection.

previous volume of these *Studies* in reference to "Love and Pain," and it is unnecessary to enter into further details here. The heroine of Kleist's *Penthesilea* remarks: "Kissing (Küsse) rhymes with biting (Bisse), and one who loves with the whole heart may easily confound the two."

The kiss, as known in Europe, has developed on a sensory basis that is mainly tactile, although an olfactory element may sometimes coexist. The kiss thus understood is not very widely spread and is not usually found among rude and uncultured peoples. We can trace it in Aryan and Semitic antiquity, but in no very pronounced form; Homer scarcely knew it, and the Greek poets seldom mention it. To-day it may be said to be known all over Europe except in Lapland. Even in Europe it is probably a comparatively modern discovery; and in all the Celtic tongues, Rhys states, there is no word for "kiss," the word employed being always borrowed from the Latin *pax*.[1] At a fairly early historic period, however, the Welsh Cymri, at all events, acquired a knowledge of the kiss, but it was regarded as a serious matter and very sparingly used, being by law only permitted on special occasions, as at a game called rope-playing or a carousal; otherwise a wife who kissed a man not her husband could be repudiated. Throughout eastern Asia it is unknown; thus, in Japanese literature kisses and embraces have no existence. "Kisses and embraces are simply unknown in Japan as tokens of affection," Lafcadio Hearn states, "if we except the solitary fact that Japanese mothers, like mothers all over the world, lip and hug their little ones betimes. After babyhood there is no more hugging or kisses; such actions, except in the case of infants, are held to be immodest. Never do girls kiss one another; never do parents kiss or embrace their children who have become able to walk." This holds true, and has always held true, of all classes; hand-clasping is also foreign to them. On meeting after a long absence, Hearn remarks, they smile, perhaps cry a little, they may even stroke each other, but that is all. Japanese affection "is chiefly shown in

---

[1] *Book of Common Prayer in Manx Gaelic*, edited by A. W. Moore and J. Rhys, 1895.

acts of exquisite courtesy and kindness."[1] Among nearly all of the black races of Africa lovers never kiss nor do mothers usually kiss their babies.[2] Among the American Indians the tactile kiss is, for the most part, unknown, though here and there, as among the Fuegians, lovers rub their cheeks together.[3] Kissing is unknown to the Malays. In North Queensland, however, Roth states, kissing takes place between mothers (not fathers) and infants, also between husbands and wives; but whether it is an introduced custom Roth is unable to say; he adds that the Pitta-Pitta language possesses a word for kissing.[4]

It must be remarked, however, that in many parts of the world where the tactile kiss, as we understand it, is usually said to be unknown, it still exists as between a mother and her baby, and this seems to support the view advocated by Lombroso that the lovers' kiss is developed from the maternal kiss. Thus, the Angoni Zulus to the north of the Zambesi, Wiese states, kiss their small children on both cheeks[5] and among the Fuegians, according to Hyades, mothers kiss their small children.

Even in Europe the kiss in early mediæval days was, it seems probable, not widely known as an expression of sexual love; it would appear to have been a refinement of love only practiced by the more cultivated classes. In the old ballad of Glasgerion the lady suspected that her secret visitor was only a churl, and not the knight he pretended to be, because when he came in his master's place to spend the night with her he kissed her neither coming nor going, but simply got her with child. It is only under a comparatively high state of civilization that the kiss has been emphasized and developed in the art of love. Thus the Arabic author of the *Perfumed Garden,* a work re-

---

[1] L. Hearn, *Out of the East,* 1895, p. 103.
[2] See, *e.g.,* A. B. Ellis, *Tshi-speaking Peoples,* p. 288. Among the Swahili the kiss is practiced, but exclusively between married people and with very young children. Velten believes they learned it from the Arabs.
[3] Hyades and Deniker, *Mission Scientifique du Cap Horn,* vol. vii, p. 245.
[4] W. Roth, *Ethnological Notes Among the Queensland Aborigines,* p. 184.
[5] *Zeitschrift für Ethnologie,* 1900, ht. 5, p. 200.

vealing the existence of a high degree of social refinement, insists on the great importance of the kiss, especially if applied to the inner part of the mouth, and he quotes a proverb that "A moist kiss is better than a hasty coitus." Such kisses, as well as on the face generally, and all over the body, are frequently referred to by Hindu, Latin, and more modern erotic writers as among the most efficacious methods of arousing love.[1]

A reason which may have stood in the way of the development of the kiss in a sexual direction has probably been the fact that in the near East the kiss was largely monopolized for sacred uses, so that its erotic potentialities were not easily perceived. Among the early Arabians the gods were worshiped by a kiss.[2] This was the usual way of greeting the house gods on entering or leaving.[3] In Rome the kiss was a sign of reverence and respect far more than a method of sexual excitation.[4] Among the early Christians it had an all but sacramental significance. It retains its ancient and serious meaning in many usages of the Western and still more the Eastern Churches; the relics of saints, the foot of the pope, the hands of bishops, are kissed, just as the ancient Greeks kissed the images of the gods. Among ourselves we still have a legally recognized example of the sacredness of the kiss in the form of taking an oath by kissing the Testament.[5]

So far we have been concerned mainly with the tactile kiss, which is sometimes supposed to have arisen in remote times to the east of the Mediterranean—where the vassal kissed his suzerian and where the kiss of love was known, as we learn from the Songs of Songs, to the Hebrews—and has now conquered

---

[1] E.g., the *Kama Sutra* of Vatsyayana, Bk. III, Chapter I.

[2] Hosea, Chapter xiii, v. 2; I Kings, Chapter xix, v. 18.

[3] Wellhausen, *Reste Arabischen Heidentums*, p. 109.

[4] The Romans recognized at least three kinds of kiss: the *osculum*, for friendship, given on the face; the *basium*, for affection, given on the lips; the *suavium*, given between the lips, reserved for lovers.

[5] In other parts of the world it would appear that the kiss sometimes has a sacred or ritual character. Thus, according to Rev. J. Macdonald, (*Journal of the Anthropological Institute*, November, 1890, p. 118), it is part of the initiation ceremony of a girl at her first menstruation that the women of the village should kiss her on the cheek, and on the mons veneris and labia.

nearly the whole of Europe. But over a much larger part of the
world and even in one corner of Europe (Lapland, as well as
among the Russian Yakuts) a different kind of salutation rules,
the olfactory kiss. This varies in form in different regions and
sometimes simulates a tactile kiss, but, as it exists in a typical
form in China, where it has been carefully studied by d'Enjoy,
it may be said to be made up of three phases: (1) the nose is
applied to the cheek of the beloved person; (2) there is a long
nasal inspiration accompanied by lowering of the eyelids; (3)
there is a slight smacking of the lips without the application
of the mouth to the embraced cheek. The whole process, d'Enjoy
considers, is founded on sexual desire and the desire for food,
smell being the sense employed in both fields. In the form
described by d'Enjoy, we have the Mongolian variety of the
olfactory kiss. The Chinese regard the European kiss as odious,
suggesting voracious cannibals, and yellow mothers in the French
colonies still frighten children by threatening to give them the
white man's kiss. Their own kiss the Chinese regard as exclusively voluptuous; it is only befitting as between lovers, and not
only do fathers refrain from kissing their children except when
very young, but even the mothers only give their children a rare
and furtive kiss. Among some of the bill-tribes of south-east
India the olfactory kiss is found, the nose being applied to the
cheek during salutation with a strong inhalation; instead of
saying "Kiss me," they here say "Smell me." The Tamils, I
am told by a medical correspondent in Ceylon, do not kiss during coitus, but rub noses and also lick each other's mouth and
tongue. The olfactory kiss is known in Africa; thus, on the
Gambia in inland Africa when a man salutes a woman he takes
her hand and places it to his nose, twice smelling the back of it.
Among the Jekris of the Niger coast mothers rub their babies
with their cheeks or mouths, but they do not kiss them, nor do
lovers kiss, though they squeeze, cuddle, and embrace.[1] Among
the Swahilis a smell kiss exists, and very young boys are taught
to raise their clothes before women visitors, who thereupon play-

[1] *Journal of the Anthropological Institute*, August and November,
1898, p. 107.

fully smell the penis; the child who does this is said to "give tobacco."[1] Kissing of any kind appears to be unknown to the Indians throughout a large part of America: Im Thirn states that it is unknown to the Indians of Guiana, and at the other end of South America Hyades and Deniker state that it is unknown to the Fuegians. In North America the olfactory kiss is known to the Eskimo, and has been noted among some Indian tribes, as the Blackfeet. It is also known in Polynesia. At Samoa kissing was smelling.[2] In New Zealand, also, the *hongi*, or nose-pressing, was the kiss of welcome, of mourning, and of sympathy.[3] In the Malay archipelago, it is said, the same word is used for "greeting" and "smelling." Among the Dyaks of the Malay archipelago, however, Vaughan Stevens states that any form of kissing is unknown.[4] In Borneo, Breitenstein tells us, kissing is a kind of smelling, the word for smelling being used, but he never himself saw a man kiss a woman; it is always done in private.[5]

The olfactory kiss is thus seen to have a much wider extension over the world than the European (or Mediterranean) tactile kiss. In its most complete development, however, it is mainly found among the people of Mongolian race, or those yellow peoples more or less related to them.

The literature of the kiss is extensive. So far, however, as that literature is known to me, the following list includes everything that may be profitably studied: Darwin, *The Expression of the Emotions;* Ling Roth, "Salutations," *Journal of the Anthropological Institute,* November, 1889; K. Andree, "Nasengruss," *Ethnographische Parallelen,* second series, 1889, pp. 223-227; Alfred Kirchhoff, "Vom Ursprung des Küsses," *Deutsche Revue,* May, 1895; Lombroso, "L'Origine du Baiser," *Nouvelle Revue,* 1897, p. 153; Paul d'Enjoy, "Le Baiser en Europe et en Chine," *Bulletin de la Société d'Anthropologie,* Paris, 1897, fasc. 2. Professor Nvrop's book, *The Kiss and its History* (translated

---

[1] Velten, *Sitten und Gebraüche der Suaheli,* p. 142.
[2] Turner, *Samoa,* p. 45.
[3] Tregear, *Journal of the Anthropological Institute,* 1889.
[4] *Zeitschrift für Ethnologie,* 1896, ht. 4, p. 272.
[5] Breitenstein, *21 Jahre in India,* vol. i, p. 224.

from the Danish by W. F. Harvey), deals rather with the history of the kiss in civilization and literature than with its biological origins and psychological significance.

APPENDIX B.

HISTORIES OF SEXUAL DEVELOPMENT.

THE histories here recorded are similar in character to those given in Appendix B of the previous volume.

HISTORY I.—C. D., clergyman, age, 34. Height about 5 ft. 8 in. Weight, 8st. 8lb. Complexion, fair. Physical infirmities, very myopic, tendency to consumption.

"My family is of old lineage on both sides. My parents were normal and fairly healthy; but I consider that heredity, though not vitiated, is somewhat overrefined, and there is a neuropathic tendency, which has appeared in myself and in one or two other members of the family. As a child, I suffered, though not very frequently, from nocturnal enuresis. My sexual nature, though normal, has been keenly alive and sensitive as far back as I can remember; and as I look back I discern within myself in early childhood what I now understand to be a decided masochistic or passively algolagnic tendency. So far as I remember, this manifested itself in me in two aspects; one psychic or sentimental and free from carnality, expressing itself in imaginative visions such as the following: I used to imagine myself kneeling before a young and beautiful woman and being sentenced by her to some punishment, and even threatened with death. At other times I would picture myself as a wounded soldier watched over on his sickbed by queenly women. These visions always included an imagination of something heroic in my own personality. No doubt they were the same kind of dreamings as are present in multitudes of imaginative children; they are only of interest in so far as a sexual element was present; and that was algolagnic in character.

"I had a small fund of natural common sense, and my surroundings were not favorable to sentimental imaginings; consequently I believe I began to throw them off at an early age, though the temperament which produced them is still a part of my nature.

"On the carnal side, the sexual instinct was decidedly algolagnic. Masturbation is one of my earliest recollections; indeed, it was not at first, so far as I remember, associated with any sexual ideas at all; but began as a reflex animal act. I do not remember its first occurrence. It soon, however, became associated in my mind with algolagnic excitement, giving rise to reveries which took the ordinary form of imagining oneself stripped and whipped, etc., by persons of the opposite sex. The *dramatis personæ* in my own algolagnic reveries were elderly women; somewhat strangely, I did not associate physical sexuality at this period with young and attractive women. If scientific light on these matters were generally available in the practical bringing up of children, persons in charge of young children might refrain from exciting an algolagnic tendency or doing anything calculated to awake sexual emotions prematurely. In my own case, I recollect acts performed by older persons in ignorance and thoughtlessness which undoubtedly tended to foster and strengthen my algolagnic instinct.

"Little or nothing was done to prevent, discover, or remedy the pernicious habit into which I was falling unknowingly. Circumcision was perhaps little thought of in those days as a preventive of juvenile masturbation; at any rate, it was not resorted to in my case. I remember, indeed, that a nurse discovered that I was practicing masturbation, and I think she made a few half-hearted attempts to stop it. It was probably these attempts which gave me a growing feeling that there was something wrong about masturbation, and that it must be practiced secretly. But they were unsuccessful in their main object. The practice continued.

"I went to school at the age of 10. There I came in contact almost without warning, with the ordinary lewdness and grossness of school conversation, and took to it readily. I soon became conversant with the theory of sexual relations; but never got the opportunity of sexual intercourse, and probably should have felt some moral restraint even had such opportunity presented itself, for coitus, however interesting it might be to talk about, was a bigger thing to practice than masturbation. I masturbated fairly frequently, occasionally producing two orgasms in quick succession. I seldom masturbated with the hand; my method was to lie face downward. There was probably little or no homosexuality at my first school. I never heard of it till later, and it was always repugnant to me, though surrounded with a certain morbid interest. Masturbation was discountenanced openly at the school, but was, I believe, extensively practiced, both at that school and at the two others I afterward attended. The boys often talked about the hygiene of it; and the general theory was that it was somehow physically detrimental; but I heard no arguments advanced sufficiently cogent to make me see the necessity for a real moral effort against the habit, though, as I neared puberty, I was indulging more moderately and with greater misgivings.

"The fact of becoming acquainted with the theory of sexual intercourse tended to diminish the algolagnia, and to impel my sexual instinct into an ordinary channel. On one occasion circumstances brought me into close contact with a woman for about three or four weeks, I being a mere boy and she very much my senior. I felt sexually attracted by this woman, and allowed myself a degree of familiarity with her which I have since recognized as undue and have deeply regretted. It did not, however, go to the length of seduction, and I trust may have passed away without leaving any permanent harm. It should, indeed, be remarked here that I never knew a woman sexually till my marriage; and with the one exception mentioned I do not recall any instance of conduct on my part toward a woman which could be described as giving her an impulse downhill.

"On the psychic side my sexual emotions awoke in early childhood; and though my love affairs as a boy were not frequent and were kept to myself, they attained a considerable degree of emotional power. Leaving out of account the precocious movements of the sexual instinct to which I have already referred as colored by psychic algolagnia, I may say that somewhat later, from the age of puberty and onward, I had three or four love affairs, devoid of any algolagnic tendency, and considerably more developed on the psychic and emotional, than on the physical, side. In fact, my experience has been that when deeply in love, when the mind is full of the love ecstasy, the physical element of sexuality is kept—doubtless only temporarily—in abeyance.

"To return now to the subject of masturbation. Here befell the chief moral struggle of my early life; and no terms that I have at command will adequately describe the stress of it.

"A casual remark heard one day as I was arriving at puberty convinced me that there must be truth in the vague schoolboy theory that masturbation was *weakening*. It was to the effect that the evil results of masturbation practiced in boyhood would manifest themselves in later life. I then realized that I must relinquish masturbation, and I set myself to fight it; but with grave misgivings that, owing to the early age at which I had formed the habit, I had already done myself serious harm.

"Before many weeks had passed, I had formed a resolution to abstain, which I kept thereafter without—so far as I remember—more than one conscious lapse into my former habit. Here it must be said at once that, so far as touches my own experience of a struggle of this kind, the religious factor is of primary importance as strengthening and sustaining the moral effort which has to be made. I am writing an account of my sexual, not my spiritual, experiences; but I should not only be untrue to my convictions, but unable to give an accurate and penetrating survey of the development of my sex life, unless I were clearly to state that it was to a large extent on that life that my strongest and most valuable religious experiences arose.[1] It is to the

---

[1] My Christian faith is of a somewhat nonemotional, intellectual type, with a considerable element of agnostic reserve.

endeavor to discipline the sexual instinct, and to grapple with the difficulties and anxieties of the sex life, that I owe what I possess of spiritual religion, of the consciousness that my life has been brought into contact with Divine love and power.

"My early habits, after they were broken off, left me none the less a legacy of sexual neurasthenia and a slight varicocele. My nocturnal pollutions were overfrequent; and I brooded over them, being too reticent and too much afraid of exposure at school and possible expulsion to confide in a doctor. Far better for me had I done so, for a few years later I received the truest kindness and sympathy in regard to sexual matters at the hands of more than one medical man. But while at school I was afraid to speak of the trouble which so unnerved and depressed me; and as a consequence my morbid fears grew stronger, being intensified by generalities which I met with from time to time in my reading on the subject of the punishment which nature metes out to impurity.

"On leaving school my sex life continued for some years on the same lines: a struggle for chastity, morbid fears and regrets about the past, efforts to cope with the neurasthenia, and a haunting dread of coming insanity. These troubles were increased by my sedentary life. However I obtained medical aid, and put as good a face on matters as possible.

"But the most trying thing of all has yet to be mentioned—the discovery that I had not yet got fully clear of the habit of masturbation. I had, indeed, repudiated it as far as my conscious waking moments were concerned, even though strongly impelled by sexual desire; but one night, about a year after I had relinquished the practice, I found myself again giving way to it in those moments between sleeping and waking when the will is only semiconscious. It was as if a race took place for wakefulness between my physical instinct, on the one side, and my moral sense and inhibitory nerves on the other; and very frequently the physical instinct won. This, perhaps, is not an uncommon experience, but it distressed me greatly; and I never felt safe from it until marriage. I resorted to various expedients to combat this tendency, at length having to tie myself in a certain position every night with a cord round my legs, so as to render it impossible to turn over upon my face.

"In my early manhood the strain on my constitution was considerable from causes other than the sexual neurasthenia, which, indeed, I am now well aware I exaggerated in importance. Medical advisers whom I consulted in that period assured me that this was so; and, though at the time I often thought that they were concealing the real facts from me out of kindliness, my own reading has since convinced me that they spoke nothing but scientific truth.

"The years went on. I went through a university course, and in spite of my poor health took a good degree. The agony of my struggle for chastity seemed to come to a climax about four years later when for a long period, partly owing to overstudy and partly to the sexual strain, I fell into a condition of severe nervous exhaustion, one of the most distressing symptoms of which was insomnia. The dreaded cloud of insanity seemed to come closer. I had to use alcohol freely at nights; and might by now have become a drunkard, had I not been casually—or I must say, Providentially—directed to the common sense plan of measuring my whisky in a dram glass; so that the alcohol could not steal a march upon me.

"This period was one of acute mental suffering. One cause of the nervous tension was—as I have now no doubt—the need of healthy sexual intercourse. I proved this eventually. My circumstances, which had long been adverse to marriage, at length were shaped in that direction. I renewed acquaintance with a lady whom I had known well some years before; and our friendship ripened until, after much perplexity on my side, owing to the uncertainty of my health and prospects, I decided that it was right to speak. We were married after a few months; and I realized that I had gained an excellent wife. We did not come together sexually for some nights after marriage; but, having once tasted the pleasure of the marriage bed, I have to admit that, partly owing to ignorance of the hygiene of marriage, I was for some time rather unrestrained in conjugal relations, requiring intercourse as often as eight or nine times a month. This was not unnatural when one considers that I had now for the first time free access to a woman, after a long and weary struggle to preserve chastity. Married life, however, tends naturally—or did so in my case—to regulate desire; and when I began to understand the ethics and hygiene of sex, as I did a year or two after marriage, I was enabled to exercise increasing self-restraint. We are now sparing in our enjoyment of conjugal pleasure. We have had no children; and I attribute this chiefly to the remaining sexual weakness in myself.[1] But I may say that not only my sexual power, but my nerve-power and general health, were greatly improved by marriage; and though I have fallen back, the last year or two, into a poor state of health, the cause of this is probably overwork rather than anything to do with sex. Not but what it must be said that, had it not been for the juvenile masturbation superadded to a neuropathic temperament, my constitution would no doubt have endured

---

[1] On having connection with my wife I frequently exhibit sufficient sexual power to produce orgasm in her; but on occasion, especially during the first year or so of married life, I have been unable to do this, owing to the too rapid action of the reflexes in myself, and have even, now and again, had emissions *ante portam.*

the general strain of life better than it has done. The algolagnia, being one of the congenital conditions of my sexual instinct, must be considered fundamental, and certainly has not been eliminated. If I were to allow myself indulgence in algolagnic reveries they would even now excite me without difficulty; but I have systematically discouraged them, so that they give me iittle or no practical trouble. My erotic dreams, which years ago were (to the best of my remembrance) frequently algolagnic, are now almost invariably normal.

"My conjugal relations have always been on the lines of strictly normal sexuality. I have a deep sense of the obligations of monogamous marriage, besides a sincere affection for my wife; consequently I repress as far as possible all sexual inclinations, such as will come involuntarily sometimes, toward other women.

"From what I have disclosed, it will be seen that I am but a frail man; but for many years I have striven honestly and hard to discipline sexuality within myself, and to regulate it according to right reason, pure hygiene, and the moral law; and I can but hope and believe that the Divine Power in which I have endeavored to trust will in the future, as it has done in the past, working by natural methods and through the current events of my life, amend and control my sex life and conduct it to safe and honorable issues."

HISTORY II.—A. B., married, good general health, dark hair, fair complexion, short-sighted, and below medium height. Parents both belong to healthy families, but the mother suffered from nerves during early years of married life, and the father, a very energetic and ambitious man, was cold, passionless, and unscrupulous. A. B. is the oldest child; two of the brothers and sisters are slightly abnormal, nervously. But, so far as is known, none of the family has ever been sexually abnormal.

A. B. was a bright, intelligent child, though inclined to be melancholy (and in later years prone to self-analysis). At preparatory school was fairly forward in studies, at public school somewhat backward, at University suddenly took a liking to intellectual pursuits. Throughout he was slack at games. Has never been able to learn to swim from nervousness. Can whistle well. Has always been fond of reading, and would like to have been an author by profession. He married at 24, and has had two children, both of whom showed congenital physical abnormalities.

Before the age of 7 or 8 A. B. can remember various trifling incidents. "One of the games I used to play with my sister," he writes, "consisted in pretending we were 'father and mother' and were relieving ourselves at the w. c. We would squat down in various parts of the room, prolong the simulated act, and talk. I do not remember what our conversation was about, nor whether I had an erection.

I used also to make water from a balcony into the garden, and in other unusual places.

"The first occasion on which I can recollect experiencing sensations or emotions similar in character to later and more developed feelings of desire was at the age of about 7 or 8, when I was a day-boy at a large school in a country town and absolutely innocent as to deed, thought, or knowledge. I fell in love with a boy with whom I was brought in contact in my class, about my own age. I remember thinking him pretty. He paid me no attention. I had no distinct desire, except a wish to be near him, to touch him, and to kiss him. I blushed if I suddenly saw him, and thought of him when absent and speculated on my chances of seeing him again. I was put into a state of high ecstasy when he invited me to join him and some friends one summer evening in a game of rounders.

"At the age of 8 I was told by my father's groom where babies came from and how they were produced. (I already knew the difference in sexual organs, as my sister and I were bathed in the same room.) He told me no details about erection, semen, etc. Nor did he take any liberties with me. I used to notice him urinating; he used to push back the foreskin and I thought his penis large.

"When about 8 years old the nursemaid told me that the boy at her last place had intercourse with his sister. I thought it disgusting. About a year later I told the nurse I thought the story of Adam and Eve was not true and that when Eve gave Adam the apple he had intercourse with her and she was punished by having children. I don't know if I had thought this out, or if it had been suggested to me by others. This nurse used often to talk about my 'tassel.'

"A family of several brothers went to the same school with me, and we used to indulge in dirty stories, chiefly, however, of the w. c. type rather than sexual.

"When I was about 10 I learned much from my father's coachman. He used to talk about the girls he had had intercourse with, and how he would have liked this with my nursemaid.

"A year later I went to a large day school. I think most of the boys, if not nearly all, were very ignorant and innocent in sexual matters. The only incident in this connection I can recollect is asking a boy to let me see his penis; he did so.

"During the summer holidays, at a watering place I attended a theatrical performance and fell in love with a girl of about 12 who acted a part. I bought a photograph of her, which I kept and kissed for several years after. About the same time I thought rather tenderly of a girl of my own age whose parents knew mine. I remember feeling that I should like to kiss her. Once I furtively touched her hair.

"When I was 12 I was sent to a small preparatory boarding school, in the country. During the holidays I used to talk about sexual things with my father's footman. He must have told me a good deal. I used to have erections. One evening, when I was in bed and everyone else out (my mother and the children in the country) he came up to my room and tried to put his hand on my penis. I had been thinking of sexual matters and had an erection. I resisted, but he persisted, and when he succeeded in touching me I gave in. He then proceeded to masturbate me. I sank back, overcome by the pleasant sensation. He then stopped and I went on myself. In the meantime he had taken out his penis and masturbated himself before me until the orgasm occurred. I was disgusted at the sight of his large organ and the semen. He then left me. I could hardly sleep from excitement. I felt I had been initiated into a great and delightful mystery.

"I at once fell into the habit of masturbation. It was some months before I could produce the orgasm; at about 13 a slight froth came; at about 14 a little semen. I do not know how frequently I did it—perhaps once or twice a week. I used to feel ashamed of myself afterward. I told the man I was doing it and he expressed surprise I had not known about it before he told me. He warned me to stop doing it or it would injure my health. I pretended later that I had stopped doing it.

"I practiced solitary masturbation for some months. At first the semen was small in amount and watery.

"I had not at this time ever succeeded in drawing the foreskin below the 'corona.' After masturbation I would sometimes feel local pain in the penis, sometimes pains in the testicles, and generally a feeling of shame, but not, I think, any lassitude. The shame was a vague sense of discomfort at having done what I knew others would regard as dirty. I also experienced fears that I was injuring my health.

"It was not long before I found a few other boys at the preparatory school with whom I talked of sexual things and in some cases proceeded to acts. The boys were between the ages of 9 and 14; they left at 14 or 15 for the public schools. We slept in bedrooms—several in one room.

"There was no general conversation on sexual matters. Few of the boys knew anything about things—perhaps 7 or 8 out of 40. Before describing my experiences at the school I may mention that I cannot remember having at this period any wish to experience heterosexual intercourse; I knew as yet nothing of homosexual practices; and I did not have, except in one case, any love or affection for any of the boys.

"One night, in my bedroom—there were about six of us—we were talking till rather late. My recollection commences with being aware that all the boys were asleep except myself and one other, P. (the son of a clergyman), who was in a bed at exactly the opposite end of the room. I suppose we must have been talking about this sort of thing, for I vividly remember having an erection, and suddenly—as if by premonition—getting out of my bed, and, with heart beating, going softly over to P.'s bed. He exhibited no surprise at my presence; a few whispered words took place; I placed my hand on his penis, and found he had an erection. I started masturbating him, but he said he had just finished. I then suggested getting into bed with him. (I had never heard at that time of such a thing being done, the idea arose spontaneously.) He said it was not safe, and placed his hand on my penis, I think with the object of satisfying and getting rid of me. He masturbated me till the orgasm occurred.

"I had no further relations with him, except on one occasion, shortly afterward, when one day, in the w. c. he asked me to masturbate him. I did so. He did not offer to do the same to me.

"He was a delicate, feeble boy; not good at work; womanish in his ways; inclined to go in for petty bullying, until a boy showed fight, when he discovered himself to be an arrant coward. Four or five years later I met him at the university. His greeting was cool. My next affair was with a boy who was about my age (13), strong, full-blooded, coarse, always in 'hot water.' He was the son of the headmaster of one of the best-known public schools. It was reported that two brothers had been expelled from this public school for what we called 'beastliness.' He told me his older brother used to have intercrural intercourse with him. This was the first I had heard of this. We used to masturbate mutually. I had, however, no affection or desire for him.

"With E., another boy, I had no relations, but I remember him as the first person of the same sex for whom I experienced love. He was a small, fair, thin, and little boy, some two years younger than myself, so my inferior in the social hierarchy of a school.

"At the end of my last term I had two disappointments. I was beaten by a younger and clever boy for the first place in the school, and also beaten by one point in the competition for the Athletic Cup by a stronger boy who had only come to the school that very term. However, as a consolation prize, and as I was leaving, the headmaster gave me a second prize. This soothed my hurt feelings, and I remember, just after the 'head' had read out the prizes, on the last day of term, E., coming up to me, putting his arm on my shoulder, looking at me rather pensively, and in a voice that thrilled me and made me wish to kiss and hug him, tell me he was so glad I had got a prize and that it was a shame that other chap had beaten me for the cup.

"I was three years (aged 12 to 15) at the preparatory school. I started in the bottom form and ended second in the school. My reports were generally good, and I was keen to do well in work. I was considerably influenced by the 'head.' He was a clergyman, but a man of wide reading, broad opinion, great scholarship, and great enthusiasm. We became very friendly.

"During the holidays I now first practiced intercrural intercourse with a younger brother. I started touching his penis, and causing erections, when he was about 5. Afterward I got him to masturbate me and I masturbated him; I used to get him into bed with me. On one occasion I spontaneously (never having heard of such a thing) made him take my penis in his mouth.

"This went on for several years. When I was about 16 and he about 10, the old family nurse spoke to me about it. She told me he had complained of my doing it. I was in great fear that my parents might hear of it. I went to him; told him I was sorry, but I had not understood he disliked it, but that I would not do it again.

"About a year later (having persisted in this promise) I made overtures to him, but he refused. I then commended his conduct, and said I knew he was quite right, and begged him to refuse again if I should ever suggest it. I did not ever suggest it again. For many years I bitterly reproached myself for having corrupted him. However, I do not think any harm has been done him. But my self-reproaches have caused me to feel I owe some reparation to him. I also have more affection for him than for my other brothers and sisters.

"At the age of 15 I went to one of the large public schools. I was fairly forward for my age, and entered high. But I made small progress. I had bad reports; I was 'slack in games,' and not popular among the boys. In fact, I stood still, so that when I left I was backward in comparison with other boys of even less natural intelligence.

"The teaching was certainly bad. Moreover, I had not any friends, and this made me very sensitive. It was to a great extent my fault. When I first went there I was taken up by a set above me—boys who were 'senior' to me in standing. When they left I found myself alone.

"My unpopularity was increased by my being considered to put on 'side'; also because I paid attention to my dress.

"At the public school I had homosexual relations with various boys, usually without any passion. With one boy, however, I was deeply in love for over a year; I thought of him, dreamed of him, would have been content only to kiss him. But my courtship met with no success.

"When carrying on with other boys the desire to reach the crisis was not always strong, perhaps out of shyness or modesty. Occasionally I had intercrural connection, which gave me the first intimation of what intercourse with a woman was like. When I masturbated in solitude I used to continue till the orgasm.

"My housemaster one day sent for me and said he had walked through my cubicle and noticed a stain on the sheet. At this time I used to have nocturnal emissions. I cannot remember whether on this occasion the stain was due to one, or to masturbation. But I imagined that one did not have 'wet dreams' unless one masturbated. So when he went on to say that this was a proof that I was immoral I acknowledged I masturbated. He then told me I would injure my health—possibly 'weaken my heart,' or 'send myself mad'; he said that he would ask me to promise never to do it again.

"I promised. I left humiliated and ashamed of myself; also generally frightened. He used to send for me every now and then, and ask me if I had kept my promise. For some months I did. Then I relapsed, and told him when he asked me. Ultimately he ceased sending for me—apparently convinced either that I was cured or that I was incorrigible.

"A year or so afterward he discovered in my study (for I was now in the upper school and had a study) a French photograph that a boy had given me, entitled '*Qui est dans ma chambre?*' It represented a man going by mistake into the wrong bedroom; inside the room was a woman, in nightdress, in an attitude that suggested she had just been relieving herself. My housemaster told me the picture was terribly indecent, and that, taken with what he knew of my habits, it showed I was not a safe boy to be in the school. He added that he did not wish to make trouble at home, but that he advised me to get my parents to remove me at the end of that term, instead of the following term, when, in the ordinary course of things, I should have left.

"I wrote to my people to say I was miserable at school, and I was removed at the end of that term.

"My first case of true heterosexual passion was with a girl called D., whom I first knew when she was about 16. My family and hers were friendly. My attraction to her soon became a matter of common knowledge and joking to members of my family. She was a dark, passionate-looking child, with large eyes that—to me—seemed full of an inner knowledge of sexual mysteries. Precocious, vain, jealous, untruthful—those were qualities in her that I myself soon recognized. But the very fact that she was not conventionally 'goody-goody' proved an attraction to me.

"I never openly made love to her, but I delighted to be near her. Our ages were sufficiently separated for this to be noticeable. I dreamed of her, and my highest ideal of blessedness was to kiss her and tell her I loved her. I heard that she had been discovered talking indecently in a w. c. to some little boys, sons of a friend of my family's. The knowledge of this precocity on her part intensified my fascination for her.

"When I left home to return to school I kissed her—the only time. Absence did nothing to diminish my affection. I thought of her all day long, at work or at play. I wrote her a letter—not openly passionate, but my real feelings toward her must have been apparent. I found out afterward that her mother opened the letter.

"When I returned home for the holidays her mother asked me not to write her any letters and not to pay attentions to her, as I might 'spoil her.' I promised. I was, of course, greatly distressed.

"D. used to come to our house to see my younger sister. She had clearly been warned by her mother not to allow me to speak to her. I was too nervous to make any advances; besides, I had promised. As I grew older, my passion died out. I have hardly ever seen her since. She married some years ago. I still retain sentimental feelings toward her.

"I was now 18; I had stopped growing and was fairly broad and healthy. Intellectually I was rather precocious, though not ambitious. But I was no good at games, had no tastes for physical exercises, and no hobbies.

"During the holidays, in my last year at school, I had gone to the Royal Aquarium with a school companion. This was followed by one or two visits to the Empire Theatre. It was then that I first discovered that sexual intercourse took place outside the limits of married life. On one occasion my friend talked to one of the women who were walking about. This same friend spoke to a prostitute at Oxford. (At this time I went up to the university.) Once or twice I met this girl. She used to ask about my friend. My feelings toward her were a combination of admiration for her physical beauty, a sense of the 'mystery' of her life, and pity for her isolated position.

"On the whole, my first university term produced considerable improvement in me. I began to be interested in my work and to read a fair amount of general literature. I learned to bicycle and to row. I also made one intimate friend.

"In my first holiday I went to the Empire and made the acquaintance of a girl there, W. H. She attracted me by her quiet appearance. I eventually made arrangements to pay her a visit. My apprehensions consisted of: 1. Fear of catching venereal disease. This I decided to safeguard by using a 'French letter.' 2. Fear that she might have a 'bully.'

"The girl showed no sexual desire; but at that time this did not attract my attention.

"I got very much 'gone' on her, paid her several visits, gave her some presents I could ill afford, and felt very distressed when she informed me she was to be married and therefore could not see me any more.

"My experiences with prostitutes cover a period of twelve years. During three years of this period I was continually in their company. I have had intercourse with some two dozen; in some cases only once; in others on numerous occasions. They have usually been of the class that frequent Piccadilly, St. James Restaurant, the Continental Hotel, and the Dancing Clubs. Usual fee, £2 for the night; in one case, £5.

"1. Not one of them, as far as I knew, was a drunkard.

"2. As a rule, they were not mercenary or dishonest.

"3. In their language and general behavior they compared favorably with respectable women.

"4. I never caught venereal disease.

"5. I twice caught pediculi.

"6. I did not find them, as a rule, very sensual or fond of indecent talk. As a rule, they objected to stripping naked; they did not touch my organs; they did not suggest masturbation, sodomy, or *fellatio*. They seldom exhibited transports, but the better among them seemed sentimental and affectionate.

"7. Their accounts of their first fall were nearly always the same. They got to know a 'gentleman,' often by his addressing them in the street; he took them about to dinners and theatres; they were quite innocent and even ignorant; on one occasion they drank too much; and before they knew what was happening they were no longer virgins. They do not, however, apparently round on the man or expose him or refuse to have anything more to do with him.

"8. They state—in common with the outwardly 'respectable' women whom I have had a chance of catechising—that before the first intercourse they did not feel any conscious desire for intercourse and hardly devoted any thought to it, that it was very painful the first time, and that some time elapsed before they commenced to derive pleasure from it or to experience the orgasm.

"E. B. was the second woman I had intercourse with. She was a prostitute, but very young (about 18) and had only been in London a few months. I met her first in the St. James Restaurant. I spoke a few words to her. The next day I saw her in the Burlington Arcade. I was not much attracted to her; she was pretty, in a coarse, buxom style; vulgar in manners, voice, and dress. She asked me to go home with her; I refused. She pressed me; I said I had no money. She still urged me, just to drive home with her and talk to her while she dressed for the evening. I consented. We drove to lodgings in Albany Street. We went in. She proceeded to kiss me. I remained cold, and told her again I had no money. She then said: 'That does not matter. You remind me of a boy I love. I want you ꜰ ꜰ my fancy boy.' I was flattered by this. I saw a good deal of her. She was sentimental. I never gave her any money. When I had some, she refused to take it, but allowed me to spend a little in buying her a present. On the night before I left London she wept. She wrote me illiterate, but affectionate letters. One day she wrote to me that she was to be kept by a man, but that she had made it a condition with him that she should be allowed to have me. I had never been in love with her, because of her vulgarity. I therefore took the earliest opportunity of letting matters cool, by not writing often, etc. The next thing I remember was my fascination, a few months later, for S. H.

"She was not a regular prostitute. She had taken a very minor part in light opera. She was American by birth, young, slim, and spoke like a lady. Her hair was dyed; her breasts padded. She acted sentiment, but was less affectionate than E. B. I met her when she was out of a job. I gave her £2 whenever I met her. She was not mercenary. She was sensual. I became very much in love with her. I discovered her, however, writing letters to a fellow whom I had met one day when I was walking with her. He was only an acquaintance, but the brother of my most intimate friend. What I objected to was that in this letter to him she protested she did not care for me, but could not afford to give me up. She had to plead guilty, but I was so fascinated by her I still kept in with her, for a time, until she was kept by a man, and I had found other women to interest me.

"Owing to the strict regulations made by the university authorities, prostitutes find it hard to make a living there, and I never had anything to do with one. My adventures were among the shopgirl class, and were of a comparatively innocent nature. One of them, however, M. S., a very undemonstrative shopgirl, was the only girl not a prostitute with whom I had so far had intercourse.

"About this time I made the acquaintance of three other prostitutes, who, however, were nice, gentle, quiet girls, neither vulgar nor mercenary. A night passed with them always meant to me much more than mere intercourse. They were—especially two of them—of a sentimental nature, and would go to sleep in my arms. There was, on my part, not any passion, but a certain sympathy with them, and pity and affection. I remained faithful to the first, J. H., until she was kept by a man, and gave up her gentlemen friends. Then came D. V. She got in the family way and left London. Last, M. P. She was not pretty, but a good figure, well dressed, a bright conversationalist, and an intelligent mind. Her regular price for the night was £5, but when she got to know one she would take one for less and take one 'on tick.' She was very sensual. On one occasion, between 11 P.M. and about midday the following day I experienced the orgasm eleven or twelve times.

"During term time I was often prevented from having women by want of money and absence from London. I considered myself lucky if I could have a woman once or twice a month. My allowance was not large enough to admit of such luxuries; and I was only able to do what I did by being economical in my general expenditure and living, and by running up bills for whatever I could get on credit. I lived in the hopes of picking up 'amateurs' who would give me what I wanted for the love of it and without payment. My efforts were not very successful at present, except in the case of M. S. I considered myself very lucky in having discovered her, and I should have stuck to her for longer but for the rival attraction of another. There was, however, no deep sentiment on either side.

"But in order to preserve a continuity in my account of the women, I have left out two cases of temporary reversion to homosexual practices. During the periods when I could not get a woman I had recourse once more to masturbation. At times I had 'wet dreams' in which boys figured; and my thoughts, in waking hours, sometimes reverted to memories of my school experiences. I think, however, that I should have preferred a woman."

The homosexual reversions were as follows:—

"1. I had arranged to meet a shopgirl one evening, outside the town. She did not turn up. The meeting place was a railway bridge. Waiting there too, a few feet from me, was a boy of about 15. He was employed (I afterward found) by a gardener, and was waiting to meet his brother, who was engaged on the line. I got into casual conversation with him, and suddenly found myself wondering whether he ever masturbated. With a feeling, that I can only describe by calling it an intuition, I moved nearer him, and asked: 'Do you ever play with yourself?' He did not seem surprised at the abruptness of my question. and answered 'yes.' I thereupon touched his penis, and *found he had an erection!* I suggested retiring to a bench that was near. We sat down. I masturbated him till he experienced the orgasm; then intercrurally. I gave him a shilling, and said good night.

"2. During my last summer at the university I took to gardening. There was a small piece of garden behind the house in which I had lodgings. My landlady suggested getting a cousin of hers, employed by a nurseryman, to supply me with plants, etc. He was a youth of about 16 or 17, tall, dark, not bad favored in looks. I forget how many times I saw him—not many, perhaps twice or thrice; but one day, when he came to see me in my room, about something connected with the garden, I gave him some old clothes of mine. He was a great deal taller than myself, and I suggested his trying on the trousers to see if they would fit. I do not know whether I made this suggestion with any ulterior motive or whether I had ever before thought of him in connection with any sexual relations. I only know that once more, as if guided by instinet, I felt he would not rebuff me, although certainly no indecent talk had ever taken place between us. I pretended to help him to pull up the trousers, and let my hand touch his penis. He did not resist; and I felt his penis for a few seeonds. I then proposed he should eome upstairs to my bedroom. No one was in the house. We went up. He did not at first have an erection. I asked why. He said 'because you are strange to me.' He then felt my penis. Eventually we mutually masturbated one another. I gave him half a erown.

"Some short time afterward he eame again to the house. On this oceasion I attempted *fellatio*. I don't think I had at that time ever heard of such a practice. He said, however, he did not like it. He masturbated interrerurally. He said he had never done this before, although he had had girls. (The other boy also told me he had had girls.)

"3. On another oecasion I was out bicyeling. A boy, of about 10 years of age, offered me a bunch of violets for a penny. I told him I would give him a shilling to pick me a large buneh. I am not sure if I had any ulterior motive. He proceeded into a wood on the side of the road; I dismounted from my machine and followed him. He was a pretty, dark boy. He made water. I went up to him and asked him to let me feel his penis. He at once jumped away, and ran off shrieking. I was frightened, mounted my bicycle, and rode as fast as I eould home.

"There was no sentiment in the above cases. It is also to be noted that in neither instance did I make any arrangements to see the person again. As far as I can remember, when once I was satisfied I felt disgust for my aet. In the case of women this was never so.

"Two of the women described in the foregoing pages stand out above the others. Perhaps I have not sufficiently shown that in the cases of W. H. and S. H. I felt a considerable degree of *passion*. W. H. was the first woman with whom I had had intercourse; this invested her in my heart, with a peculiar sentiment. In neither case can I be accused of fickleness. Indeed, I may say that up to this time I had had no opportunity of being fickle. I never saw enough, or had enough, of a woman to get a surfeit of her.

"The ease I now come to presents the features of the cases of W. H. and S. H. in a stronger form. I was then 20; I have since then married; I am a father; my experiences have been many and varied; but still I must confess that no other woman has ever stirred my emotions more than—I doubt if as much as—D. C. Up to date, if there has been any grand passion in my life, it is my love for her. D. C., when I got to know her—by talking to her in the street—was a girl of about 20. She was short and plump; dark hair; dark, mischievous eyes; a fair complexion; small features; quiet manners, and a sensual *ensemble*. I do not know what her father was. He was dead, her mother kept a University lodging house. She spoke and behaved like a lady. She dressed quietly; was absolutely unmercenary; her intelligence—*i.e.*, her intellectual calibre—was not great. Her master-passion was one thing. The first evening I walked out with her she put her hand down on my penis, before I had even kissed her, and proposed intercourse. I was surprised, almost embarrassed; she herself led me to a wall, and standing up made me do it.

"Next day we went away for the day together. I may say she was *always* ready and never satisfied. She was sensual rather than sentimental. She was ready to shower her favors anywhere and to anyone. My feelings toward her soon became affectionate and sentimental, and then passionate. I thought of nothing else all day long; wrote her long letters daily; simply lived to see her.

"I found she was engaged to be married. Her *fiancé*, a schoolmaster, himself used to have intercourse with her, but he had taken a religious turn and thought it was wicked to do it until they married. I had intercourse with her on every possible occasion: in private rooms at hotels, in railway carriages, in a field, against a wall, and—when the holidays came—she stayed a night with me in London. She had apparently no fear of getting in the family way, and never used any precaution. Sensual as she was, she did not show her feelings by outward demonstration.

"On one occasion she proposed *fellatio*. She said she had done it to her *fiancé* and liked it. This is the only case I have known of a woman wishing to do it for the love of it.

"The emotional tension on my nerves—the continual jealousy I was in, the knowledge that before long she would marry and we must part—eventually caused me to get ill. She never told me she loved me more than any other man; yet, owing to my importunity, she saw much more of me than anyone else. It came to the ears of her *fiancé* that she was in my company a great deal; there was a meeting of the three of us—convened at his wish—at which she had formally, before him, to say 'good-bye' to me. Yet we still continued to meet and to have intercourse.

Then the date of her marriage drew near. She wrote me saying that she could not see me any more. I forced myself, however, on her, and our relations still continued. Her elder sister interviewed me and said she would inform the authorities unless I gave her up; a brother, too, came to see me and made a row.

"I had what I seriously intended to be a last meeting with her. But after that she came up to London to see me, we went to a hotel together. We arranged to see one another again, but she did not write. I had now left the university. I heard she was married.

"It was now four years since I had first had intercourse with a woman. During this time I was almost continually under the influence, either of a definite love affair or of a general lasciviousness and desire for intercourse with women. My character and life were naturally affected by this. My studies were interfered with; I had bcome extravagant and had run into debt. It is worthy of note that I had never up to this time considered the desirability of marriage. This was perhaps chiefly because I had no means to marry. But even in the midst of my love affairs I always retained sufficient sense to criticise the moral and intellectual calibre of the women 1 loved, and I held strong views on the advisability of mental and moral sympathies and congenial tastes existing between people who married. In my amors I had hitherto found no intellectual equality or sympathies. My passion for D. C. was prompted by (1) the bond that sexual intercourse with a woman has nearly always produced in my feelings, (2) her physical beauty, (3) that she was sensual, (4) that she was a lady, (5) that she was young, (6)that she was not mercenary. It was kept alive by the obstacles in the way of my seeing her enough and by her engagement to another.

"The D. C. affair left me worn out emotionally. I reviewed my life of the last four ycars. It seemed to show much more heartache, anxiety, and suffering than pleasure. I concluded that this unsatisfactory result was inseparable from the pursuit of illegitimate amors. I saw that my work had been interfered with, and that I was in debt, owing to the same cause. Yet I felt that I could never do without a woman. In this quandary I found myself thinking that marriage was the only salvation for me. Then 1 should always have a woman by me. I was sufficiently sensible to know that unless there were congenial tastes and sympathies, a marriage could not turn out happily, especially as my chief interests in life (after woman) were literature, history, and philosophy. But I imagined that if I could find a girl who would satisfy the condition of being an intellectual companion to me, all my troubles would be over; my sexual desire would be satisfied, and I could devote myself to work.

"In this frame of mind I turned my thoughts more seriously in the direction of a girl whom I had known for some two years. Her age was nearly the same as mine. My family and hers were acquainted with one another. I had established a platonic friendship with her. Undoubtedly the prime attraction was that she was young and pretty. But she was also a girl of considerable character. Without being as well educated as I was, she was above the average girl in general intelligence. She was fond of reading; books formed our chief subject of conversation and common interest. She was, in fact, a girl of more intelligence than I had yet encountered. On her side, as I afterward discovered, the interest in me was less purely platonic. Our relations toward one another were absolutely correct. Yet we were intimate, informal, and talked on subjects that would be considered forbidden topics between two young persons by most people. I felt she was a true friend. She, too, confided to me her troubles.

"We corresponded with one another frequently. Sometimes it occurred to me that it was rather strange she should be so keen to write to me, to hear from me, and to see me; but I had never thought of her, consciously, except as a friend; I never for a moment imagined she thought of me except as an interesting and intelligent friend. Nor did the idea of illicit love ever suggest itself to me. She was one of those women whose face and expression put aside any such thought. I was, indeed, inclined to regard her as a good influence on me, but as passionless. I confided to her the affair of D. C., which took place during our acquaintance. She was distressed, but sympathetic and not prudish. I did not suspect the cause of her distress; I thought it was owing to her disappointment in the ideals she had formed of me. She invited me to join her and her family for a part of the summer (I had now left the university, having obtained my degree in low honors) and I decided to join them. At this stage there began to impress itself on my mind the possibility that she cared for me; also the desirability, if that were so, of becoming engaged to her. I found my feelings became warmer. On several occasions we found ourselves alone. Then, one day, our talk became more personal, more tender; and I kissed her. I do recollect distinctly the thought flashing through my mind, as she allowed me to kiss her, that she was not after all the passionless and 'straight' girl I had thought. But the idea must have been a very temporary one; it did not return; she declared her love for me; and without any express 'proposal' on my part we walked home that afternoon mutually taking it for granted that we were engaged. I was happy, and calmly happy; proud and elated.

"Circumstances now made it necessary for me to make money for myself and I was forced to enter a profession for which I had never felt any attraction; indeed, I had never considered the possibility of it, until I became engaged, and saw I must support myself if I were ever to marry. I worked hard, and rapidly improved my position.

"I think I am correct in stating that from the day I became engaged my sexual troubles seemed to have ceased. My thoughts and passions were centred on one woman. We wrote to one another twice every week, and as far as I was concerned every thought and feeling I had I told her, and the receipt of her letters was for me the event of my life for nearly three years. My anxiety in connection with my work used up a great deal of my energy, and, although I looked forward to the time when I should have a woman at my side every night, my sexual desires were in abeyance. Nor did I feel any desire or temptation for other women.

"I masturbated, but not frequently. Generally I did it to the accompaniment of images or scenes associated with my betrothed, sometimes the act was purely auto-erotic. My leisure time was devoted to reading.

"On only one occasion did I have intercourse with a woman during my engagement (three years); it was with a girl whose acquaintance I had made at the university and who asked me to come to see her.

"I married at the age of 24. Looking back on the early days of my married life it is now a matter of surprise to me that I was so far from exhibiting the transports of passion which since then have accompanied any intercourse with a new woman. Partly I was frightened of shocking her; partly my three years of comparative abstinence had chastened me. It was some weeks before I ever saw my wife entirely naked; I never touched her parts with my hand for many months; and after the first few weeks I did not have intercourse with her frequently.

"Perhaps this was to be expected. The basis of my affection for her had always been a moral or mental one rather than physical, although she was a handsome, well-made girl. Besides, money and other worries kept my thoughts busy, as well as struggles to make both ends meet.

"Indeed, I may say my sexual nature seemed to be dying out. When I had been married less than six months I discovered that sexual intercourse with my wife no longer meant what sexual intercourse used to mean—no excitement or exaltation or ecstasy. My wife perhaps contributed to this by her attitude. She confessed afterward to me that for the first week or so she positively dreaded bedtime, so physically painful was intercourse to her; that it was many weeks, if not months, before she experienced the orgasm. For the first year and more of marriage she could not endure touching my penis. This at first disappointed me; then annoyed and finally almost disgusted me.

"Later on, she learned to experience the orgasm. But she was very undemonstrative during the act, and it was seldom that the orgasm occurred simultaneously; she took a much longer time.

"I ceased to think about sexual matters. When I had been married about three years I was aware that, in my case, marriage meant the loss of all mad ecstasy in the act. I knew that if I had no work to do, and plenty of money, and temptation came my way, I should like to have another woman. But there was no particular woman to enchain my fancy and I did not have time or money or inclination to hunt for one.

"At times I masturbated. Sometimes I did this to the accompaniment of homosexual desires or memories of the past. Then I got my wife to masturbate me.

"About four years after my marriage I got a woman from Piccadilly Circus to do *fellatio*. I had never had this done before. She did not do it genuinely, but used her fingers.

"As stated above various anxieties, the fact that I could always satisfy my physical desires, all served to calm me. I was also interested in my work and had become ambitious to improve my position and was very energetic.

"On the whole, notwithstanding money worries, the first four or five years of my married life were the happiest in my life. Certainly I was very free from sexual desires; and the general effect of marriage was to make me economical, energetic, ambitious, and unselfish. I was certainly overworked. I seldom got to bed before 1 or 2; my meals were irregular; and I became worried and nervous. At the beginning of my fifth year of married life I got run down, and had a severe illness, and at one time my life was in danger, but I had a fairly rapid convalescence.

"My illness was critical, in more senses than one. My convalescence was accompanied by a remarkable recrudescence of my sexual feelings. I will trace this in detail: 1. As I got well—but while still in bed—I found myself experiencing, almost continually, violent erections. These were at first of an auto-erotic character, and I masturbated myself, thus gaining relief to my nerves. 2. I also found my thoughts tending toward sexual images, and I felt a desire toward my nurse. I first became conscious of this when I noticed that I experienced an erection during the time that she was washing me. I mentioned the matter to my doctor, who told me not to worry, and said the symptoms were usual in the circumstances. 3. When I got up and about I found myself desiring very keenly to have intercourse with my wife. I can almost say that I felt more sexually excited than I had done for four or five years. As soon, however, as I had had intercourse with my wife a few times I felt my desire toward her cease. 4. My thoughts now centered on having a woman to do *fellatio*, and as soon as I was well enough to go out I got a prostitute to do this.

"Just before I was ill my wife had a child, which was born with more than one abnormality. No doubt the shock and worry caused by this got me into a low state and predisposed me to my illness. But the consequences were farther reaching still. The child underwent an operation, and my wife had to take her away into the country for nearly six weeks, so as to give her better air. I was left alone in London, for the first time since my marriage. The worry in connection with the child, and the heavy expenses, served to keep me nervously upset after I had apparently recovered physically from the illness. Once more I found myself thinking about women. As an additional factor in the situation I became friendly with an old college-chum whom I had not seen much of for many years. He lived the life of a fashionable young bachelor and was at the time keeping a woman. The only common interest between us was women. I found myself reverting to the old condition of rampant lust that had been such a curse to me in my university days. Some books he lent me had a decided effect. They gave me erections; and it was on top of the excitement thus engendered that one day I got a woman to do *fellatio*, as already mentioned. Moreover, since my illness, I found all my previous energy and ambition had gone.

"I have stated that I was in London alone with two servants. The housemaid was a young girl; nice looking, with beautiful eyes and a sensual expression. She had been with us for about a year. I cannot remember when I first thought of her in a sexual way. But one evening I suddenly felt a desire for her. I talked to her; I found my voice trembling; I let my hand, as if by accident, touch hers; she did not withdraw it; and in a second I had kissed her. She did not resist. I took her on my knee, and tried to take liberties, which she resisted, and I desisted.

"Next day I kissed her again, and put my hand inside her breasts. The same evening I took her to an exhibition. On the way home, in a hansom cab, I made her masturbate me. This was followed by a feeling of great relief, elation, and *pride*.

"Next morning, when she came up to my bedroom to call me, I kissed and embraced her; she allowed me to take liberties, and, reassuring her by saying I would use a preventive, I had intercourse with her. She flinched somewhat. She then told me she was at her period and that she had never had intercourse with a man before.

"During the next few weeks I found her an adept pupil, though always shy and undemonstrative. I took her to a hotel, and experienced the intensest pleasure I had ever had in undressing her. I had lately heard about *cunnilingus*. I now did it to her. I soon found I experienced very great pleasure in this, as did she. (I had attempted it with my wife, but found it disgusted me.) I also had intercourse *per anum*. (This again was an act I had heard about, but had never been able to regard as pleasurable. But books I had been reading stated it was most pleasant both to man and woman.) She resisted at first, finding it hurt her much; it excited me greatly; and when I had done it in this way several times she herself seemed to like it, especially if I kept my hand on her clitoris at the same time.

"My relations with the housemaid, with whom I cannot pretend that I was in love, were only put an end to by satiety, and when I went away for my holidays I was utterly exhausted. This was, however, only the first of a series of relationships, at least one of which deeply stirred my emotional nature. These experiences, however, it is unnecessary to detail. There have also been occasional homosexual episodes.

"I think I am now in a much healthier condition than I have been for some years. (I assume that it is *not* healthy for all one's thoughts to be always occupied on sexual subjects.) The conclusion I come to is that I can live a normal, healthy life, devoting my thoughts to my work, and finding pleasure in friendship, in my children, in reading, and in other sources of amusement, as long as I can have occasional relations with a young girl—*i.e.*, about once a week. But if this outlet for my sexual emotions is stopped sexual thoughts obsess my brain; I become both useless and miserable.

"I have never regretted my marriage. Not only do I feel that life without a wife and home and children would be miserable, but I entertain feelings of great affection toward my wife. We are well suited to one another; she is a woman of character and intelligence; she looks after my home well, is a sensible and devoted mother, and understands me. I have never met a woman I would have sooner married. We have many tastes and likings in common, and—what is not possible with most women—I can, as a rule, speak to her about my feelings and find a listener who understands.

"On the other hand, all passion and sentiment have died out. It seems to me that this is inevitable. Perhaps it is a good thing this should be so. If men and women remained in the state of erotic excitement they are in when they marry, the business and work of the world would go hang. Unfortunately, in my case this very erotic excitement is the chief thing in life that appeals to me!

"The factors that in my case have produced this death of passion and sentiment are as follows:—

"I. Familiarity. When one is continually in the company of a person all novelty dies out. In the case of husband and wife, the husband sees his wife every day; at all times and seasons; dressed, undressed; ill; good tempered, bad tempered. He sees her wash and perform other functions; he sees her naked whenever he likes; he can have intercourse with her whenever he feels inclined. How can love (as I use the expression—*i.e.*, sexual passion) continue?

"2. Satiety. I am of a 'hot,' sensual disposition, inclined to excess, as far as my health and nerves are concerned. The appetite gets jaded.

"3. Absence of strong sexual reciprocity on the part of my wife. I have referred to this above. She likes intercourse, but she is never outwardly demonstrative. She has naturally a chaste mind. She never is guilty of those little indecencies which affect some men a great deal. She does not like talking of these things; and she tells me that if I died, she would never want to have intercourse again with anyone. At times, especially recently, she has even asked me to have intercourse with her, or to masturbate her; but it is seldom that the orgasm occurs contemporaneously. In this respect she is different from other women I knew, in whom the mere fact that the orgasm was occurring in me at once produced it in them. At the same time I doubt whether even strong sexual reciprocity would have retained my passion for long.

"4. During the early years of our married life money worries caused at times disagreements, reproaches and quarrels. Passion and sentiment are fragile and cannot stand these things.

"5. The fact that I had already had other women diminished the feeling of awe with which many regard the sexual act and the violation of sexual conventions.

"6. Loss of beauty. Loss of figure is, I fear, inseparable from childbearing especially if the woman works hard. We have always had servants, still my wife has always worked hard, at sewing, etc.

"I have stated that I entertain feelings of respect and admiration for my wife. But I almost *loathe* the idea of intercourse with her. I would sooner masturbate, and think of another woman than have intercourse with her. It causes nausea in me to touch her private parts. Yet with other women it affords me mad pleasure to kiss them, every part of their bodies. But my wife still feels for me the love she had when we first married. There lies the tragedy."

The following narrative is a continuation of History XII in the previous volume:—

HISTORY III.—I had become good looking. For a time I knew what it was to have loving looks from every woman I met, and being saner and healthier I would seem to be moving in a divine atmosphere of color and fragrance, pearly teeth and bright eyes. Even the old women with daughters looked at me amiably—married women with challenge and maidens with Paradise in their eyes.

"I was standing one morning at St. Peter's corner, with two young friends, when a girl went by, coming over from the Roman Catholic cathedral. When she had passed she looked back, with that imperious swing that is almost a command, at me, as my friends distinctly admitted. They advised me to follow her; I did so, and she turned a pretty, blushing face and pair of dark gray eyes, with just the kind of eyebrows I liked: brown, very level, rather thick, but long. Her teeth and mouth were perfect, and she spoke with a slight Irish brogue. She let me do all the talking while she took my measure.

God knows what she saw in me! I spoke in an affected manner, I remember, imitating some swell character I had seen on the stage a night or two before, but I was wise enough not to talk too much and to behave myself. She promised to meet me again and made the appointment. She was a school-teacher and engaged to be married to some one else. She meant to amuse herself her own way before she married. The second night I met her she allowed me to kiss her as much as I liked and promised all her favors for the third night. We took a long walk, and in the dark she gave herself to me, but I hurt her so much I had to stop two or three times. She had had connection only once, years before, when at school herself. She was inclined to be sensual, but she was young, fresh, and pretty, and her kisses turned my head. I fell genuinely in love with her and told her so, one night when she was particularly fascinating, with the tears in my eyes; and her face met mine with equal love. The first night or two I had felt no pleasure—whether through years of self-abuse or not I do not know,—but this night my whole being was excited. I met her once and sometimes twice a week and was always thinking of her. My sister saw me looking love-sick one day and I heard her say 'He's in love,' which rather flattered me, and I looked more love-sick and idiotic than ever. It was all wrong and perverted. She continued to meet her *fiancé*, and intended to marry him. We both spoke of 'him' as an adultress speaks of her husband. That high level of tears and childlike joy in our youth and love was never reached again. But I realized her *sex*, her kisses, her presence—after all those years of horror (if she had only known)—more even than the sexual act itself; while she, as time went on, commenced to show a curiosity which I thought desecrating; she liked to examine—to 'let her hand stray,' were her words. Even her beauty seemed impaired some nights and I caught a gleam in her eye and a curve of her lip I thought vulgar. But perhaps the next night I met her she would be as bright as ever.

"I introduced her to my friends, who knew our relations, for I blabbed everything. But she did not mind their knowing and if we met would give them all a kiss, so that I felt I had been rather too profuse in my hospitality, though I still would say: 'Have another one, Bert; I don't mind.' But whatever ass I made of myself she forgave me anything, and was fonder of me every time we met, while I, although I did not know it for a long time, was less fond of her. She knew how to revive my love, however. Some nights she would not meet me, and I would be like a madman. Other nights she would meet me, but not let me raise her dress. She would lie on me, on a moonlit night, and her young face in shadow like a siren's in its frame of hair, merely to kiss me. But what kisses! Slow, cold kisses changing to clinging, passionate ones. She would leave my mouth to look around, as if frightened, and come back, open-mouthed, with a side-contact of lips that brought out unexpected felicities.

"One night her *fiancé* saw us together, and followed me after I left her, but on turning a corner I ran. I ridiculed him to her and despised him. I should have found it difficult to say why. Another night her brother attacked me, and it would have gone hard with me, but Anne pulled me in and banged the door. We were in a friend's house, but her father came around soon and laid a stick about her shoulders, in my presence. I tried to talk big, and said something idiotic about being as good a man as her betrothed, as though my intentions were honorable, which for one brief moment made Anne look at me, paler faced and changed, such a strange glance. But he beat her home, enjoying my rage, and she went away, crying in her hands. I was allowed to go unmolested.

"I soon received a letter from her asking me not to mind and making an appointment, at which she turned up cheerful and unconcerned. She went to confession, and would meet me afterwards; and her faith in that, and the difference of our religions (if I had any religion) would make her seem strange and alien to me at times, even banal. At last our meetings became a mere habit of sensuality, with all charm, and suggestion of better things eliminated. . . .

"I went with my friend George (who shared my room) one afternoon and called at Annie's school; she kept an infants' school of her own. She came to the door herself. It was the first time I had seen her in daylight, and I thought her cheek-bones bigger; she certainly was not so pretty as on the first evening I met her. George had told me he would sleep away if I wanted the room, and when next I met her she promised to come and sleep with me. Before I had always met her on the grass, under trees. She came, and the sight of her young limbs and breasts revived something of my love for her, my better love. But she was insatiable and more sensual every day. One day she came when I was not well, and would not go away disappointed. I had met a very pretty girl about this time, and now resolved to give Annie up, which I did in the cruelest manner, cutting her dead, and refusing to answer her letters and touching messages. I heard that she would cry for hours, but I was harder than adamant. . . .

"I thought myself very much in love with the very pretty girl for whom I had thrown up Annie. She lived with her mother and two sisters, one older than herself, the other a mere child. The eldest sister, a handsome, dark girl like a Spaniard, was not virtuous. She was good natured; too much so, and took her pleasure with several of us, dying, not long after, of consumption. I thought her sister, my girl, was virtuous, and I meant to marry her—some day. At any rate, I saw her mother, who lived in a well-furnished house and was a superior woman.

This did not prevent my trying to seduce her daughter. I did not succeed for a long time, though she did not cease meeting me. The sisters came to see us. I knew, one night, her sister was upstairs with D. and I guessed what they were at, so I suggested to her she should creep up on them for fun. She did so, came back, excited and pale—and gave herself to me. But she was not a virgin and in time I had a glimpse of her unhappy fate and her mother's position. Her father was dead or divorced, and her mother, I believe, was mistress to some wealthy bookmaker. I am not sure, there was always a mystery hanging over the mother, nor am I certain that she connived at her daughter's seduction, but the girl's account was that after some successful Cup day there had been too much champagne drunk all around, and that a man she looked on as a friend came into her bedroom that night when she was *tête montée* and seduced or violated her—whichever word you like to choose. Since then his visits had been frequent until she met me, she said, and if I would be true to her she would be a true wife to me, and I believed her and still believe she meant what she said. But I left Melbourne shortly after this, our letters got few and far between, and ultimately I heard she was married to a young man who had always been in love with her. . . .

"Among the inmates of the boarding house was a 'married' couple who stayed for some time; he was an insignificant, ugly, little, cross-eyed commercial traveler; she was a pretty, little creature who looked as innocent and was as merry as a child; we all vied in paying her attentions and waited on her like slaves, the husband always smiling a cryptic smile. After they had left it was hinted they were not married at all; the oldest hands had been taken in. . . . One afternoon I met Dolly, the commercial traveler's wife, and she stopped and spoke to me. I remembered what I had heard and ventured on some pleasantry at which she laughed, and on my proposing that we should go for a walk she consented. She had left the commercial traveler, it came out in conversation, and we went on talking and walking, one idea only in my mind now: could I detain her till dark? Dolly, who was very pretty indeed, amused herself with me for hours, playing hot and cold, snubbing me one minute, encouraging me with her eyes another. Hour after hour went and she found this game so entertaining that she accompanied me to the park behind the Botanical Gardens, and it was not until it was too late for me to catch a train home that she gave herself to me. In fact, we stayed out the whole of that warm summer night. As the hours went by she told me of her home in London and how she first went wrong. She had been a good girl till one day on an excursion she drank some rum or gin, which seemingly revived some dormant taint of heritage; when she went home that night she fell flat at her mother's feet. Her parents, well-to-do shopkeepers, who had forgiven her several times before, turned her out. She became one man's mistress and then another's. She began early, and was scarcely 19 now. She would leave off the drink for a time and try to be respectable. She loved her father and mother, but she could not help drinking at times. She spoke cheerfully and laughingly about it all; she was young, strong, good natured, and careless. We went to sleep for a little while and then wandered in the early morning down toward the cemetery, when she tried to tidy her hair, asking me how I had enjoyed myself and not waiting for an answer. She was thirsty, she said, and when the public houses opened we went and had a drink. It was the first time I had seen her drink alcohol,—at the boarding house she had always been the picture of health and sweetness,—and I saw a change come over her at once, so that I understood all that she had told me. The sleepless night may have made it worse, but the look that came into her eyes, and the looseness of the fibres not only of her tell-tale wet mouth, but of every muscle of her face was startling and piteous to see. She saw my look and laughed, but her laugh was equally piteous to hear, and when she spoke again her voice had changed too, and was equally piteous. She asked for another. 'No, don't,' I begged, for the pretty girl I had flattered myself I had passed a summer's night with that most young men would envy, showed signs of changing, like some siren, into a flabby, blear-eyed boozer. That hurt my vanity.

"I met her another night and she took me to her lodgings, and I slept with her all night. I no longer tried to stop her drinking, but drank with her. I ceased to treat her with courtesy and gallantry; she noticed it, but only drank the more, drank till she became dirty in her ways, till her good looks vanished. I left her, too drunk to stand, as some friend, a woman, called on her.

"She came to see me once more, like her old self, so well dressed and well behaved, and chatted so cheerfully to my landlady that the latter afterward congratulated me on having such a friend. Dolly carried a parcel of underclothing she had made, with a few toys, for the children of a poor man in the suburbs, and I accompanied her to the house. There was great excitement among the ragged children; in fact, the atmosphere became so dangerously full of love and charity that I commenced to feel uncomfortable,—the shower of roses again,—and was glad to find myself in the open air. We went for a walk and had several drinks, which made the usual change in Dolly. I got tired of her, determined I would leave her, spoke cruelly, and finally—after having connection with her on the dry seaweed—rose and left her brutally, walked away faster and faster, deaf to her remonstrances, and careless whether or how she reached the station. . . .

"I had gone to lodge with a family whom I had been accustomed to visit as a friend; there were two daughters; the elder, engaged to a young German who was away with a survey party, had a rather plain face, but a strong one and was herself a strong character, and I came to like her in spite of myself; the second girl had light golden hair, a fresh complexion, a short nose, and rather large mouth, which contained beautiful teeth; they were both good, obedient, innocent church-going daughters. As there was plenty of amusement there of an evening, singing and dancing, I did not go out, got into better ways, and gradually gave up drinking to excess. I was so improved in appearance that an old acquaintance did not recognize me. My anecdotes and fun amused Mrs. S., the mother of the girls. She could be very violent on occasion, I found, and I learned that there had been terrible scenes at times, and that from time to time it had been necessary to place her in an asylum. I went for drives with the girls and to theatres, and ought to have been happy and glad to find myself in such good quarters. The mother trusted me so entirely that she left me for hours with the girls, the younger one of whom I would kiss sometimes. She was engaged to a young fellow whom I spoke to patronizingly, but whose shoes I was not worthy to fasten. I was the cause of quarrels between them. They made it up again, but I think he noticed the change that was taking place in Alice. For from kissing her I had gone on—all larking at first. We formed the habit of sitting down on the sofa when alone and kissing steadily for ten minutes or more at a time. She was excited without knowing what was the matter with her—but I knew. And one day when our mouths were together I drew her to me and commenced to stroke her legs gently down. She trembled like a string bow, and allowed my hand to go farther. And then she was frightened and ashamed and commenced to laugh and cry together. She had these hysterical attacks several times and they always frightened me. It ended in my seducing her. She broke off her engagement, and then was sorry; but soon she thought only of me. . . . One day Alice and I were nearly caught. I had just left her on the sofa and had commenced drawing at a table with my back to her when suddenly her mother came in without her shoes, while Alice had one hand up her clothes arranging her underclothing. The mother stopped dead and shot me one glance I shall never forget. 'Why, Alice, you frighten me!' she said. I feigned surprise and asked 'What is the matter?' Alice, although she was frightened out of her wits, managed to stammer: 'He couldn't see me—you couldn't see me, could you?' appealing to me. But I had managed to collect my senses a bit and although still under that maternal eye I asked,—at last turning slowly around to Alice: 'See? What do you mean? See what?' And I looked so mystified that the mother was deceived, and contented herself with scolding Alice and telling her to run no risks of that sort. I breathed again.

"But I was near the end of my tether. Alice and I talked about everything now. She told me about her life at boarding school and the strange ideas some of the girls had about men and marriage. After leaving school she had been sent to a large millinery or drapery establishment to learn sewing and dressmaking. Here, she said, the talk was awful at times, and one girl had a book with pictures of men's organs of generation, which was passed around and excited their curiosity to the highest pitch.

"I had days of tenderness and contrition, and even told her I would get on and marry her. Then the tears would come into her eyes and she would say: 'I seem to feel as if you were my husband now.' . . .

"I had to see a man on business and went to his cottage. The door was opened by his wife, a handsome, dark-eyed young woman, who looked as if butter would not melt in her mouth. After leaving a message I went on talking to her on other subjects. She piqued my vanity in some way, and made me feel curious and restless. I found myself thinking of her after I left and looking back I saw she was still looking at me.

"To make a long story short, she encouraged me. It ended by my leaving the S. family and going to board with them. T. D., the husband, was glad of my company and my money. They had a little boy—whose father T. was not. I soon understood her inviting looks at me. For she was a general lover, and an old man, in a good government billet, visited her often when T. D. was away: I will call him Silenus. There was also a dark, handsome man who built organs. The latter came one day and sent for some beer. I was working in my room, and it so happened that before he knocked she had been going further than usual in her talk with me; in fact, as good as giving me the word. When her friend was admitted he had to pass my open door and he gave me a look with his black eyes and I gave him a look which told each what the other's game was. It is wonderful what a lot can be learned from a single glance of the eyes. When I saw the little boy bringing in the beer I felt that he had bested me. But she brought me in a glass first, and putting her down on the sofa I scored first. It was done so suddenly, so brutally, that, accustomed as she must have been to such scenes she turned red and bit her under lip. But she sent the other man away in a few minutes. After that she was insatiable; it was every day and sometimes twice in one day. I commenced to be gloomy and miserable again. And there was not even a pretense of love. There was no deception about her; she even introduce me to Silenus and we made excursions together, for which he paid, as he had plenty of money. We were always drinking, until at last I could eat nothing unless I had two or three whiskies. I became very thin, my horizon seemed black and all things at an end. (But T. D. enjoyed his meals and was really fond of his wife and her boy and his work; life was pleasant to him.) She would go up to town with me and to a certain hotel; after drinking she would leave me waiting while she retired with the handsome young landlord for a short time. She told me when she came back that he was a great favorite with married women.

"She told me that Silenus visited a woman who practiced *fellatio* on him. Mrs. D. thought such practices abominable and could not imagine how a woman could like doing such a thing.

"When she was out walking with me one day T. D.'s name came up and she said in a slightly altered voice: 'He told me he loved me!' It was a word seldom used by her except in jest. I threw a startled look at her and caught an inquisitive and apologetic look in return, such a strange and touching glance that I saw I had not yet understood her,—there was an enigma somewhere. When, bit by bit, she told me her life, I understood, or thought I understood, that strange childlike glance in this young woman steeped to her eyes in sin. No one had even made love to her or spoken to her of love in her life.

"It had commenced at school. She must have been a particularly fine and handsome girl, judging from her photographs. She had seen boys playing with girls' privates under the form and felt jealous that they did not play with her's. She had no mother to look after her and she soon found plenty of boys to play with her, and young men, too, as she grew older. She took it as she took her meals. She had been really fond of her child's father, but as he had shown no tenderness for her, nothing but a craving for sensual gratification, she would rather have died than let him know. She soon tired of her attachments, she told me. She did not like T. D. He was not the complacent husband; he was spirited enough, but he believed everything she told him. One day he came home unexpectedly when we were together on the bare palliass in her room. It was a critical moment when his knocks were heard, and in the hurry and excitement some moisture was left on the bed. The knocks became louder, but she was calmer than I, and bade me run down to the closet. I could hear her cheerful and chaffing voice greeting him. When I walked in back to my own room she called out: 'Here's T. home!' I learned afterward that he had been surly and suspicious, and had seen the moisture on the bed, and asked about it, whereupon she had turned the tables upon him completely: he ought to be ashamed of himself; she knew what he meant by his insinuations; if he must know how that moisture come on the bed, why she put the soap there in a hurry to catch a flea. He believed her and brought her a present next day in atonement for his suspicions.

"During her monthly periods, when I could not touch her, she would come in and play with me until emissions occurred, and my feelings had become so perverted that I even preferred this to coitus. The orgasm would occur twice in her, to once in me, and though her eyes were rather hard and her mouth too, she always looked well and cheerful, while I was gloomy and depressed. In her side, however, was a hard lump, which pained her at times, and which, doubtless, was waiting its time. . . .

"One day I felt so low in health that I proposed to T. D. that we should take a boat and sail out in the bay for a day or two. The sea, the change, the open air revived me, and I even made sketches of the black sailor as he steered the boat. One day when I was left alone in charge of the boat, as I felt the time hanging on my hands, for the sea, the blue sky, the lovely day gave me no real pleasure, I remember abusing myself, the old habit reasserting itself as soon as I was alone and idle. When T. D. came back he brought Mrs. D. with him, laughing and jolly as usual. She was surprised when lying next to me under the deck on our return I did not respond to her advances. It would have pleased her, with her husband only a few feet away. After that I spent a night with her, but she was getting tired of me. I did not care for her, but it hurt my vanity and I made a few attempts to be impertinent. She looked at me coldly and threatened to complain to T. . . .

"I want to relate an impression I received one night about this time when with several friends we called at a brothel. I forget my companion, but I remember two faces. It was winter, and great depression prevailed in Adelaide. We had been talking to the mistress as we drank some beer and were pretending to be jolly fellows, although we were wet, cold, and had not enjoyed ourselves (at least, I had not), and she was speaking harshly and jeeringly about two girls she had now who had not earned a penny for the past week. Just then we heard footsteps and she said in a lower tone: 'Here they are.' They came in, unattended, having ascertained which the brothel-keeper snorted and turned her back to them. The faces of the girls, who were quite young, looked so miserable that even I pitied them. The look on the face of one of those girls as she stood by the hearth drawing off her gloves lives in my memory. Too deep for tears was its sorrow, shame, and hopelessness. . . .

"I had given up drink and was living in the bush. To anyone with normal nerves it would have been a happy time of quiet, rustic peace, beauty, and relief from city life. With me it was restless vanity amounting to madness. In every relation, action, or possible event in which I figured or might figure in the future, I always instantaneously called up an imaginary audience. And then this imaginary audience admired everything I did or might do, and put the most heroic, gallant, and romantic construction on my acts, appearance, lineage, and breeding. Suppose I saw a pretty girl on a bush road. Instead of thinking 'There is a pretty girl; I should like to know her or kiss her,' as I suppose a healthy, normal young man would think, I thought after this fashion: 'There is a pretty girl; now, as I pass her she will think I am a handsome and aristocratic-looking stranger, and, as I carry a sketch-book, an artist—"A landscape painter! How romantic!" she will say, and then she will fall in love with me,' etc. This preoccupation with what other people might think or would think so engrossed all my time that I had no means of enjoying the presence, thought, or favor of the divine creatures I met, and I must have appeared 'cracked' to them with my reticence, pride, and silly airs.

"I met girls as foolish as myself sometimes. Once at a *table d'hôte* I met a young girl who went for a walk with me and let me know her carnally although she was little more than a schoolgirl. She was going down to town soon, she said, and would meet me at a certain hotel (belonging to relations of hers) in Adelaide on a certain date, some time ahead; if I took a room there she would come into it during the night. In the meanwhile I had given way to drink again and abused myself at intervals. I came down to town, drunk, in the coach, and kept my appointment with the young girl at the hotel, expecting a night of pleasure; but she merely stared at me coldly as if she had never seen me before. I abused myself twice in my solitary room. . . .

"I met a middle-aged schoolteacher (who had once been an officer in the army) down for his holidays. As he spoke well, and was a 'gentleman,' I cultivated him. One night he asked me to meet a girl he had an appointment with and tell her he was not well enough to meet her. He foolishly told me the purpose of their intended meeting. I went to the trysting-place, at the back of the hotel, and met the girl. On delivering my message she smiled, made some joke about her friend, and looked at me as much as to say: 'You will do as well.' I had been drinking, and in the most brutal manner I took her into a closet. By some strange chance or state of nerves she gave me exquisite pleasure, but the orgasm came with me before it did with her, and in spite of her disappointment and protests I stood up and pulled her out of the place for fear some one should find us there. Still protesting she followed me, but her foot slipped on the paved court, and she fell down on her face. When she rose I saw that her front teeth were broken. I looked at her without pity, with impatience, and abruptly leaving her I went into the hotel to 'the colonel.' I commenced to tell him lies, when he asked me with a weak laugh what had been keeping me. I smiled with low cunning and drunken vanity, evading the question. Then he accused me directly. I only laughed; but, drunk as I was, I remember the look of the ageing bachelor as he saw he had been betrayed by a younger man. He had known her for years. . . .

"I was now living in the home of a woman who was separated from her husband and kept lodgers. She had a daughter, with whom I walked out, a pretty girl who drank like a fish, as her mother also did. There were other lodgers coming and going. I would lie down all day and keep myself saturated with beer. I commenced to get fat and bloated, with the ways of a brothel bully. A broken-down, drunken old woman who visited the house and had been a beautiful lady in her youth told me I should end my days on the gallows trap. The same woman when drunk would lift up her dress, sardonically, exposing herself. Other old women would congregate in the neglected and dirty bedrooms and tell fortunes with the cards. One little woman, an onanist, was like a character out of Dickens, exaggerated, affected, unnatural, with remains of gentility and society manners. Amidst all this drunkenness and abandonment May, the landlady's daughter, preserved her virginity. Young lodgers would take liberties with her, but at a certain stage would receive a stinger on the face. The girl liked me and would kiss me, but nothing else. And then—out of this home of drunkenness and shame—May fell in love with some pretty boy she met by chance, whom she never asked to her home. She began to neglect me, even to neglect drink, and to dream, preoccupied. I felt a restless jealousy, but she would look at me, without resentment, without recognition, without seeing me, look me straight in the eyes as I was talking to her, and dream and dream. This same pretty boy seduced her, I believe. When next I met her she was 'on the town,' her one dream of spring over. . . .

"About this time I had one of those salutary turns that have marked epochs in my life, and as a result I left that house and resolutely abstained from drink. . . . I was now in a small up-country town. I commenced to play croquet and to ride out. Sometimes I was invited to dinner by a young man at the bank, whose house was kept by his sister. She had a small figure, a pretty but rather narrow face, and well-bred manners; but there was a look in her asymmetrical eyes, in the shape of her thin hands, even in the stoop of her shoulders, that seemed passionate. One day—when her brother, a fine, sweet-blooded manly young athlete, was absent—I commenced to pull her about. She gave me one passionate kiss, but said: 'No! Do you know what keeps me straight? It is the thought of my brother.' I refrained from molesting her further. I met other girls, some pretty and arrogant, others plain and hungry-eyed; it was a country town where there were four or five females to every male. But I could not speak frankly and candidly to a young woman as the young banker did. . . .

"I remember that one night, when I was living at the Port, I slept all night with a prostitute who had taken a fancy to me and who used to cry on my shoulder, much to my impatience and annoyance. In the same bed with us, lying beside me, was a girl aged about 12. On my expressing surprise I was told she was used to it and noticed nothing. But in the morning I turned my head and looked at her, and even in the dim light of that dirty bedroom I could see that her eyes had noticed and understood. She pressed herself against me and smiled; it was not the smile of an infant. I could record many instances I have observed of the precocity of children.

"At one time I made the acquaintance of three young men, two in the customs, the other in a surveyor's office. At the first glance you would have said they were ordinary nice young clerks, but on becoming better acquainted you would notice certain peculiarities, a looseness of mouth, a restless, nervous inquietude of manner, an indescribable gleam of the eye. They were very fond of performing and singing at amateur minstrel shows and developed a certain comic vein they thought original, though it reminded me of professional corner-men. However, I enjoyed their singing and drinking habits and went to their lodgings several nights to play cards, drink beer, and tell funny stories. One night they asked me to stay all night and on going to a room with two beds I was told to have one. Presently one of the young men came in and commenced to undress. But before going to his bed he made a remark which, though I had been drinking, opened my eyes. I told him to shut up and go to bed, speaking firmly and rather coldly, and he went reluctantly to his own bed. But another night when they had shifted their lodgings and were all sleeping in the same room I was drunk and went to bed with the same fair-haired young man. On waking up in the night I found my bedmate tampering with me. The old force came over me and I abused him, but refused to commit the crime he wanted me to. His penis was small and pointed. I rose early in the morning, sobered, suffering, and covered with shame, and went hastily away, refusing to stay for breakfast. I thought I caught an amazed and evil smile on the faces of the other two. Meeting the three the same evening in the street, I passed them blushing, and my bedmate of the previous night blushed also. . . . .

"I now took cheap lodgings in North Adelaide. Here I had slight recurrences of the strangeness and fear of going mad which I had experienced once before. I led such a solitary life and fell into such a queer state that I turned to religion and attended church regularly. It was approaching the time for those young men and women who wished to be confirmed to prepare themselves, and a struggle now ensued between my pride and my wish to gain rest and peace of mind in Jesus. I was self-conscious to an incredible degree, and dreaded exposure or making an exhibition of myself, but still went to church, hoping the grace of God would descend on me. I had no other resource. I had no pleasure in life, and was so shattered and in such misery of dread that I welcomed the only refuge that seemed open to me. At last, one Sunday, I had what I thought was a call; I shed a few tears, and although tingling all down my spine I went up in the cathedral and joined those who were going to be confirmed. I attended special meetings and shocked the good bishop very much by telling him I had never been baptized. I had to be baptized first and went one day to the cathedral and he baptized me. When the critical awful moment came the bishop, whose faith even then surprised me somehow, held my hand in his cold palm, and gave it a pressure, eyeing me, expectantly, inquisitively, to see any change for the better. But, it so happened, that morning I was in a horrible temper and black mood, hard and dry-eyed, and no change came. Still, I tried to believe there was a change.

"I was confirmed with others, had a prayer-book given me with prayers for nearly every hour in the day, and was always kneeling and praying. I procured a long, white surplice, and assisted at suburban services, even conducting small ones myself, reading the sermons out of books. But my mood of rage increased, and one Sunday I had to walk a long way in a new pair of boots. I shall never forget that hot Sunday afternoon. My feet commenced to ache and a murderous humor seized me. I swore and blasphemed one moment and prayed to God to forgive me the next. When I reached the chapel where I had to assist the chaplain I was exhausted with rage, pain, fear, and religious mania. I thought it probable I had offended the Holy Ghost. When, next Sunday, I went to try my hand at Sunday-school teaching I wore a pair of boots so old that the little boys laughed. I was always talking of my conversion and the spirit of our Saviour. I do not know what the clergymen I met thought of me. I thought I should like to be a minister myself, and questioned a Church of England parson as to the amount of study necessary. He received my question rather coldly, I thought, which discouraged me. As my dread gradually diminished, though I still felt strange, I made excuses for not conducting services, although I continued to read my Bible and prayer-book, and really believed I had been 'born again.'

"Surely now, I thought, that I had Christ's aid, I shall be able to break off my habit of self-abuse that had been the curse of my youth. What was my horror and dismay to find that, when the mood came on me next, I went down the same as ever. And after all my suffering and dread and fear of fits! What could I do? Was I mad, or what? I was really frightened at my helplessness in the matter and decided on a course of conduct that ultimately brought me past this danger to better health and comparative happiness. I said to myself that there is always a certain amount of preliminary thought and dalliance before I do this deed; doubtless this it is that renders me incapable of resisting. I decided, therefore, never to let my thoughts *commence* to dwell on lustful things, but to think of something else on the *first* intimation of their appearance in my mind. I rigorously followed this rule; and it proved successful, and I recommend it to others in the same predicament as myself. After suffering weeks and months of dread and illness once more, falling away in flesh and turning yellow, I gradually mended a little. I had a better color and tone, and was something like other young men, barring a strange alternate exaltation and depression. Even this gradually became less noticeable, and my moods more even and reliable."

INDEX OF AUTHORS.

INDEX OF SUBJECTS.

Reprint Publishing

FOR PEOPLE WHO GO FOR ORIGINALS.

This book is a facsimile reprint of the original edition. The term refers to the facsimile with an original in size and design exactly matching simulation as photographic or scanned reproduction.

Facsimile editions offer us the chance to join in the library of historical, cultural and scientific history of mankind, and to rediscover.

The books of the facsimile edition may have marks, notations and other marginalia and pages with errors contained in the original volume. These traces of the past refers to the historical journey that has covered the book.

ISBN 978-3-95940-272-9

Made in Germany

www.reprintpublishing.com